the traditional NEWFOUNDLAND kitchen

Roger Pickavance

BOULDER BOOKS

Library and Archives Canada Cataloguing in Publication

Pickavance, Roger, 1943-, author
The traditional Newfoundland kitchen / Roger Pickavance.

Includes bibliographical references and index.
ISBN 978-1-927099-92-6 (softcover)

1. Cooking, Canadian--Newfoundland and Labrador style.
2. Cooking, Canadian--Newfoundland and Labrador style--History.
3. Cooking--Newfoundland and Labrador--History. 4. Cookbooks--
I. Title.

TX715.6.P5 2017 641.59718 C2017-904398-6

Published by Boulder Publications
Portugal Cove-St. Philip's, Newfoundland and Labrador
www.boulderpublications.ca

Design and layout: Todd Manning
Editor: Stephanie Porter
Copy editor: Iona Bulgin
Printed in China

We acknowledge the financial support of the Government of Newfoundland and Labrador through the Department of Tourism, Culture and Recreation.

Newfoundland Labrador

Funded by the Government of Canada | Financé par le gouvernement du Canada | Canada

For Priscilla

Contents

Introduction . . . vii
Chapter 1. The Kitchen and the Meals . . . 1
Chapter 2. Gardens and Root Cellars . . . 9
Chapter 3. The Community Store . . . 19
Chapter 4. Breads . . . 25
Chapter 5. Soups and Dumplings . . . 43
Chapter 6. Cod . . . 53
Chapter 7. Fish other than Cod . . . 71
Chapter 8. Shellfish . . . 91
Chapter 9. Domestic Meat . . . 101
Chapter 10. Salt Meats: Pork, Fatback, and Beef . . . 119
Chapter 11. Wild Meat from Land and Sea . . . 127
Chapter 12. Domestic Poultry, Eggs, and Wild Birds . . . 141
Chapter 13. Miscellaneous Savoury Dishes . . . 151
Chapter 14. Dairy: Milk, Butter, and Cheese (and Margarine) . . . 163
Chapter 15. Vegetables . . . 173
Chapter 16. Steamed Puddings and Duffs . . . 183
Chapter 17. Sweet Pies (or Tarts) and Pastry . . . 193
Chapter 18. Cakes . . . 201
Chapter 19. Miscellaneous Sweet Things . . . 219

Chapter 20. Preserves: Jams, Jellies, and Pickles . . . 233
Chapter 21. Canning and Bottling . . . 249
Chapter 22. Sauces . . . 255
Chapter 23. Drinks . . . 267
Bibliography . . . 277
Appendix 1. Formal Names of Animals and Plants with Common Names . . . 282
Appendix 2. Measures: Volume, Weight, Currency, Oven Temperature, and Barrels . . . 288
Appendix 3. Food in the Stores . . . 291
Index . . . 298
About the Author . . . 307

Introduction

When I arrived in Newfoundland from Wales in 1968, cod was king, Joey was still emperor, and I was amazed by all the foods I had never seen before. Cod tongues were hawked by small boys on the side of the road, "watered fish" was advertised on downtown corner-store windows, and partridgeberry pie was cooked by the mothers of new friends. It slowly dawned on me that these were traditional foods still being cooked alongside the pizzas and barbecues of the modern world. I was intrigued and I asked questions, and that led to my habit of talking to older people about what they had cooked early in the 20th century, or what their parents and grandparents had cooked before that. As my accumulated memories and notes from those conversations evolved into this book, I was faced by the obvious questions: how can traditional Newfoundland food be defined? What should be included? What left out?

My first inclination was to simply include any recipe that used traditional ingredients, but that idea rapidly turned into a minefield of the unexpected. We might all agree on cod tongues and bakeapples as being traditional fare, but what about olive oil? One older man I talked to had fished on the Grand Banks and traded with Portuguese and Spanish fishermen. As a result, olive oil was commonplace in some homes in his area (Elliston, Trinity Bay), and Spanish brandy was the tipple of choice around Christmas. Neither of these springs to mind as traditional ingredients but nevertheless were part of his Newfoundland life.

So I thought instead to focus on a time period of traditional cooking, with a beginning and end marked by some notable event.

What should mark the beginning? Any definition of traditional food must include the impressive array of baked goods—cakes, tea buns, and squares. But these were not characteristic of the cooking of the early 17th- and 18th-century settlers, who brought with them the cooking of late-medieval Europe, where meats were roasted in front of an open fire and bread was baked in an iron pot if you had one (or on a flat hearthstone if you didn't) and in an oven only if you were wealthy. Where was the transition? Starting around 1850, the free-standing cookstove with its built-in oven made baking possible for the general population of Newfoundland. Baking powder arrived around 1880, dramatically expanding the limits of what could be baked.

What should mark the end? It seems to me that the huge influx of American and other servicemen to Newfoundland during and after World War II, followed by Confederation with Canada, ended the domination of traditional cooking. Traditional dishes still existed after that time, but in modern Newfoundland they are diluted and overshadowed by stir-fries, lasagnas, and the casual use of exotic ingredients borrowed from the general homogenization going on around us. Although exact demarcation is impossible, overall I will call the time span of traditional food as shortly after the middle of the 19th century through to World War II, a period of fewer than 100 years.

Sources

Virtually all of my information is from primary sources. The first and by far the most important is a diverse cross-section of Newfoundlanders. I have poked my nose into many kitchens and chatted to many cooks, who are acknowledged generally and specifically below. I have relied particularly on those who grew up before World War II, because they learned to cook in the 1920s and 1930s from mothers and grandmothers who, in turn, had learned their cooking in the 19th or very early 20th century. A second primary source is newspaper advertisements of wholesale and retail merchants from the late 19th and early 20th centuries. A third is handwritten ledgers and account books of 19th-century Newfoundland merchants, and two handwritten, personal recipe collections from the early 20th century, the Ayre and the Lillico manuscripts.

Early cookbooks published in Newfoundland provided another source. The very first of these was *The Art of Cooking Made Easy*, published in 1900 by O'Mara's Drug Store, St. John's, but this was essentially a reprint of an 1890 publication from Ontario advertising Emerald Baking Powder. Other early publications contained little or no original material.

The first truly Newfoundland cookbooks were put out by ladies' associations of three major religious denominations. *The L.C.A.S. Cook Book* was published in 1905 by the Ladies College Aid Society of the Methodist Church. Then came *Tested Recipes* by the Presbyterian Ladies' Aid in 1924, which was retitled and reissued in 1925 as *The P.L.A. Cook Book*, by the Ladies' Aid Society of St. Andrew's Presbyterian Church. A second edition of this was put out in 1928, and a third in 1939. The Catholic ladies also contributed in 1926: *The C.L.A. Cook Book* from the Columbus Ladies' Association. Thereafter came a succession of compilations under various auspices, which has continued to the present day. Of all these, I have paid particular attention to the 1905 *L.C.A.S. Cook Book* and the 1928 edition of *The P.L.A. Cook Book*, for the unscholarly but pragmatic reason that I have both in my collection and so reference to them was easy. In the text I occasionally refer to these as the 1905 or 1928 cookbook. The sources for all my second-hand information are listed in the Bibliography.

The Recipes

This book is not intended as an encyclopedia of every version of every traditional Newfoundland recipe I have encountered. That would be impossibly long, tedious, and repetitive. Instead, I give a cross-section of what was cooked in the traditional food period I have defined by presenting typical examples. At first I thought I would put recipes in my sources' own words, but this was not possible. Although all my informants knew exactly what they meant, they were astonished when I did not. A typical conversation:

Mrs. Smith (in the middle of a recipe): "… and then you add some flour …"
Me (scribbling furiously): "How much?"
Mrs. Smith: "Oh, you know, a good bit."
Me (an educated guess): "Say, half a cup?"
Mrs. Smith: "Oh, gracious, no, more than that—a good bit."
Me (guessing wildly): "Maybe 2 or 3 cups?"
Mrs. Smith: "Oh no, not that much; like I said, you just need a good bit."

I quickly learned to skate over such approximations and focus on the essential ingredients and method from which eventually to create a finished recipe. Some recipes were given to me in a very condensed fashion, with few quantities and scanty instructions; in such cases, I had to experiment to find a working recipe. Another difficulty, particularly with popular recipes, was hearing many slightly different versions, each with its own ambiguities. The finished recipes in this book are often a composite of different sources.

For oven temperatures, my sources talked about hot, medium, or slow ovens, which I have approximated to degrees. Some sources used other archaic measures—soup spoon, serving spoon, coffee cup, and breakfast cup—which I have converted into the standard US teaspoon, tablespoon, cup, quart, and gallon. And if, for example, a 10-cent package of something was mentioned, that has also been converted into standard units. Metric equivalents, temperatures, and standard US measures are in Appendix 2.

I have tested almost all of the recipes in this book, in part out of curiosity but also to check on quantities and methods. Only a few I have not, and so I am unable to confirm the details. I have neither boiled a seal's head nor smoked a ham in a wooden barrel, although I hope to attempt both in the future. Many of my sources, recalling days of large families, gave me recipes that served 10 or more people. Such quantities are often unnecessary; except in cases where a whole unit such as a ham is involved, or a dish such as a boiled dinner can really only be cooked for a crowd, I have reduced the quantities to feed four to six people.

Apart from such necessary interpretations and reductions, I have tried to editorialize as little as possible. Much of the reason for writing this book was simply to record both *what* was cooked and *how* it was cooked in the traditional period. Although I occasionally comment on the recipes, I have not tried to alter them to suit modern tastes and methods, because by those standards, almost all the recipes here could be improved.

Acknowledgements

I have talked about food to so many Newfoundlanders over the years that unfortunately they are too numerous to mention individually. In many cases, particularly from earlier days when my notes were more perfunctory or non-existent, I have lost their names. But I am truly grateful for all those conversations and kitchen visits, not only for the chats about food and cooking but also for the glimpses into a way of life that had its own rewards while being incomprehensibly difficult to our modern sensibilities—imagine having no electricity, no appliances; having to get water from the well, wash everything by hand, heat water on the stove, and of course, make and mend everything, milk the cow, tend the garden, look after the children …

A few people were exceptionally generous with their time and talked to me about food and cooking sometimes for several days on end. I want to particularly acknowledge these few, and they are listed here in alphabetical order. The place names refer to where they grew up and learned about food, not necessarily where they lived in later life: Kathleen Atkins (née Gaslard), Eddie's Cove West, Northern Peninsula; Mary Courage (née Keeping), Lally's Cove, Fortune Bay; Jane Mifflin (née Lodge), Catalina South (now Port Union), Trinity Bay; Hilda Quinton (née Gould), Open Hall and Red Cliff, Bonavista Bay; Ada Samms (née Laing), Norris Point, Bonne Bay; Reuben Samms, Norris Point, Bonne Bay; and Mary Tapp (née Bishop), Grand Falls.

Apart from all the cooks, a number of people have helped greatly in the long gestation of this work. In particular, this book would have been impossible without the generous help provided by the staff of the Centre for Newfoundland Studies and of the Archives and Special Collections, both divisions of the Memorial University of Newfoundland

Libraries. I would also like to thank the Maritime History Archive (Memorial University), The Rooms Provincial Archives Division, and the City of St. John's Archives for providing invaluable assistance. All newspaper advertisements throughout this book were taken from the *Evening Telegram*, 1879–1929.

This book would also have been impossible without the support and encouragement, through good times and bad, of Frances and Augustus Oldford, Red Cliff, Bonavista Bay.

Over: "Janet the Invaluable," likely a cook with the Grenfell Mission in St. Anthony, 1908, in a well-equipped kitchen. *From the International Grenfell Association Photographs. The Rooms Provincial Archives Division, VA 118-62.2.*

Roger Pickavance

Chapter 1

The Kitchen and the Meals

THE KITCHEN

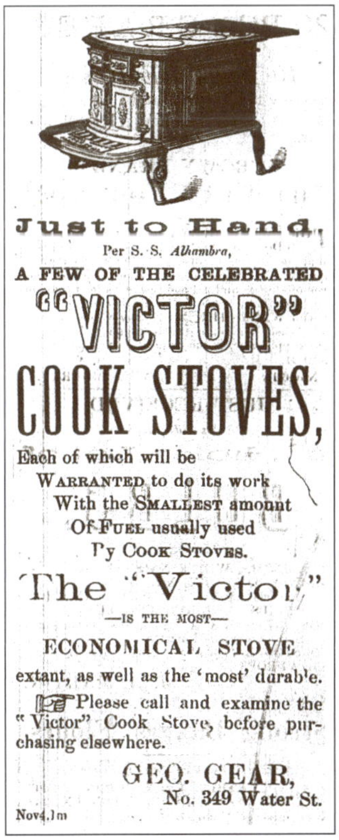

Until the middle of the 19th century in Newfoundland, an open fire in the hearth was all most people had to cook their food. At best, there were andirons to hold the fire together, a spit in front of it, and a crane to suspend a cooking pot. Under those conditions, cooking was necessarily restricted. Stews and soda bread were made in iron pots suspended from the crane, meat was roasted on the spit, and griddle cakes or flatbreads cooked on a hearthstone. Ovens in Newfoundland in those days were strictly for the wealthy.

Early in the 19th century, European improvements in cooking technology reached Newfoundland. The cooking range replaced the open fire and was inserted into the hearth under the chimney. The central grate contained the fire, focused the heat, and used fuel more efficiently. Food was cooked in pots hung over the fire, placed on an iron cover on top of it, or cooked in the ovens alongside. Ranges were imported or made by local blacksmiths, but they were expensive and never in general use.

The turning point was around 1850 with the introduction of the free-standing cast-iron cookstove. These had enclosed fires with cooktop and oven, were bought ready-made, and did not have to be custom-fitted. Given such advantages, it is not surprising that they were adopted so enthusiastically. By 1860, for example, George Gear, a St. John's merchant, offered seven British and 12 American free-standing cookstoves, and demand was such that, by 1863, he offered the "Terra Nova," a British-made model named specifically for the local market. Local foundry owners sensed an opportunity, and by 1870 locally made cookstoves were being produced. As so often is the case, however, imported stoves were cheap and plentiful, and in 1880 the government imposed a protective tariff to help foster the local industry. Free-standing cast-iron cookstoves continued to be made in St. John's well into the 20th century.

Those cookstoves were things of beauty. Casting techniques allowed detail and ornamentation to run rife, and the smooth cast iron was burnished to a fine polish. With their details glowing in the lamplight, they looked magnificent, and several women told me they had lingered with the stove polish a little longer than strictly necessary, just for the pleasure of it.

A small free-standing cast-iron cookstove.
Archives and Special Collections Division, Memorial University, 27 02 004.

Free-standing cookstoves revolutionized the Newfoundland kitchen. In practical terms, the first major benefits were a totally enclosed fire and an iron chimney at the back, a blessing after the heat and smoke of an open fire. The flat, upper surface had circular openings, typically four (one or two in smaller models), each closed with a loose disk of iron—the damper—which, when removed, exposed the pot to the direct heat of the fire below. The cook could have several pots cooking at the same time at different heats. The oven (or ovens) meant that bread, cakes, and buns could be baked, and meat roasted or braised. The oven temperature could be regulated by feeding or starving the fire or, in fancy models, by opening or closing vents. Compared to the open fireplace this must have been a revelation for those cooks who experienced the transition. Later models had refinements such as warming drawers over the stove or adaptations to burn oil instead of wood or coal. From the early 19th century—and possibly earlier, but records are scarce—an extensive range of cooking utensils was available, although affording any of it was another matter.

Ryan and Sons (of St. John's and Liverpool) imported into Newfoundland between 1812 and 1814: iron pots, 4 gallon, 3 gallon, 2½ gallon, 2 gallon, 1½ gallon, 1¼ gallon, and 1 gallon; three-legged iron pots, iron bake-pots and covers, and iron ladles; tin tea kettles, 8 quart, 5 quart, and 4 quart; various sizes of boat kettles; tin saucepans and covers nos. 1, 2, and 3; tin round pudding pans nos. 1 and 2; colanders no. 3; and blue-edged baking dishes, 9 inch, 11 inch, 12 inch, and 14 inch.

THE MEALS

There was a traditional, set pattern of meals in Newfoundland. Such a fixed but flexible schedule was a boon to women who were also in charge of cleaning and scrubbing, polishing and waxing, making and mending clothes, washing and ironing, looking after children, some or all of the gardening, milking the cow, feeding the chickens, drying fish on the flakes, and other chores essential to running a household. A fixed plan meant knowing what had to be done each day and allowed for small grace notes to the fare, an occasional cake or a batch of buns or cookies.

Meal plans could never be totally rigid—seasonal events like the glut of fresh wild or domestic meat in the fall would require flexibility, or some unexpected event would require a change of plan. One woman remembered fondly the day a schooner from outside the area came into the harbour and dumped a huge mound of freshly caught halibut on the foreshore with the invitation to everyone to help themselves. Meal plans were forgotten as everyone scrambled to take advantage of this windfall.

Although families and communities differed in their meal planning, I have been struck more by the broad similarity of meal sequence across the island than by the diversity. I have seen an account of a meal pattern in St. John's in the 1960s remarkably similar to the typical sequence set out below, based on outports in the 1920s and 1930s. Traces of this pattern can still be found in the early 21st century.

Breakfast

Breakfast varied in timing and substance. Men going out early on the boats often had two breakfasts, an early, lighter one and a more substantial affair later on. A busy housewife might have hers before she fed the children in time to get them to school, or afterwards, before she started her daily chores.

Tea was consumed everywhere, drunk from a large mug, hot and sweet, black or with a slug of fresh or tinned milk. Bread was a breakfast staple, with molasses or jam, sometimes toasted, often not. Eggs, bacon, and sausages were always popular. Salt fish was a favourite, whether as leftovers or freshly cooked (after soaking overnight).

Sunday breakfast was often special. Many families had fish and brewis (or another salt fish dish) every Sunday morning, quite independently of having the same thing at one or more meals during the week. Or this would be the morning to have bacon and eggs, or brewis and bacon. Families in more affluent circumstances might have a more elaborate Sunday breakfast involving a steak of fresh meat, usually beef, but sometimes pork. In many places, steak and brewis (page 40) was the Sunday breakfast of choice.

Dinner

The principal meal of the day was dinner, typically eaten between noon and 1 p.m.

Sunday

A cooked, meat-based meal. If fresh meat was available, this would be the day to have mutton, pork, beef, rabbit, or a fresh bird—perhaps a gull or a wild duck. Fresh meat was available year-round in towns, so for the affluent denizens it was a routine on Sundays. When fresh meat was not available, a boiled dinner with salt beef or salt pork would be the usual meal.

Monday

Leftovers from Sunday, reheated with extra vegetables and/or bread and butter. If leftovers were in short supply, fish was the usual alternative.

Tuesday

Boiled dinner of salt beef and vegetables.

Wednesday

Fish of some sort, or a stew of fish or meat according to availability.

Thursday

Boiled dinner of salt beef and vegetables (if not already eaten on Tuesday), or any kind of meat, such as rabbit in season.

Friday

Always fish, for Catholic and non-Catholic families alike, fresh or salted according to availability, with vegetables and bread and butter.

Saturday

Pea soup, usually made from split yellow peas and containing chunks of vegetables (carrot, potato, and particularly turnip), sometimes with dumplings, and almost always eaten with bread and butter. Baked beans were an alternative.

Supper

This was the evening meal, typically eaten between 5 p.m. and 6 p.m. Suppers were more varied than dinners; the thrifty cook took advantage of seasonally available foods or made creative use of leftovers. Hash was a favourite, made from leftover meat or fish with potatoes and vegetables, augmented, if necessary, by soaking torn-up bread in water or milk and then stirring it in. Soup was also popular, or sometimes baked potatoes if the oven had been on for baking bread. If the midday meal had been soup, supper might be more substantial—perhaps baked beans that had been in the oven for most of the day, or salt fish with bread or raisin buns.

Lunch

Beware of the word *lunch* in Newfoundland. Traditionally it meant (and often still does) a snack or small meal taken at any time of day between the main meals, and particularly snacks just before bed, which were not surprising given the active way of life and the early supper. Lunches could be as simple as a few spoonfuls of leftovers or slices of cold roast. Bread was a mainstay, either in a sandwich or as backup to leftovers.

SPECIAL OCCASIONS

Christmas Eve

Salt fish, the traditional Christmas Eve meal for most Newfoundlanders, was eaten either as the regular evening supper, much later in the evening, or very early on Christmas Day morning, perhaps after church and alongside the opening of gifts. It was served either plain, with bread and butter, or as a full meal with boiled potatoes and boiled onions with white sauce. The fish dish was often followed by sweet raisin bread, often called Christmas sweet bread (page 33).

Christmas Day

Christmas Day dinner was either eaten at the usual dinner time, or later if the household had been awake late the night before. Some households treated it as just another Sunday dinner, so it would be a meat-based cooked meal or a simple boiled dinner based around

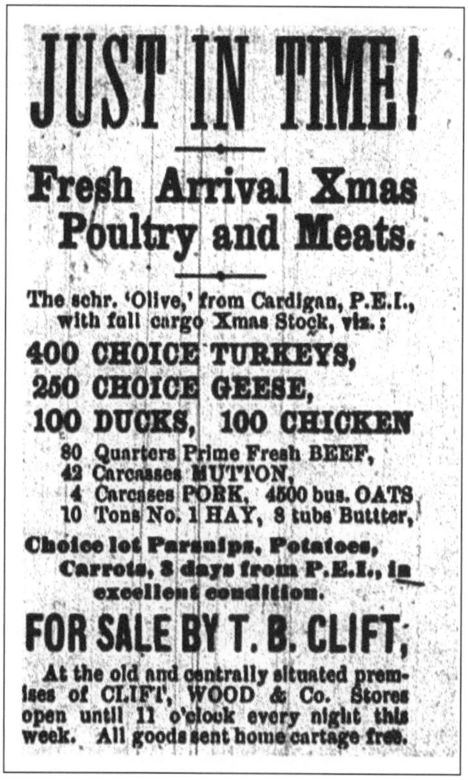

salt beef or salt pork. But for most families it was a special occasion, and sometimes it was the only special dinner of the year. Fresh meat was obtained if possible, and in some areas the annual fall slaughter of livestock was delayed until just before Christmas. The meat—beef, pork, mutton, goat, rabbit, chicken, or duck—was served with boiled vegetables (often boiled with salt beef for flavour). As on Christmas Eve, sweet bread was often part of the meal.

For more affluent households in towns, imported poultry was an option year-round, but especially over the Christmas to New Year's season, frequently advertised in the local press.

The meat main course was often followed by some sort of duff (see Chapter 16) or a plum pudding. The English tradition of hiding a silver coin (never copper, which was considered poisonous) in the pudding or duff was adopted across the island, and the lucky finder kept the coin and made a wish.

New Year's Day

If observed, the main course was similar to that served on Christmas Day, ranging from a meat meal—fresh if available, salt if not—to expensive poultry such as a fresh goose with sage and onion stuffing.

Pancake Day (Shrove Tuesday)

The custom of eating pancakes on Shrove Tuesday was widespread. Usually, thin English-style pancakes (page 155) were served, rather than the thick mainland Canadian style. They were typically spread with jam or molasses, or in the English style simply sprinkled with sugar, or with sugar and lemon juice.

Many families enjoyed the custom of hiding fortune-telling tokens in the pancakes: the finder of a coin would become wealthy, of a ring would soon marry, of a nail would become a carpenter, of a piece of straw a farmer, and so on. Cooks who prided themselves on their thin pancakes were obliged to make pancakes thicker than normal to disguise the embedded tokens.

Ash Wednesday and Lent

Some families observed the first day of Lent as a meat-free day. The rest of Lent was rarely totally meat-free (a difficult diet in traditional Newfoundland), but there was often a sense of eating simply, without such extras as cakes and cookies.

Good Friday

Good Friday was a day to eat fish, usually salted because fresh fish was rarely available at Easter time. The majority of households had salt codfish, but others always had salt herring, while a few would save salt salmon fillets for this day.

Easter Sunday

The main meal on Easter Sunday was either nothing special—just the usual Sunday meat-based dinner—or it was treated like Christmas Day, with special fresh meat or poultry when available. Where ham was popular, this was the day for it. In towns, ham could be bought from the store, but in rural areas it was the custom to smoke one's own for Easter Sunday. Very often a pork leg was left in salt until a week before Easter, and then smoked for that occasion (page 110).

Birthdays

Birthdays were celebrated for children, less so for adults. Perhaps a chicken would be killed for the occasion, and a cake baked. Children with birthdays in Lent were particularly popular, because the general frowning upon of indulgence was ignored for the celebration.

Over: Fred Sears (left) holds a cabbage, with Sir Wilfred Grenfell, St. Anthony, 1930. *The Rooms Provincial Archives Division, VA 94-31.5.*

Chapter 2

Gardens and Root Cellars

Gardens and root cellars were essential to the traditional mixed economy of rural Newfoundland, where survival as a fishing family was really only possible if supported by gardening and woodcutting. Urban areas had access to imported produce, but still relied heavily on the agriculture and horticulture surrounding them.

The famously rocky terrain of Newfoundland usually meant that gardens were built up over the years by laborious, careful husbandry. Adding seaweed to soil built its quantity and quality. In some places, gales pushed extensive drifts of seaweed onto the shore, where it was usually left for a season to let the excess salt leach out in the rain. Then it was collected and placed directly on the soil, in the soil in trenches, or made into part of a giant compost heap.

Another traditional way to improve the soil was by adding domestic livestock manure, often mixed with sawdust or peat, readily available for most people. Where clay was part of the soil, peat was often dug in to lighten it. Capelin (a small fish) were gathered on beaches where they congregated to spawn in early summer and either dug directly into the soil or covered in pits adjacent to the garden. In due course the pits were opened up and the richly perfumed slurry was dug into the ground or simply spread on it. Domestic compost heaps were present but not universal—the abundance of seaweed, for example, so completely outstripped the production of domestic vegetable waste that composting was hardly worthwhile and, in any case, most such waste went straight to the pig or chickens.

There was usually division of labour in the garden. Typically, men began the yearly cycle in the spring with the heavy work of turning over the soil, gathering seaweed, and digging capelin pits. Women planted seeds, tended the garden through the growing season, and then made preserves from the garden produce. The whole family pitched in for the harvest and to fill the root cellar.

Anybody with a garden probably grew at least four mainstays: potatoes, carrots, turnips, and cabbage. These were also the principal occupants of the root cellar, and together with salt fish, wild berries, and a little meat, kept families alive over long winters. What else was in a garden varied according to individual tastes. For example, Mrs. Stein, the proprietor of a plant nursery on what is now Kenna's Hill in St. John's, advertised in March 1897 that she was taking orders for cauliflower, cucumber, vegetable marrow, and lettuce plants, among others. In April 1902 she advertised that her celery, cauliflower, and cabbage plants would be ready on May 15.

Locally grown vegetables are listed alphabetically, but this is no reflection of their relative popularity. Beets, onions, and parsnips were almost as popular as potatoes, turnips, carrots, and cabbage, but not quite so widespread. A long list of other crops was grown according to individual tastes, such as cucumbers, lettuce, pumpkins, and tomatoes.

Vegetables

Beans were often called green beans to distinguish them from their dried relatives, or sometimes string beans because most varieties had fibrous strings on both sides of the pod that needed removing before cooking.

Beets—rarely but occasionally called beetroot—were widely but not universally grown. Like turnips, beets were a double-duty crop: leaves were harvested as a green vegetable early in the season and the roots gathered at the end.

Cabbages were a primary crop, and both early and late varieties were typically grown. The former, often called spring cabbage, was planted at the beginning of the season to be eaten in the summer. They were considered more watery than late cabbage, which made them unsuitable for keeping over the winter; they were all eaten fresh in season. Late cabbage was planted after the early variety, grown late into the fall, and stored as well as eaten fresh. The crinkly leaved Savoy cabbage as well as the smooth-leaved types were grown. Advertisements showed a wide range of varieties available in the last decades of the 19th century and the beginning of the 20th, including Webb's Drum Head, Large York, Ox Heart, Little Wonder of Savoy, Imperial, Henderson's Succession, Early Spring, Jersey Wakefield, Charleston Wakefield, Flat Dutch, and Winningstadt.

Carrots were found in every community and virtually every garden, but apart from a general distinction between long, thin carrots and short, fat ones, it seems that carrots were always just carrots. Cauliflower and celery were grown here and there, but few of my sources remembered them. Cucumbers were not generally popular, but those who prized them took considerable trouble to grow them. Several people described cucumbers being grown in cold frames made from storm windows taken off the house in the spring and put back after the cucumbers had been harvested in the fall.

Herbs were grown across the island and used both fresh and dried. Typically, they were tied in bunches, hung up by the stalks in a corner of a shed, and left to dry. The leaves were then crumbled into a paper bag and stored in a cool, dry place for year-round use. Savoury, also called summer savory, was particularly widespread, and sage, thyme, and chives were frequently grown. Many people grew mint, but not those with a wild crop nearby.

Hops grow all over Newfoundland, clinging to the sides of buildings and twining around utility poles, and sometimes an abandoned community will be marked by hops clambering over old fence posts. The hardy vines spread easily and needed little attention once established, so people were often hazy about whether the hops in their gardens were there by accident or design. It is uncertain if the plants are the European hop or the native North American variety. Recent information indicates that both may grow on the island; just to complicate matters, they may have hybridized.

Lettuce, often called leaf lettuce, was grown, if rarely. Onions were almost as popular as the big four. After being harvested in the fall, onions were surface-dried and stored in a cool, dry place, but never in a root cellar because the dampness would rot them. Parsnips, also very popular, were kept over the winter either in a root cellar or left in the ground until spring, when they were considered particularly sweet. Peas, usually called green peas to distinguish them from dried peas, were planted by some.

Potatoes were the most popular crop. Every garden had at least white potatoes and frequently a red and a blue type as well—the exact varieties remain mostly unknown, as people simply grew what their parents had grown or what neighbours had given them. One notable exception came from a woman who was perfectly clear that Black Minguns were grown by her family and most of the community. The name was a corruption of Black Mignion, also called Cups, a once-popular potato now only known as a heritage variety. Black Minguns were a floury, dry potato, but they were not a blue potato as the name suggests (the skin of blue potatoes often looks almost black). Newspaper advertisements of the period hint about the varieties available in the last decades of the 19th century. Swinden and Co. (No. 4 New Gower Street, St. John's) offered Prolifics, Early Rose, and Prince Alberts, while John Wills (Water Street west, St. John's) advertised an extensive selection of seed potatoes: Early Ashleaf Kidneys, Early Rose, Goodrich, Snowballs, Jacksons, Victorias, and Prince Alberts. Other merchants offered Chilis, Prolifics,

The International Grenfell Association promoted cold frames as a means of extending the growing season. Here a volunteer works at one in St. Anthony, 1910. *The Rooms Provincial Archives Division, VA 94-31.5.*

Calicoes (Nova Scotian), Early Alpha (round white), Early Vermont (earlier than Rose), Paterson's Regents, White Dalmahoys, Perth Reds or True Scotch Apples, and Scotch Champion. By the first decade of the 20th century, Beauty of Hebron, White Elephants, Dakota Reds, and Prince Edward Island Blues were also on the market.

Pumpkins, squash, and vegetable marrows were grown here and there. Pumpkins were described as big and orange, the squash usually as green with longitudinal ridges, and the marrow as just "marrow" (essentially a gargantuan zucchini).

Shallots were frequently grown, as much for their superior keeping qualities as for their good flavour. They were the real thing—double-lobed, diminutive onions with brown outer skins and red-rimmed interior layers. After being harvested in the fall, they were treated like onions: surface-dried and kept in a cool, dry place but not a root cellar, where they would rot in the dampness.

Tomatoes were grown by some, often in a cold frame with cucumbers. The popularity of green tomato pickles (page 244) is likely based on an abundance of unripe tomatoes.

"Turnips" in Newfoundland are not Eurasian turnips, but Swedish turnips, often called just that in 19th-century advertisements. They are called swedes for short in

Europe, or rutabaga in the US, where they are also called Canadian turnips, after the principal source of imports. As they are tough and frost-hardy, ideal for Newfoundland, they were another mainstay grown all over the island in large quantities. They were particularly enjoyed because turnips—like beets—did double duty: young leaves were harvested as a green vegetable in the beginning of the year, bulbous roots dug up in the fall. Nineteenth-century varieties grown in Newfoundland included Webb's Green Globe, Champion Purple Top, Devonshire Grey Stone, and Beef Heart.

Fruit

Hardy garden fruits (blackcurrants for example) were grown across the island, while more delicate fruits were found only where local conditions favoured them. Some places were well known for their microclimates favourable for fruit, such as Clarenville, Shoal Harbour, Deer Lake, Cormack, and Woody Point.

Apples were widely grown, and gnarly old apple trees are a feature of abandoned communities. Cherries were grown in favourable places, particularly south-facing, sheltered locations. Blackcurrants were grown across the island; redcurrants were second in popularity and white a distant third. Damsons were so widespread and needed so little care that they were often considered wild fruit. In years when they were plentiful, they were sold by the sack to merchants. Gooseberries, both big purple and smaller green types, were popular.

Pears grew well in a sunny, south-facing corner of the garden. Plums (as distinct from damsons) thrived in many places in Newfoundland, and in good years crops were large. Locally, the word *plums* denoted any variety, or they were distinguished as egg (large, purple), blue (medium, blue-black), greengage (medium, green-yellow), or yellow (small, yellow) plums.

Rhubarb became popular in Britain in the first half of the 19th century, and the first printed recipe using this ingredient in America appeared in 1850. When it arrived in Newfoundland is uncertain, but it was well known by 1879, when Swinden & Co. in St. John's advertised 1,000 bundles of rhubarb, just received via the SS *Alhambra*. By the first decades of the 20th century rhubarb was widely grown across the island, and remnants of extensive rhubarb patches can still be seen in abandoned communities.

Root Cellars

Vegetables held in root cellars kept body and soul together through long winters and lean springs for generations of Newfoundlanders. The root cellar was a pivotal piece of technology in the settlement of Newfoundland.

Root cellars are scattered throughout rural Newfoundland, most in ruins but some still in use. They are preserved in part as a labour of love, but also because homegrown vegetables overwintered in a root cellar are preferable to commercial crops shipped halfway across the continent. To the unaccustomed eye they are unexpected and mysterious structures in a forbidding landscape—small wonder that they have been reported as everything from medieval dungeons to Viking longhouses. Some abandoned cellars have returned to the earth, mouldering away, leaving at best a depression and ordered shapes of stones to mark their passing. Other disused cellars are more obvious because they were well-made stone or concrete structures, now sticking out of the ground like snaggleteeth, their overburden of soil and sod washed away. These are particularly poignant when encountered in some lonely cove. There they stand, gravestones of a dead community, vanished houses marked by level patches of ground, sheds and wharves totally gone. They are the last witnesses of vanished lives, of the unremitting hard work, but also of children playing, and laughter and love and happiness.

Root cellars were often better built than houses, and with good reason. If a cellar collapsed in the middle of winter a family was in serious trouble, but if the wooden post of a house gave way at the same time, well, it could be propped up and fixed the next summer.

The primary function of a root cellar is to keep vegetables semi-underground, below the frost line, to prevent them from freezing and spoiling. In essence, the vegetables are held in high-humidity cold storage. The essential principle, from which all construction details follow, is to get at least the bottom half—preferably more—of the cellar under the frost line. The exact depth depends on local conditions, but as a rule of thumb in Newfoundland it is 4 feet below the surface.

The description below covers the principles of traditional root-cellar construction and is a distillation of the wisdom of two men who described how cellars were built in the 1920s and 1930s.

Building a New Root Cellar: A Traditional Account

First, find a good place, ideally close to the house for easy access, but the local terrain will be the deciding factor. Perhaps the easiest to deal with is sloping ground, up to about 45 degrees, with some depth of soil, so you can dig back into the hill by 8 or 10 feet. The back of the cellar will thus be essentially underground, and the excavated soil can be used to cover the front half, leaving the door exposed on the downhill side.

With rocky ground it will be impossible to dig to any depth, but in compensation there will usually be an outcrop of rock to form a very convenient back cellar wall. The door will be in the wall opposite this. Most of the cellar will have to be buried by soil carried from elsewhere.

A fenced garden and root cellar in Conche, 1932. *The Rooms Provincial Archives Division, VA 92-122.*

If the ground is more or less flat, find a place to dig down about 4 feet, more if possible. Six feet would eliminate the need to build up much, so the cellar can be accessed through a hatch in the roof with a ladder inside. If the whole cellar has to stick out of the ground by several feet, then put a low door at one end. (Sometimes, when deep excavation was possible, the cellar was put under a shed, or under the house itself, with a trapdoor and ladder access.)

Assume that a piece of ground, backing onto a rocky outcrop, which slopes enough to give sufficient headroom for a low door on the downhill side, can be found. In other situations, modify the building style as necessary. A good minimum size for a cellar is about 8 feet by 8 feet, adequate for a family of six to eight. Make the cellar bigger for a larger family, but don't make it smaller for a smaller family; it will need to accommodate bigger crops in some years, and surplus vegetables are easy to give away or feed to the pig.

Dig a hole about 9 feet by 9 feet; this leaves a clear square about 8 feet by 8 feet inside, allowing for the thickness of the logs that will make the walls. Ideally, dig down about 6 or 7 feet. On the downhill side, dig out a patch for the porch outside the door. Line all four sides of the hole with slender logs, about 6 inches or a little less in diameter at the thicker end, and a little over 8 feet long. Lay the logs horizontally head-to-tail, a thicker end over a thinner end below it, to maintain approximately the same height. At corners notch the logs at their ends so they fit together neatly. Build these walls 4 or 5 feet high on all sides.

One gable wall will usually be the side deepest into the slope, against the rocky outcrop, with the other gable opposite on the downward slope. Build these gable walls higher, about 7 or 8 feet or more off the floor of the cellar. They can narrow toward the top, so a few shorter logs can be used. Choose a good straight log for the ridge pole, long enough to easily span from one gable wall to the other, and with less taper than others, perhaps cut from the middle of the trunk of a taller tree. Put the top of this ridge pole about 8 feet from the floor. Use more logs to build a pitched roof from the tops of the walls and over the ridge pole. Each side of the roof will slope about 7 or 8 over 12, but this is flexible, and reverse the taper on adjacent logs to keep them more or less parallel to the gable-end walls and to minimize the spaces between them.

Make a vent pipe about 6 inches square and about 6 feet long from available boards. It has to be long enough to project below the ridge pole inside the cellar and protrude 1 foot above the approximately 2 feet of soil and sods being laid on the roof. Cut a square hole, which fits the vent, through the roof poles just to one side of the ridge pole toward the end that is tucked into the slope. Reinforce the rafters with boards nailed on each side of the hole parallel to the ridge, and wedge the vent upright in the hole. Make a little wooden cap for the top of the vent to keep out the rain, and fix it on short legs so that it sits a few inches above the top of the vent.

In the downhill gable wall, cut a hole for an inner door and frame it up with boards. Make it as small as can be comfortably used, but no more than about 2 feet by 5 feet, and make a door to fit the opening. Outside this inner door, build a little porch to provide a barrier between the inner and outer doors. In particularly cold weather pack this space with hay to provide extra insulation. The shape and size of the porch can vary, but typically there is a secondary wall about 3 feet from the main gable wall, and maybe 6 feet high to accommodate an outer door about the same size as the inner one. For that size door, a wall only needs to be 4 or 5 feet wide and 6 feet tall. It can have its own short ridge pole and roof rafters or a flat roof. Either way, it will be covered by soil and sod like the principal roof.

Now lay two layers of birch rind over the roof poles, starting at the lower ends above the side walls. Overlap the pieces of rind like roof shingles, so that they shed water outside the walls rather than into the cellar. Birch rind is quite waxy, so it takes a long time to rot. It is just the thinner outer layers of bark that can be peeled off without harming the tree. Plaster the roof with 2 feet of soil and sods if possible. Use the excavated soil and sods, and bring in more from elsewhere as needed. Make sure the final layer is a thick layer of sods so that the earth roof will hold together in the rain until roots of the sods have bound it all together.

If the land is flat and a low door has not been added, a hatch in the roof is required. First reinforce the roof poles close to the gable at the opposite end to the vent. Use two or more boards about 4 feet long, one nailed close to the ridge, the other about 3 feet down the slope of the roof. Then cut a hole just over 2 feet square straight down through the roof poles, between the reinforcements, and alongside both the ridge and the interior side of the gable.

Within that hole build a sturdy box which projects just below the ridge on the inside and sticks up above the ridge on the outside by a little more than 2 feet. Fix rims at the top and bottom of this box, and make two hatches with handles to fit snugly on the rims. Now make a ladder for climbing down into the cellar after removing the hatches.

In very cold weather pack the space between the two hatches with hay for extra insulation (or old clothes if hay is not available). After opening the cellar in the winter, make sure to pack snow over the top hatch or around the outer door to keep the cold and wind out.

This structure will need repairing at intervals because it is made of wood. But it should last for 10 years, perhaps as many as 20. If stone walls would be as cheap as those built from logs, use stone to build a structure that will last longer than a wooden cellar and require less repair.

Inside the cellar make a series of wooden bins to fit the space. A useful arrangement in a typical 8 feet by 8 feet cellar is six or seven bins, with two larger than the others, which can be as wide as space allows, but no more than about 3 feet from the wall to facilitate easy reaching. Smaller bins can be about 2 feet by 2 feet. Make the bins by nailing boards to corner posts, leaving a little gap between each board. Make them about 30 inches deep, but leave the corner posts longer than that so extra boards can be slipped in to hold a larger-than-expected crop. Put a floor of boards in each bin to keep the vegetables at least a few inches off the floor. If wall space is available, put shelves to hold jars of pickles and such.

Usually a root cellar has at least two varieties of potato loose in bins. Turnips are also kept loose in bins. Both beets and carrots are sometimes loose, but often packed in sand or sawdust in one bin. Parsnips are often left in the ground over winter, but can also be loose in bins. Cabbages are trimmed and kept on trays or racks, or sometimes pulled up roots and all and planted in troughs of earth in the cellar.

Over: Possibly a Job Brothers & Company store, likely a dry goods and general merchandise store, ca. 1905. *Maritime History Archive, Memorial University, PF-315.371.*

GILLETT'S
LYE.
KOPS
FRUIT WINES
Cordials
GILLETT'S
LYE.
GILLETT'S
LYE.
GRAN. SUGAR

Chapter 3

The Community Store

The word *store* in Newfoundland means not only a private building where the necessities of life, from firewood to fishing gear, are stored (elsewhere called a shed), but also retail premises, which is how it is used here.

The community store was a common feature of both towns and outports until the second half of the 20th century, when the advance of supermarkets drove most of them out of business. However, in the period up to World War II, the store was an essential ingredient of community life. It was not just a source of supplies but also a social centre where neighbours gossiped, local affairs were discussed, and the government of the day damned or praised, according to one's politics.

An outport was small indeed if it did not have at least one or two stores, which of necessity were general stores stocking a wide range of goods, from groceries to boots to kettles. Some outports were served by trader boats that visited four or five times in the summer and fall. Bigger communities had several stores, and in St. John's and other towns they were numerous. This meant that competition was fierce and the St. John's press was full of advertisements promising the highest quality and the lowest prices—and the most convenient locations. Many retailers offered free delivery to anywhere in town.

In towns there was also more specialization, so grocery stores would not stock clothes or boots, which were carried by specialist stores. But eclectic mixtures could still be found. For example, Wood's Candy Store in St. John's advertised in 1896 not just their candy ("Our own make: Caramels, Taffies, Mixtures and Nobs. Fresh Chocolate Creams and Bon Bons") but also apples, lemons, Spanish grapes, hot lunches, tea, chocolate,

AUCTION SALE.

To-Morrow, THURSDAY, at 12 o'clock.

ON THE PREMISES OF

GOODFELLOW & Co.,

1 CASE marked triangle G., No. 155
1 ditto ditto ditto No. 155
1 Brl ditto ditto No. 146

All cont'g Confectionery.

Landed in a damaged state from on board the S.S. "Bear," Ash, Master, from Greenock; surveyed and ordered to be sold by Public Auction for the benefit of whom it may concern.

AUGUSTUS O. HAYWARD,
march14 Not. Pub.

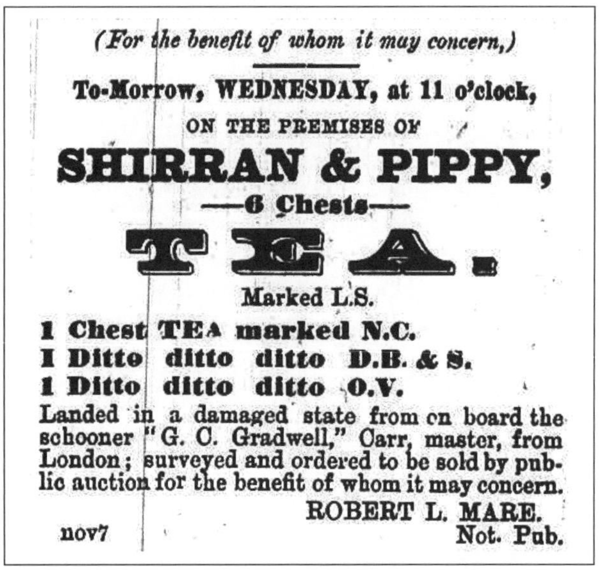

(For the benefit of whom it may concern,)

To-Morrow, WEDNESDAY, at 11 o'clock,

ON THE PREMISES OF

SHIRRAN & PIPPY,

—6 Chests—

TEA.

Marked L.S.

1 Chest TEA marked N.C.
1 Ditto ditto ditto D.B. & S.
1 Ditto ditto ditto O.V.

Landed in a damaged state from on board the schooner "G. C. Gradwell," Carr, master, from London; surveyed and ordered to be sold by public auction for the benefit of whom it may concern.

ROBERT L. MARE.
nov7 Not. Pub.

coffee, venison, beefsteaks, baked beans, cold meat, and fresh oysters.

Wholesalers were an important part of the system, and regular advertisements for bulk supplies such as barrels of flour, puncheons of molasses, and hogsheads of ale were frequent. Regular auctions of damaged or salvaged goods were held, a reflection of the perils of shipping at that time. Advertisements for these auctions were in a standardized format: the time and place, any identifying marks on the containers, a brief description of the goods, the name of the vessel concerned, the name of its master and port of origin, and finally authorization by a notary public.

Appendix 3 lists most foods mentioned in newspaper advertisements in Newfoundland before World War I, but no single store ever carried all those items at the same time.

In a small general store, regular customers had accounts and transactions were noted in large ledgers. Many merchants also bought goods from customers, everything from a firkin of damsons to the year's harvest of salt fish, and these were credited to the provider's account. If a customer was selling produce or fish to a merchant, he could walk away with goods of equivalent value—a barter system, but one based strictly on cash values.

Central to any store was a long counter where business was transacted. In an isolated location, or if stocking a schooner for a summer's fishing, whole sacks and barrels of food were purchased. But for most people most of the time, purchases were weighed on a scale on the counter. The most common scale was a beam balance: a large scooped pan at one end, a sliding weight on the beam, and counterweights added on the other end to cope with heavier items.

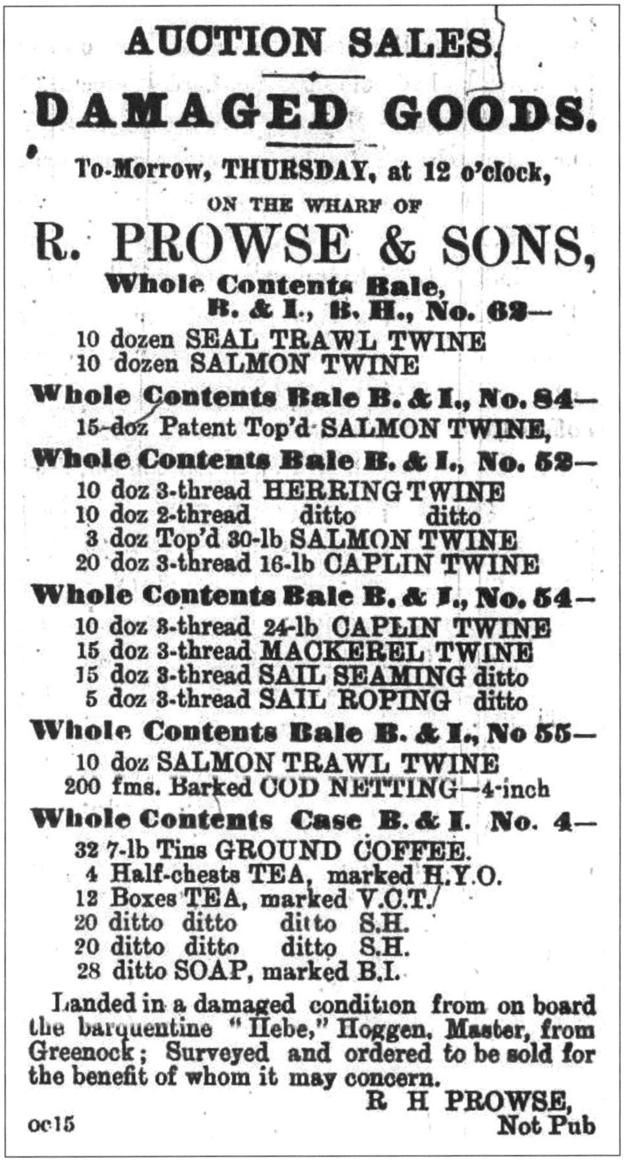

AUCTION SALES.

DAMAGED GOODS.

To-Morrow, THURSDAY, at 12 o'clock,

ON THE WHARF OF

R. PROWSE & SONS,

Whole Contents Bale,
B. & I., S. H., No. 63—
10 dozen SEAL TRAWL TWINE
10 dozen SALMON TWINE

Whole Contents Bale B. & I., No. 84—
15-doz Patent Top'd SALMON TWINE,

Whole Contents Bale B. & I., No. 52—
10 doz 3-thread HERRING TWINE
10 doz 2-thread ditto ditto
3 doz Top'd 30-lb SALMON TWINE
20 doz 3-thread 16-lb CAPLIN TWINE

Whole Contents Bale B. & I., No. 54—
10 doz 3-thread 24-lb CAPLIN TWINE
15 doz 3-thread MACKEREL TWINE
15 doz 3-thread SAIL SEAMING ditto
5 doz 3-thread SAIL ROPING ditto

Whole Contents Bale B. & I., No 55—
10 doz SALMON TRAWL TWINE
200 fms. Barked COD NETTING—4-inch

Whole Contents Case B. & I. No. 4—
32 7-lb Tins GROUND COFFEE.
4 Half-chests TEA, marked H.Y.O.
12 Boxes TEA, marked V.C.T.
20 ditto ditto ditto S.H.
20 ditto ditto ditto S.H.
28 ditto SOAP, marked B.I.

Landed in a damaged condition from on board the barquentine "Hebe," Hoggen, Master, from Greenock; Surveyed and ordered to be sold for the benefit of whom it may concern.

R H PROWSE,
oc15 Not Pub

Goods were arranged around the room: bulky items on the floor, smaller packaged goods on shelves behind the counter, and anything with a hook or a handle hung from the ceiling. A heavy object like a whole cheese would be kept handy to the scale for convenience, either on the counter itself or a side table. Cheese, affectionately called rat trap, was a staple. Pieces were cut from the block and laid on small squares of plain paper in the scale pan.

The process illustrates the widespread ritual between assistant and customer enacted many times daily for many different goods in all the stores in Newfoundland: The customer would request, for example, "about half a pound," or "a large piece," or "just a wafer." The assistant then laid the edge of a large knife on the cheese to indicate where he or she thought the cut would yield the amount requested. Then the customer, with pursed lips and quizzical eye, carefully scrutinized the position of the knife and usually asked for an adjustment. The cut was made and the portion weighed. At this juncture it was considered rather beneath one's dignity to quibble, but occasionally a customer would indicate dissatisfaction with the portion on the scale and so a part was shaved off, an extra slice added, or a whole new piece cut. Once weighed, the portion was wrapped in brown paper and tied—a ball of shop twine was a feature of all stores, the end dangling from the suspended ball, and experienced assistants expertly tied a knot and snapped the string. Metal scoops were used to fill paper bags with dry goods like rice and dried peas.

On the shelves were packaged goods such as chocolate and cocoa, tinned goods like meats, milk, and fruit, and jars of jams and preserves. Baking powder and baking soda were always present, and usually a selection of herbs and spices such as savory, thyme,

A small general store in Fortune, ca. 1950. *Archives and Special Collections Division, Memorial University, 08 03 001.*

caraway seed, pepper, nutmeg, cinnamon, cloves, turmeric, and mixed pickling spices. Small bottles of flavourings such as vanilla, lemon, ginger, and others were also regularly part of the inventory.

Much of the store was given over to bulk goods in crates, barrels, or sacks. Flour was kept close to the scale for ease of frequent purchases. Flour came in barrels containing 200 pounds, or sacks nominally holding 100 pounds but which actually contained 7 stone (98 pounds), or sacks that really did contain 100 pounds and were marked accordingly. Some stores also had a sack of brown or graham flour and, during the 1930s, sacks of dole flour (page 26). Flour sacks were made of a heavy calico, necessarily of a fine weave to hold the milled flour, with the manufacturer's name stencilled on it. These sacks were much in demand. After the seams had been unpicked, the sacks were bleached by boiling with lye, and re-sewn into underwear, shirts, blouses, and other items. One woman in Norris Point showed me her flour-sack tablecloths, soft and worn after 50 years of use, but still in fine condition.

Split yellow peas, whole dried peas, dried beans, rice, cornmeal, oatmeal, and sometimes rolled oats were kept in sacks or barrels. Table butter (real butter), cooking butter (margarine), and usually lard were kept in smaller tubs.

The molasses barrel, usually a puncheon, typically rested on the edges of two notched boards. As the barrel emptied, it was tipped by wedging boards under the rear—only those who have waited for a gallon jug to fill on a winter's day truly understand the expression "as slow as cold molasses." Molasses was typically bought by the gallon. Some customers brought jugs with them to be filled; others borrowed containers from the merchant and returned them the next time they shopped.

Larger stores often had two barrels of molasses: a dark, thick blackstrap and a lighter, fancy molasses. If the option was available, people tended to use the blackstrap for brewing beer and the lighter for cooking. Molasses sugar, widely known as lassie sugar, was the thick, sticky, partly crystalline paste left in the molasses barrel after it had yielded all it could by standing on end. The molasses sugar was scraped from the bottom of the barrel through the fill-hole with a long spoon or flat-ended stick. It was sometimes sold, but usually given away, particularly to children, to be eaten by the spoonful, or spread on a slice of buttered bread as an after-school snack widely called lassie bread.

Salt beef and salt pork were held in 200-pound barrels. Bigger stores had several barrels, each holding a different cut of meat. The salt pork might be mess pork, or heads, or jowls (see Chapter 10). There was also bologna sausage, packed in salt in wooden boxes for a long shelf life, six sausages in a box, each sausage about 8 pounds. Bologna was weighed out by the slice or portion of the whole. The empty boxes and the loose salt they contained were used for many other purposes.

Sugar came in 100-pound sacks and was weighed out to order. Mostly this was white sugar, used for general baking and jam-making. Larger stores often had brown sugar as well, used for dark cakes or anything containing molasses, or sometimes sprinkled on bread and butter for a child's snack.

Crammed between everything else were crates of currants, raisins, eggs, vegetables, imported apples and oranges, and seasonal local fruit. In places where many customers did not fish for themselves, there were also crates of salt fish.

Any general store worth the name carried everything from boots to wallpaper, including cooking and kitchen equipment. A big-ticket item like a kitchen stove was sometimes stocked by the biggest general stores, but usually had to be special-ordered from St. John's or elsewhere. But general stores had selections of smaller items: cast-iron bake-pots, frying pans, and kettles; tinware such as slope-sided dough-mixing pans and bread pans; earthenware cylindrical crocks, bean pots, and baking dishes. Enamelware was relatively cheap and very popular, so an extensive range was carried, including many sizes of kettles, teapots, saucers, plates, serving platters, mugs, saucepans with lids, large boilers with lids, pie plates, and slant-sided rimmed basins with lids. There was also an assortment of small miscellaneous items such as rolling pins, box-graters, kitchen knives, sharpening steels, and flour sifters. Many Newfoundlanders lived near a port of call of one of the coastal boats that carried passengers and freight around the island, so it was easy to order special supplies from St. John's.

Over: A domestic cooking range, manufacturer unknown, ca. 1840, with a central fire in a grate flanked by a pair of ovens. *Courtesy of Dr. P. J. Wells, by kind permission of Shane and Maire O'Dea, St. John's.*

Chapter 4

Breads

The first grist mill in North America was built in Newfoundland in John Guy's settlement at Cupids sometime between 1610 and 1613. Wheat was impossible to grow on the island, and flour mills in Newfoundland have always used imported grain. Steel-roller mills, perfected in 1834, produced flour on a modern, industrial scale, and the resulting bulk imports of cheap flour presented stiff competition for Newfoundland mills, which only survived until the end of the 19th century.

Whether they used domestically milled or imported flour, early commercial bakers in Newfoundland primarily baked unleavened, dry hard bread. The Rennie brothers in 1836 were probably the first, at their Rennie's River mill. Robert Vail found a poor market for soft (leavened) bread when he opened his first bakery on Water Street in St. John's in the early 1850s. After perfecting a method of making hard bread, Vail opened Vail's Steam Bakery, and became a wealthy man by capturing 75 per cent or more of the market. Soft bread was made domestically from the earliest days of settlement, but was not available commercially until the second half of the 19th century in St. John's and not until the 1930s in other towns, such as Grand Falls.

Steel-roller flour mills greatly simplified the process of separating the germ and bran from the rest of the grain, which made refined white flour easily available, and it soon became the popular taste. White flour and hence white bread had long been expensive, and therefore only for the rich. When the new mills made it cheap enough, white flour was quickly adopted by the poorer classes because of its association with wealth and privilege. This was reinforced by the association of whole wheat flour with hard times: during the depression of the 1930s the government became concerned with diseases of malnutrition such as beriberi. The only flour it made available to those "on the dole" (receiving relief) was a nutritious but coarse-grained whole wheat flour, known as "dole flour." This was widely disliked, and attempts to get people to embrace it were in vain. No less a person than Joey Smallwood (who later led Newfoundland into Confederation with Canada) reported favourably in 1938 on bread made with dole flour in his column "The View from Here," a regular feature in the St. John's *Daily News*.

Dole flour was disliked because it behaved differently from white flour in the kitchen, so those accustomed to putting a dozen or more white loaves on the table every week struggled to do the same with dole flour. Perhaps more importantly, it was disliked for its association with charity. To the typically self-reliant Newfoundlander, taking rations came with a certain stigma. All of which explains why most Newfoundlanders, when asked about "traditional homemade bread," talk about the warm security of Nan's kitchen and the anticipation as freshly baked fluffy white loaves with their brown tops rubbed with butter were slipped from their pans. Such bread has a certain charm when straight out of the oven and, with the lingering smell of freshly baked bread in the air, can be delicious as a vehicle for butter and a generous slather of blueberry jam.

BREAD LEAVENED WITH BARM

Any risen bread, except soda bread, needs yeast in some form. Before modern commercial yeast was available, either a sourdough starter or a by-product of brewing, like the yeast-laden foam on top of fermenting beer, was used. That foam is generally called barm, but in Newfoundland "barm" took on the particular meaning of a leavening agent based on hops. In that sense, it was the same as a sourdough starter, and kept in a barm-crock in a warm spot in the kitchen, and a portion taken out for each batch of bread.

Commercial yeast arrived in Newfoundland in the 1880s and became popular quickly because of its ease and convenience, but the habit of keeping a barm-crock persisted, an example of taste triumphing over expediency.

BARM traditional style, for leavening bread

I gleaned some details from cooks who used barm in bread-making in the 1920s and 1930s. First, dry hops were stewed in water, and then one or more of sugar, potatoes, flour, molasses, salt, and grounds or lees (the residues from beer-making) was added. Most of those ingredients were not required. Hops were not the source of wild yeasts for the barm, as some claimed, because all recipes boiled the hops, which would kill any yeasts. All that is required to start a barm is flour with wild yeast on it (organic, unbleached flour is an excellent source), and water. In the interest of historicity, however, this recipe is a traditional style starting with hops.

Always use boiled, cooled water in barm at any stage. Boiling gets rid of the chlorine in tap water, which was added to kill microbes—but you are trying to encourage them. In the initial barm starter mixture, use organic flour, which will contain wild microbe spores. Once the barm is established, unbleached white flour can be used. If you want to use hops and cannot find whole cones (bunches of female flowers shaped like cones), use pellets of dried hops available in brewing supply stores. A useful rule of thumb: 1 ounce of dried hop pellets equals 1 cup of lightly crumbled, whole, dry hop cones.

2 cups water
½ cup crumbled dry hop cones
1 tablespoon sugar
2½ cups organic flour
extra flour and cooled, boiled water

DAY 1: Simmer the dry hops in water for 5 minutes, then let the mixture cool. Strain through a cloth or fine sieve; discard the solids but keep the liquid. Dissolve the sugar in this liquid. Stir in the flour to make a batter. Cover with a cloth. Leave undisturbed at room temperature.

DAY 3: Inspect the mixture carefully. It should show signs of gentle bubbling and have a slightly sweet, yeasty smell. If it smells unpleasant or has patches of mould on the surface, discard and start again. If the mixture is good, stir in about ½ cup flour and about ¼ cup water to make a loose batter.

DAY 4: Stir in another ½ cup flour and ¼ cup water.

DAYS 5, 6, and 7: On each day, stir in about 1 cup flour and about ½ cup water.

DAY 8: This should now yield about 2 quarts of gently bubbling barm, the consistency of a thick batter. It is ready to use.

Established barm may be kept alive indefinitely by feeding it flour and water. The general aim is to feed the barm regularly while maintaining approximately the same volume. The above recipe makes enough barm to make one loaf three or four times a week, while maintaining an adequate reservoir. If barm is removed, make up the volume taken by adding flour and water (two to one by volume). To make more loaves in a week, maintain a larger reservoir of barm.

Keeping barm in a graduated vessel makes it easy to monitor the volume. If you are not making bread regularly, discard some of the barm at intervals lest it take over your kitchen. For example, every second day scoop out and discard 2 cups of barm and stir in enough flour and water (two to one by volume) to maintain the same volume. The barm can be refrigerated for extended periods, but it should be occasionally taken out of the refrigerator, and about half of the volume discarded (including any crusty, discoloured top layers). Feed it for two or three days before using or putting back in the refrigerator.

WHITE BREAD made with barm

makes 1 loaf

From start to finish this is a lengthy process, at least 18 hours. If you want to bake bread around noon, make the initial batter in the late afternoon of the previous day and let it rise during the evening. Make the dough and knead it late in the evening and let it rise in a greased bowl overnight. Next morning, give it the final brief knead, and let it rise in a loaf pan until baking it in the middle of the day.

The finished loaf is far superior to any risen with commercial yeasts. Such yeasts, like race horses, have been bred purely for speed—speed of gas generation in the case of the yeast—which makes for fast-rising, fluffy bread that can be made in less than a day. Wild yeasts, on the other hand, are slower to generate gas, but what they lack in speed, they make up for in personality—those yeasts and their symbiotic bacteria give the bread character, taste, and texture.

2 cups barm
1 cup flour
½ cup water
1 cup water
1 teaspoon salt
3 cups flour
¼ to ½ cup flour for kneading

Thoroughly mix the first three ingredients to form a batter. Cover and set aside in a warm place for 6 or more hours.

Make the dough by stirring the next three ingredients into the batter. Start by mixing in the water and salt, then portions of the flour until it becomes too stiff to stir. Turn out onto a well-floured surface and slowly knead in the rest of the flour. Knead the dough about 10 minutes, using enough extra flour to keep it from sticking. Put the dough in a greased bowl, cover with a cloth, and leave to rise for about 8 hours.

Grease a loaf pan. With floured hands, turn the risen dough out onto a floured surface and knead it a few times to smooth it out. The dough will be very sticky; use extra flour as required. Tuck the ragged edges underneath and form it into a log roughly the size of the loaf pan. Put it in the loaf pan. Cover with a cloth, and let it rise until it is above the rim of the pan, about 4 hours. Bake at 400°F for about 1 hour or until the top is well browned and the loaf sounds hollow when tapped.

BREAD LEAVENED WITH COMMERCIAL YEAST

Barm can be used to leaven any of the breads described in the yeast-leavened section below, as would have been done until the late 19th century. As a general rule, substitute 2 cups of barm for about one-third of the volume of flour called for in a one-loaf recipe and reduce the amount of fluid by about one-third. The final amounts of flour used at the kneading stage can be juggled. Bear in mind the extra time needed for barm-leavened bread.

Commercial yeast, in the form of little cakes, hit the American market in the late 1870s, arriving in Newfoundland around 1880, and from 1881 onward became the standard bread-leavener. There were many brands: Surprise Yeast Cakes, Royal Yeast Cakes, Barm Yeast Cakes, Foam Yeast Cakes, Victoria Yeast Cakes, and Jersey Cream Yeast Cakes. Granular, dry yeast did not appear until after World War II. For these yeast-risen recipes I specify modern, granular yeast because it has the same properties as the yeast cakes that arrived in the 1880s.

Loaf pans varied, but were typically about 5 by 10 inches, and 2½ inches deep. A well-used and well-seasoned loaf pan was a treasure which became perfectly non-stick with only a light greasing, and these were often handed down from generation to generation.

BASIC WHITE BREAD

makes 2 loaves

The ingredients for the basic, much-loved white bread were standard, though techniques vary.

- 3 cups milk and water mixed, about half and half
- 2 teaspoons sugar
- 3 teaspoons dry yeast
- ¼ cup butter
- 2 teaspoons salt
- 7 cups flour, plus a little extra for kneading

Gently warm 1 cup of the milk and water mixture until tepid. Dissolve the sugar into this liquid, sprinkle the yeast on top, and leave until frothy. In a separate bowl, mix the salt into about 2 cups flour and rub in the butter.

When the yeast mixture is ready, mix in the buttered flour. Stir in the rest of the milk and water; add flour gradually, until too stiff to stir with a spoon. Turn the mixture out onto a floured surface and knead in the rest of the flour. Knead about 10 minutes or until the dough is smooth and elastic, using enough extra flour to keep the dough from sticking. Put the kneaded dough into a greased bowl large enough to allow the dough to expand, cover with a cloth, and leave in a warm, draft-free place to rise for 1½ to 2 hours, or until the dough has clearly risen and is about doubled in size. Push the dough down to deflate it, fold it a few times in the bowl, then cover and leave to rise again for about the same length of time.

Divide the dough into two portions. Fold the cut edges under to make a smooth top, then place each portion in a greased loaf pan and cover with a cloth. Let rise again until the dough has risen well above the rim of the pan. Bake at 400°F for 35 minutes or until the tops are dark brown and the loaves sound hollow when tapped. Turn out on a rack to cool. Brush the tops with melted butter for an attractive glaze.

Basic white bread lends itself to many savoury and sweet variations. Savoury pork bread and pork buns are typical of the habit of including cubes of fatback pork (either raw or lightly cooked) in bread or buns as a means of packing extra calories and flavour into a basic food. Sweet variations, starting with raisin bread, follow these two savoury options. Recipes for damper bread and toutons, made from bread dough, are found in Chapter 13.

PORK BREAD

makes 1 loaf

1½ cups water
½ teaspoon sugar
1 teaspoon dry yeast
2 tablespoons rendered pork fat
1 teaspoon salt
3 cups flour, plus extra for kneading
1 cup finely diced fatback pork

Warm 1 cup of the water and dissolve the sugar in it. Sprinkle the yeast on top and leave for 10 minutes or more, until frothy. Add the pork fat to the remaining water and warm just enough to melt the fat. Set aside to cool but do not allow the fat to solidify.

When the yeast is ready, gradually stir in some of the flour and add the cooled water and fat. Stir in the cubes of fatback and then the rest of the flour. Turn out onto a lightly floured surface and knead for about 10 minutes, kneading in more flour as needed to make a smooth, elastic dough that does not stick to the surface. The little cubes of fatback tend to pop out as it is being kneaded; just poke them back into the dough.

Put the kneaded dough in a greased bowl, cover

with a cloth, and leave in a warm, draft-free place to rise for 2 hours, or until the dough has about doubled in size. Push the dough down with one hand, knead a few times in the bowl, then cover and leave to rise a second time for about another 2 hours. Grease a loaf pan. Shape the dough into a small loaf, turning the ragged edges under to leave a smooth top, and place in the loaf pan. Cover with a cloth and leave in the pan for another 2 hours or until risen well above the rim. Bake at 400°F about 35 minutes or until well browned on top. Turn out on a rack to cool.

PORK BUNS

makes 12

½ teaspoon sugar
1 cup tepid water
1 teaspoon dry yeast
1 tablespoon butter
2 cups flour, plus extra for kneading
½ teaspoon salt
½ cup finely diced fatback pork

Dissolve the sugar in the water, sprinkle the yeast on top, and leave for 10 minutes or so until it starts to froth.

Rub the butter into the flour. Add the salt and diced fatback. Add the yeast mixture, mix well, and turn out onto a floured surface. Knead the dough for about 10 minutes, kneading in extra flour as needed to make a smooth and elastic dough that does not stick to the surface. Grease the bowl with a small piece of fatback, put in the dough, cover with a cloth, and leave in a warm place to rise for 1½ to 2 hours or until about doubled in size.

Remove the dough from the bowl and give it several quick kneads. Return it to the bowl, cover with a cloth, and leave to rise until about doubled in size again. Divide the dough into 12 portions, roll each into a ball, and tuck the ragged edges underneath to make a smooth top. Lay them smooth-side up, with spaces between them, on a greased baking tray. Cover with a cloth and let rise another hour or more. Bake at 400°F for about 25 minutes or until the tops are medium brown.

Double this recipe to make another style of pork bread. Proceed exactly as above (double all the ingredients) but, instead of dividing into small rolls, divide the finished dough into three balls, and tuck these into a greased loaf pan. Let rise in the pan, then bake at 400°F for about 45 minutes or until the top is nicely browned.

RAISIN BREAD

makes 1 loaf

Raisin bread is halfway between the basic white loaf above and the full-blown sweet bread of the next recipe, but both are sweet variations of the basic white bread. This bread is excellent toasted.

1 cup milk
¼ cup sugar
2 teaspoons dry yeast
3 cups flour
½ teaspoon salt
2 cups raisins
1 tablespoon butter
1 egg

Gently heat the milk to tepid. Stir in the sugar and then the yeast, and leave in a warm place until frothy. Beat the egg and mix it into the yeast mixture. Add the butter and salt. Mix about 2½ cups flour into the yeast mixture. Stir in the raisins. Turn out onto a lightly floured surface and knead the dough for about 10 minutes, kneading in as much of the remaining flour as needed to make a smooth, elastic dough.

Grease a bowl, put the kneaded dough in, cover with a cloth, and leave in a warm, draft-free place to rise for about 2 hours, or until the dough is about doubled in size. Push the dough down with one hand, give it a few folds in the bowl, then cover again and leave to rise a second time, for about another 2 hours. Grease a loaf pan. Shape the dough into a small loaf, turning the ragged edges under to leave a smooth top, and place this in the greased pan. Let rise a third time in the pan, for about another 2 hours, or until risen well above the rim. Bake at 350°F for about 50 minutes or until well browned on top. Turn out on a rack to cool.

SWEET BREADS

Sweet breads in this context are not animal glands ("sweetbreads") but sweetened white loaves, containing raisins and/or other dried fruit, and a spice or two. They were also known as sweet raisin bread, fruit bread, or plum bread, and also as Christmas or Easter bread—although other celebratory occasions such as birthdays were often reason enough to indulge. In many parts of Newfoundland, the Christmas Eve traditional meal of salt fish was followed by slices of Christmas sweet bread, buttered or not. The rest of the sweet bread was eaten over the course of the 12 days of Christmas.

Sweet breads were typically baked in multiples, as appropriate for the size of family or the visitors expected. Leaving the yeast to ferment overnight subtly alters the flavour of the bread and allows it to last longer without spoiling than a plain white loaf.

CHRISTMAS SWEET BREAD

makes 1 loaf

1 cup water
2 teaspoons dry yeast
3 tablespoons sugar
2½ cups flour, plus ¼ to ½ cup for kneading
2 tablespoons butter
½ teaspoon salt
2 tablespoons molasses
½ teaspoon nutmeg
½ cup raisins
½ cup candied peel, chopped
½ cup candied cherries, chopped

Mix the water, sugar, and dry yeast with about 1 cup flour in a large bowl to make a smooth batter. Cover and leave it to work overnight at room temperature (traditionally, the bowl was put behind the stove in cold weather).

The next day, mix the butter, salt, nutmeg, and molasses into the yeast batter; stir in the remaining flour in batches. Mix in the raisins, peel, and cherries. Turn out onto a lightly floured surface and knead for about 10 minutes, using just enough extra flour to stop the dough from sticking to the surface. Grease a bowl, put in the kneaded dough, cover with a cloth, and leave in a warm, draft-free place to rise for about 2 hours.

Briefly knead the dough in the bowl, turn it over to present a smooth side on top, and leave to rise another 2 hours. Grease a loaf pan, lift the dough out of its bowl, and shape it roughly into the shape and size of the pan. Lay it in the pan and leave to rise another 2 hours. Bake at 350°F for about 50 to 60 minutes or until well browned on top. Turn out on a rack to cool.

WHOLE WHEAT BREAD

makes 1 loaf

Some traditional recipes for "brown" bread are simply white flour loaves with the addition of molasses to give it colour—which is not what I am talking about here. True brown bread is made with whole wheat flour, and despite the stigma of dole flour, there was always a minority of Newfoundlanders who preferred whole wheat bread, both before and after the Great Depression. Graham flour was also available, and here I treat it as a variant of whole wheat flour, and will use the latter name. Whole wheat breads were leavened with either yeast or baking soda.

2 cups milk and water (about 1 cup of each)
2 tablespoons molasses
2 teaspoons dry yeast
3 cups whole wheat flour
1½ cups white flour
1 teaspoon salt
extra flour as needed

Warm the milk, water, and molasses together to make sure the molasses dissolves completely. Let cool to no more than body temperature and then stir in the yeast and let it stand until frothy. Mix both flours and the salt into the yeast mixture to make a stiff but slightly sticky dough. Turn out onto a floured surface and knead for about 10 minutes, using a little extra flour to keep the dough from sticking to the surface. Grease a large bowl, put in the dough, cover with a cloth, and leave in a warm, draft-free place to rise for about 1 hour, or until the dough is about double in size.

Grease a loaf pan. Shape the dough into a loaf, turning the ragged edges under to leave a smooth top, and place in the greased pan. Leave to rise in the pan for about 45 to 60 minutes or until risen well above the rim, but do not let it flow over the edge. Bake at 400°F for 50 to 60 minutes or until well browned on top and pulling away from the sides of the pan. Turn out on a rack to cool.

BREAD LEAVENED WITH SODA

Sodium bicarbonate (bread soda, baking soda, or simply soda) generates carbon dioxide when mixed with an acidic liquid. The acids used in cooking are typically sour milk, vinegar, lemon juice, molasses, or cream of tartar. The reaction is quick, so bread made with baking soda has to be baked fairly soon after mixing before too much gas escapes, although the dough retains the gas bubbles to some extent. The heat of baking both accelerates the reaction between soda and acid and expands the bubbles of gas to leaven the bread. Baking powder differs from baking soda—it is still sodium bicarbonate, but ready mixed with a dry acid which releases gas when heated in the presence of liquid.

The use of soda to leaven bread was well established in Ireland by 1840 and soda bread became a fixture of the Irish diet. Baking soda was used in England about the same time. For example, Mrs. Beeton, that doyenne of 19th-century British cookery, has a recipe in her 1861 book for soda bread, with no hint that it was a novel idea. Her basic recipe used milk, which is not sufficiently acidic to activate the sodium bicarbonate, so she added cream of tartar (tartaric acid) to release the carbon dioxide, just as in some early baking powders. Irish and English settlers in Newfoundland of that period brought the soda bread habit with them; plenty of records exist of retail trade in bread soda from the second half of the 19th century. Soda breads were alive and well in the 20th century but masquerading under different names, such as quick breads or no-yeast breads. As baking powder became popular, many of these soda-leavened breads became baking powder breads. But there was a long transition period during which people used both soda and baking powder, a classic case of hedging one's bets when faced with new technology, just as early steam ships still had masts for sails—just in case. For bread, either the soda with an acidic ingredient or the baking powder would leaven efficiently, but many such hybrid recipes persist to the present day.

Some bakers used a mixture of whole wheat and white flour for soda bread, from about half to two-thirds whole wheat; this mixture makes a superior bread. Slashing the loaf is important because it controls where the loaf will expand. An uncut loaf can blow out in unpredictable ways as it expands and ruin the looks of the loaf and how it finishes baking.

Traditionally soda bread was made with sour milk, all too common in pre-refrigeration days, or with buttermilk. In the 21st century, commercial buttermilk is rarely acidic enough to make the soda work properly. Modern homogenized and pasteurized milk does not go gracefully sour—instead, add 2 teaspoons of lemon juice or vinegar to 1 cup of milk.

SODA BREAD

makes 1 loaf

2 cups flour
extra flour, about ½ cup
1 teaspoon baking soda
½ teaspoon salt
1 cup sour milk

Mix the salt and soda, then mix thoroughly with 2 cups flour. Stir in the sour milk to make a wet paste. Mix in extra flour to make it just dry enough to handle and roll into a ball. Place the dough in a greased iron pot (or on a greased baking sheet) and slash a cross deeply into the top with a sharp knife. Bake at 400°F for 35 to 45 minutes or until well browned.

QUICK CURRANT BREAD

makes 1 loaf

¾ cup sugar
2 tablespoons butter
¾ teaspoon salt
1 egg
1½ cups water
4 cups flour, plus more if needed
2 cups currants
3 teaspoons baking powder
1 teaspoon baking soda

Mix the butter and sugar, then beat in the egg and salt. Mix in the water and about 2 cups flour. Sprinkle the soda and baking powder over the mixture, and stir in the rest of the flour to make a dough. Stir in the currants, and place in a greased loaf pan. Bake at 350°F for 60 to 70 minutes or until well risen and browned on top.

CORNMEAL

Early 17th-century settlers in America adopted the Native Americans' grain and initially called it Indian corn to distinguish it from their European grains. When ground, it was naturally called Indian corn meal, rapidly shortened to simply cornmeal or Indian meal. Here I will call it all cornmeal.

Cornmeal was an early import to Newfoundland and became a minor staple in the diet, as witnessed by the dole ration of the 1930s—unlikely to include any extras—which included 2 pounds of cornmeal per adult per month.

Bread made with cornmeal alone won't rise; corn lacks gluten, which is what traps the gas bubbles to make it rise, so the very first corn breads of America were unleavened. Soon, on both sides of the Atlantic, people began mixing in wheat flour, which provided enough gluten to enable rising. For example, Boston brown bread, typically rye and wheat flours with some cornmeal, was made by the Puritans in New England, and from the middle of the 19th century the Irish baked corn bread containing a proportion of wheat flour. Newfoundland most likely picked up corn bread from its Irish connection.

Early corn breads used baking soda. The Puritans used molasses as the necessary acid, and the Irish sour milk or buttermilk. But when baking powder arrived, molasses or any form of milk could be dispensed with.

CORN BREAD

makes 1 small loaf

This is by no means a fluffy bread, but it has a pleasingly dense texture, if somewhat crumbly—and delicious with a little butter and jam.

2 cups cornmeal
2 cups white flour
1 teaspoon salt
6 teaspoons baking powder
2 tablespoons sugar
1¼ cups water

Thoroughly mix together the cornmeal, flour, salt, sugar, and baking powder. Stir in the water, adding a little more if necessary to make a loose but manageable dough. Grease a loaf pan, put in the dough, and bake at 350°F for 50 to 60 minutes or until the top is lightly browned.

HARD BREAD

Hard bread in Newfoundland is a species of unleavened bread, and so ubiquitous in the 19th and early 20th centuries it was simply called "bread." Hard bread was also known as ship's biscuit, hard biscuit, and hard tack, among other names.

Hard bread is perhaps the most striking anachronistic culinary survivor in Newfoundland. Ever since sailors ventured away from the coast, provisions at sea were modelled on staple foods on land, and bread was an obvious candidate for western seafarers. But leavened bread goes mouldy quickly, and the logistics of bread baking in ovens with large fuel demands generally meant that fresh bread was not baked at sea. Methods of drying bread or bread dough to the point where it would keep indefinitely—or at least until it got damp or ridden with insects—were developed.

Before the 1850s, huge quantities of hard bread were imported, mostly from England and Germany, especially from Hamburg (many records simply called it Hamburg bread). Local production started in 1835 at Rennie's Mill in St. John's, and most of the market for hard bread was captured by local manufacturers before the end of that century. One of the larger manufacturers, Browning Harvey, stopped making hard bread in the early 1960s, and in 2017, the sole surviving local manufacturer is Purity Factories. The company opened in the 1930s, and its hard bread is widely available in supermarkets and corner stores, with significant local demand. A 2010 industrial dispute at the factory caused much local consternation: bags of hard bread were hoarded, prices soared, other commercial bakers threatened to make their own versions, and there was a flurry of interest in how to make it at home. The natural order of things was only restored when the strike was settled and Purity hard bread was back on the shelves. Hard bread has survived from a time when it was a necessary part of seafaring life and is retained not out of necessity but from a love of its distinctive taste and texture.

Before it can be eaten, hard bread is almost always soaked and usually cooked, at which point it becomes *brewis*, which in Newfoundland rhymes with *bruise*, although variants can be heard. The word comes from Middle English, and by the early 16th century one of its meanings was a broth thickened with meal or bread. The word survived in general use until the end of the 19th century. For example, Fanny Farmer, the most famous 19th-century American cookery writer, gave a recipe in 1896 for brewis: equal parts stale white and brown bread covered with equal parts of milk and water, cooked until soft with butter and salt added to taste. The word *brewis* survives only in Newfoundland and Labrador and some parts of Britain; elsewhere it is obsolete.

At least two grades of hard bread were available for purchase: if No.1, the best unblemished bread, was beyond a person's budget, No. 2 might be an option. If even that was too expensive, broken pieces from the bottom of the bag would be sold for almost nothing or given away. Some Newfoundlanders made hard bread at home, in times when they had more flour than cash.

For casual use, hard bread might be carried, unsoaked, on berry-picking trips, and then dipped into a mug of tea and slowly gnawed as the edges softened. But the principal use at home was as a starchy accompaniment to a smaller amount of more expensive food, as one might use potatoes. In this chapter are several recipes which only have the brewis in common. For recipes with fish and hard bread, see Chapter 6.

HARD BREAD

makes 6 cakes

This is a domestic formula and may be different from industrial methods used in bulk production. The main idea is to make a dough as stiff as possible. Aim for getting the full amount of flour into the dough (or more if possible), but I gave up just short of that. The pricking all over is supposed to help release the moisture from the dough; this may or may not be necessary, but it does make the finished breads look like store-bought hard bread.

1 cup water
2½ cups flour
¾ teaspoon salt

Mix about 2 cups flour with the salt and water into a stiff dough. Turn out onto a floured surface and knead in as much of the remaining flour as possible. Make as stiff a dough as possible. Roll out into a circle about ½ inch thick and cut into six wedges. Prick all over with the point of a small knife, skewer, or sliver of wood. Place on an ungreased baking sheet and bake at 300°F to 350°F for 2 hours, or until the breads are lightly browned. At this point they are still not totally dry, so store them in a warm dry place for several days or a week until they are. When properly dried, hard bread will keep indefinitely if kept dry and away from insects.

BREWIS and SCRUNCHIONS

serves 4

Brewis and scrunchions was typically eaten for breakfast, and any leftovers would make a nice snack or bedtime lunch. A common variation on this recipe is to use a little sugar and perhaps a pat of butter instead of the molasses.

4 cakes hard bread
1 cup cubed fatback pork
salt and pepper
molasses to taste

Soak the hard bread in water overnight. Drain well. Fry the fatback to make rendered fat and scrunchions (page 121). Put this fat in a large frying pan, add the bread, and fry on medium heat for about 10 minutes. Sprinkle generously with salt and pepper, and turn the mixture over frequently to heat through. Chop up any big pieces with a spoon—no pieces should be more than about 1 inch square. After about 10 minutes, or when the bread is well heated and starting to brown on the bottom, add the reserved scrunchions and mix well. Serve with molasses.

BREWIS and BACON

serves 4

Another brewis dish typically eaten for breakfast.

4 cakes hard bread
8 slices bacon (about ½ pound), in 1-inch pieces

Soak the hard bread in water overnight. Drain well. Fry the bacon on low to medium heat until the fat has rendered and the bacon has crisped. Add the bread; cook together to thoroughly heat through. Break up any big pieces of bread with a spoon. Serve with molasses if desired.

BREWIS with MEAT and GRAVY

serves 4

A good way of making another meal out of leftovers was brewis with meat and gravy.

4 cakes hard bread
2 medium onions, chopped
2 cups leftover meat, cut in small pieces
leftover gravy
4 tablespoons rendered pork fat

Soak the hard bread in water overnight. Drain the soaked bread, cover with fresh water, and bring to a boil. Cook 2 or 3 minutes, drain well. Fry the onions gently in the pork fat for 5 or 10 minutes or until cooked. Add the bread and fry gently until it is hot, chopping with a spoon to ensure that the bread pieces are about the same size as the meat. Add the meat and any leftover gravy and fry until the meat is hot. If the gravy is thick and the mixture starts to stick, add a little hot water.

STEAK and BREWIS

serves 4

Steak and brewis was never everyday food—most people ate it only when fresh beef was available. For wealthier folks it was sometimes the preferred Sunday breakfast.

Steak and brewis was sometimes on the menu in the dining car of The Newfoundland Railway during its heyday. This might have reflected the "special occasion" nature of this meal for some on board the train, for it was not just the affluent who would eat in the dining car.

4 cakes hard bread
2 onions, chopped
½ cup fatback pork cubes
4 beefsteaks

Soak the hard bread in water overnight. Drain, then bring to a boil in salted water and simmer for 4 to 5 minutes. Drain. Fry fatback to make rendered fat and scrunchions (page 121). Fry the onions in the fat. When the onions are soft and golden, add the bread and fry on a low heat for about 10 minutes, breaking up any lumps. Add the scrunchions.

Cook the steaks according to individual preference. If they are fried, use a little of the rendered fat. If roasted, do so ahead of time and keep warm.

To serve, put a portion of the brewis and onion mixture on each plate with a steak.

BREWIS and CHEESE

serves 4

Brewis and cheese was an interesting variation on toasted bread and cheese. It is far from fancy food, but it likely had great appeal to someone who had worked outdoors all day on short food rations.

6 cakes hard bread (about 1 pound)
3 cups grated cheddar or other hard cheese
1 onion, finely chopped
salt and pepper

Soak the hard bread in water overnight, then drain it well and squeeze gently to get the excess water out. Layer about half the bread in the bottom of a greased 9 by 9-inch pan. Break up any large pieces of bread so that no lump is bigger than about 1 inch square. Sprinkle with about half the onion, and salt and pepper, then lay about half the grated cheese on top of the onion. Repeat this layering with the remaining ingredients, ending with a layer of cheese. Bake at 350°F for 1 hour or more, until the cheese has melted and the edges of the top layer of brewis are browned and crisp.

Serve with pickles.

Over: A kitchen in Pool's Island, Bonavista Bay, 1939. *The Rooms Provincial Archives Division, VA 14-18.*

Chapter 5

Soups and Dumplings

■ SOUPS

Newfoundland cooks made a limited range of soups. Pea soup was the favourite and the only one considered suitable as a main meal. Meat-and-vegetable soups, made from beef or mutton or game, according to season and circumstance, were usually considered a supper dish or an occasional snack. A few others, such as clam or mushroom soup, were made by a small number of households. All soups were served with bread and butter. The recipes in this chapter are listed alphabetically and do not reflect the order of popularity.

BEEF BONE SOUP

serves 10

Beef bones with varying amounts of meat on them were available when cattle were slaughtered in the fall; if a community was big enough to support a full-time butcher, beef bones might be available year-round. Bones were prized for making soup. Recipes were necessarily flexible, but all followed the general pattern of simmering the bones before cooking vegetables in the resulting broth. Bones from any other animal can be made into soup in the same fashion. Lamb- or mutton-, and later moose-, bone soup was popular.

- about 3 gallons mixed beef bones, with as much meat on as possible (about 10 pounds)
- 2 onions, chopped
- ½ cup pot barley
- 5 carrots, diced
- 5 potatoes, diced
- 3 parsnips, diced
- salt

Cut any significant amount of meat off the bones and reserve. Cover the bones with water in a large stockpot, bring to a boil and let simmer all day on a low heat. Top up with boiling water every few hours as necessary.

Strain off the broth and put in a cool place overnight or until the fat sets hard. Remove the solid fat, which can be kept and used as lard. Bring the broth back to a boil and add salt to taste. Cut any reserved meat into small pieces and simmer in the broth with the onion for 1 hour or more. Then add the barley, carrots, potatoes, and parsnips and simmer 30 minutes or so. Salt to taste. Dumplings can be cooked in this soup.

CHICKEN and VEGETABLE SOUP

serves 4 to 6

The bones of roast birds were made into soups in the same fashion as meat bones. The choice and quantity of vegetables were always flexible. Some people added potatoes, others parsnip. Dumplings could stretch a limited pot of soup.

- 1 chicken carcass, with as much meat left on it as possible
- about 2 quarts water
- any leftover stuffing
- 1 onion
- 1 carrot
- ½ turnip
- salt and pepper

Break up the leftover chicken carcass into large chunks, cutting off all scraps of meat. Chop and reserve the chicken. Cover the carcass with water in a large saucepan, bring to a boil, then simmer 3 or 4 hours until the bones fall apart. Strain off the liquid and discard the bones. Put the liquid back in the pot and add the vegetables. Chop up the stuffing and add to the pot. Bring to a boil and simmer about 1 hour or until the vegetables are totally cooked. Add the chicken, and salt and pepper to taste.

CLAM SOUP

serves 4 to 6

Clams, found around the island, are easily dug up at low tide (see Chapter 8). If not enough were gathered for a main meal, then soup was the answer. This recipe illustrates the frugal use of crumbs of hard bread, always found at the bottom of a bread bag. Provided they are pre-soaked or cooked long enough to soften them, hard bread crumbs can be used anywhere that regular bread crumbs might be used. If you don't have a bag of hard bread with copious crumbs at the bottom, fold a cake of hard bread in an old cloth and pound it with a rolling pin. The chunks should be smaller than a small bean.

2 tablespoons rendered pork fat or butter
1 onion, chopped
1 potato, in ½-inch chunks
1 cup cooked clams, out of the shell
¾ teaspoon salt
¼ teaspoon pepper
¼ teaspoon dried thyme
1½ cups water
¼ cup hard bread crumbs
1½ cups milk

Put the pork fat, onion, potato, clams, salt, pepper, and thyme in a medium saucepan; add just enough water to cover. Bring to a boil and simmer about 15 minutes or until the potatoes are cooked. Add the crumbs and simmer 10 to 15 minutes or until the largest crumbs are soft. Add milk and simmer another 5 minutes.

MUSHROOM SOUP

serves 4 to 6

A few people picked wild mushrooms, traditionally only the white field mushroom with pink to brown gills. There was a firmly entrenched belief that if they peeled easily they were safe to eat. I cannot emphasize strongly enough how erroneous and potentially deadly this belief was and is. Have all mushrooms verified by an expert—Newfoundland has poisonous lookalikes.

4 cups chopped wild meadow mushrooms
1 onion, chopped fine
2 tablespoons butter
3 tablespoons flour
3 cups milk
½ teaspoon salt
pepper

Fry the onion and s in the butter on a low heat until the onion is soft and the mushrooms have released all their juices. Stir in the flour slowly to make a smooth paste. Add the milk and salt. Bring to a boil and simmer for 10 or 15 minutes. Sprinkle with pepper and serve.

OYSTER SOUP

serves 4

Oysters were popular, at least in urban areas, in the 19th century and the beginning of the 20th, even though they are not native to Newfoundland (see Chapter 8). Oyster soup was popular enough to make it into the 1905 cookbook, but it fell out of favour—or oysters became too expensive—because the 1928 cookbook contains only a recipe for Mock Oyster Soup, a mixture of potatoes and cabbage stewed in milk, strained, and drunk as a thin soup.

2 cups oyster meat, out of the shell
1 cup water
2 cups milk
2 tablespoons butter
salt and pepper
2 slices bread, toasted and buttered

Strain the oysters to separate the liquid from the meat. Reserve the meat. Mix the liquid and water and bring to a boil. Add the milk, butter, salt, and pepper. Simmer for 5 minutes, then add the meat and simmer another 5 minutes. Divide the soup between bowls. Cut the toasted, buttered bread into squares and divide these between the bowls of soup.

PEA SOUP

serves 8

Newfoundland pea soup was primarily made from dried yellow split peas, and although an iconic Newfoundland food, variations are found across the rest of North America and much of Europe. Before refrigeration, dried peas were an ideal standby food, and perfect as ship's supplies as long as they were kept dry.

Both yellow and green dried peas were available whole or split, and soup was made from all four types. Split yellow peas were almost always available, and so most frequently used, primarily for soup but also as pease pudding (page 123). Split green peas were also used in soup, and whole green peas often used as a cooked vegetable with main meals. Any of the dried peas, split or whole, can be substituted for the split yellow. Split peas can be cooked without soaking; add an extra 30 minutes or so to the cooking time. Whole peas need soaking overnight or will need to be cooked for hours to get them soft.

Meat was usually added to pea soup for flavouring. Salt beef was most often used (and is listed in the recipe below). Salt pork was treated the same way as beef. Salt pork tongues are very lean, so less than the amount specified was used. They were soaked in a similar fashion and trimmed carefully after the initial simmering. A ham bone, from which a few scraps of ham have been carved, was a great substitute, though a rare treat in most households. Traditionally pea soup was served with dumplings.

2 cups dried split yellow peas (about 1 pound)
1 medium-sized piece of salt beef
(about 1 to 1½ pounds)
1 onion, chopped
1 potato, chopped
1 carrot, chopped
1 parsnip, chopped
½ turnip, chopped
salt to taste

Soak the salt beef in water overnight, changing the water two or three times. Soak the peas separately in water overnight (there is no need to change the water on the peas).

Bring the soaked beef to a boil in about 3 quarts water and simmer 3 hours. Remove the beef and leave until cool enough to handle. When it is, remove and discard the bone, gristle, and most of the fat (some of the fat can be kept, according to taste). Chop the beef and any fat into small dice and return to the pot.

Drain the peas and discard the soaking water. Put the peas in the beef pot and bring to a boil. Add the onion and simmer for about 1 hour. Add the other vegetables and simmer 30 minutes or until tender. Taste and add salt as desired. Thin the soup with extra water as needed.

If cooled and reheated another day, the soup will be quite thick. Heat gently and add water as needed, stirring frequently.

RABBIT SOUP

serves 4 to 6

Rabbits were usually made into stews and pies (see Chapter 11), but rabbit rib cages had so little meat that they were usually reserved for soup. Sometimes the heads also went in the soup pot, although many people liked them in a stew. The components of rabbit soup entirely depended on availability and usually consisted of one or more whole rabbits with an assortment of rabbit parts.

1 rabbit, plus rib cages of other rabbits,
plus heads (about 2 pounds total)
water to cover
1 onion, chopped
2 carrots, chopped
2 potatoes, chopped
salt and pepper

Cut the rabbit into pieces (4 legs, loin, rib cage, and head), place in a large stockpot, and just cover with water. Add the onion, bring to a boil, and simmer for 1 to 2 hours or until the meat is starting to fall off the bones. Remove the rabbit pieces from the stockpot and pick all the meat from the bones. Discard the bones. Coarsely chop the meat and put it back in the stockpot. Add the carrots and potatoes. Simmer 30 minutes or until the vegetables are tender.

Serve with dumplings or additional vegetables if desired.

SEAL SOUP

serves 4 to 6

Seal soup was made in the same fashion as beef-bone soup. Any part of the seal was used, but as for rabbits, seal ribs were particularly favoured because, with so little meat, they had less value in a stew. Usually seal ribs have very little fat, but if another part of the seal is used, pick off as much fat as you can before simmering, and then skim off as much as you can before adding the vegetables.

1 ½ to 2 gallons seal ribs or other parts (about 4 or 5 pounds)
4 or 5 quarts water
2 or 3 onions, chopped
3 or 4 carrots, chopped
1 turnip, chopped
salt and pepper

Wash the pieces of seal well, and place them with the onions and water in a pot big enough to hold them with lots of headroom so that it will not easily boil over. Bring to a boil and simmer for 2 to 3 hours, or until the meat is falling off the bones.

Lift out all the pieces of seal. When cool enough to handle, remove and discard the bones and gristle. Coarsely chop the meat and return to the pot. Add the carrot and turnip. Bring back to a boil and simmer for 30 minutes or until the vegetables are tender. Add salt and pepper to taste.

Dumplings were usually served with this soup. Add balls of dumpling dough 5 to 10 minutes (according to size) before serving the soup. In addition to carrots and turnip, potatoes were often added to this soup.

DUMPLINGS AND DOUGHBOYS

Both of these names were used in Newfoundland, but both are of uncertain origin. *Dumplings* appeared early in the 17th century, and *doughboys* was in use by the late 18th century, long before it was applied to American soldiers in World War I. The idea that it is a corruption of dough-buoy is appealing, because a ball of dough bobbing in the soup certainly resembles a buoy, but this seems without foundation. Some say a doughboy is a hard or tough dumpling, or one made without any fat, but this usage does not seem widespread. In this book the two words are treated as entirely interchangeable, except when dumpling is applied to sweet steamed puddings containing dried fruit.

Before the arrival of baking powder in the 1880s, dumplings were made from pieces of yeast-risen dough, as they still are in parts of Britain. Since then, making dumplings with baking powder has been standard in Newfoundland. Dumplings are often used as fillers in soups and stews, but when made with a careful hand they are wonderful comfort food.

Recipes were broadly similar but differ in details such as whether to include fat. Dumplings with fat were more popular, and butter, pork fat, or suet could be used. Suet, the hard fat from around the kidneys of animals, gives food a rich, savoury but slightly sweet taste, particularly suited to dumplings and steamed puddings. Other variations included the use of milk or water (or both), and the quantities of sugar and salt.

Most cooks simply dropped the dumpling dough into the simmering pot, clapped on the lid, and left it. The timing is important: too long in the pot and dumplings become soggy. For the simmering times given here, I think the shorter is always better, although the longer may be more traditional.

DUMPLINGS without any fat

makes 8 to 16 or more

1 cup flour, plus extra for dusting
2 teaspoons sugar
2 teaspoons baking powder
¼ teaspoon salt
½ cup water

Mix the flour, sugar, baking powder, and salt. Stir in enough (or all) of the water to make a sticky dough. Turn out onto a floured surface, using just enough extra flour to prevent it from sticking. Divide the dough into 8, 12, 16, or even 32 portions, but make them all the same size. Roll each portion into a ball. Toward the end of the cooking time of the soup or stew, drop in the balls and cover.

Eight dumplings will take 8 to 10 minutes; 12, 6 to 8 minutes; 16, 4 to 6 minutes; and 32, 3 to 5 minutes.

DUMPLINGS with some fat

makes 8 to 16 or more

1 cup flour, plus extra for dusting
1½ teaspoons baking powder
½ teaspoon salt
1 tablespoon rendered pork fat or butter
½ cup water

Mix the flour, baking powder, and salt. Rub in the fat until no lumps remain. Stir in enough (or all) of the water to make a sticky dough. Turn out onto a floured surface, using just enough extra flour to prevent it from sticking. Proceed as above.

SUET DUMPLINGS

makes 8 to 16 or more

- 1 cup flour, plus extra for dusting
- 1½ teaspoons baking powder
- ½ teaspoon salt
- 1 cup finely shredded suet
- ½ cup water

Mix the flour, baking powder, and salt. Rub in the suet until no lumps remain. Stir in enough (or all) of the water to make a sticky dough. Turn out onto a floured surface, using just enough extra flour to prevent it from sticking. Proceed as above.

DUMPLING as pie topping

plenty for one 9-inch round pie

A dumpling dough was also used to make a paste topping for savoury pies, much akin to what is called a biscuit topping in the United States.

- 2 cups flour
- 2 tablespoons butter
- ¾ teaspoon salt
- ½ teaspoon sugar
- 3 teaspoons baking powder
- 1 cup milk

Mix the flour, salt, sugar, and baking powder. Melt the butter and stir into the milk. Stir the liquid into the flour to make a smooth, thick paste. Turn out onto a floured surface and roll it out to fit the pie dish, dusting with extra flour as needed to stop it from sticking.

Over: A man cutting codfish on a barrow on the St. John's harbourfront in 1939, with the usual crowd of onlookers. *The Rooms Provincial Archives Division, VA 14-57.*

Chapter 6

COD

Cod created Newfoundland, or at least the European version of the last half millennium. It was the pursuit of codfish that created a way of life and pattern of settlement that for centuries defined what it meant to be a Newfoundlander. St. John's residents, many never having caught a codfish in their lives, still see the outport way of life as quintessential Newfoundland: self-reliant people engaged in a mixed economy based on the seasonal cycles of fishing, gardening, and wood-cutting.

Because cod was so central, it was simply referred to as "fish," a habit that persists to this day (apparently contradictory phrases like "we have no fish, but we've got lots of halibut" are still heard). Similarly, "salt fish" means salt cod; any other species will be named, such as salt turbot or salt herring. This use of the term *salt fish* spread to Britain sometime before the mid-19th century, presumably because of the extensive trade in this commodity with Newfoundland.

For people who made a living from fishing, salt fish was the product they made and sold. Cod for salt fish were headed, gutted, and split. Splitting was the removing of just that part of the back bone (the sound bone) above the belly cavity, and then cutting the flesh open down to the tail, with a special splitting knife—short, square-ended, and very sharp. The fish were then splayed open in a kite shape, stored in excess salt for a time, rinsed, and dried in the open air on platforms of branches (flakes). The quality of the finished product depended on the care taken when splitting the fish, the time spent in salt, and the degree of drying. Eventually the salt fish was sold to a merchant, and arguments on the wharf were frequent when fishermen and merchants

Fishermen sold salt cod to a merchant or his agent, who sorted (left) and weighed (background) it, as seen here at Port au Choix, ca. 1913–1915. *Archives and Special Collections Division, Memorial University, 1.01.148.*

disagreed over the quality of the merchandise being bought and sold.

The merchant sorted salt fish into grades and shipped it to customers either in large rectangular boxes or pressed into casks. In smaller businesses, the pressing was often done by hand, the salt fish pounded into casks with a 28-pound weight from the weigh-scale. In more technically sophisticated premises, a fish-screw, a plunger on the end of a stout, threaded post, would be turned by hand to slowly compress the salt fish into a cask. Bulk salt fish was measured in quintals of 112 pounds. Shipping casks typically held 2½ or 5 quintals (280 to 560 pounds). The principal markets for Newfoundland salt fish shifted according to the vagaries of politics, but were primarily Europe (Spain, Portugal, France, Britain), the West Indies, and Brazil. The two-way trade with the West Indies created a taste for salt fish in the Caribbean, and Newfoundland's thirst for rum.

Both fresh and salt fish were fixtures in the kitchens of Newfoundland. Fresh fish was enjoyed in season, and every part of the fish was used. Heads, cheeks, tongues, sounds, britches, and hearts, among other parts, were all prepared by Newfoundland cooks. Salt fish was a reliable food for the winter, and most families salted their own in the fall. Fish for personal use were carefully treated and then salted and dried according to individual preferences. Rounders or leggies (fish too small to be worth splitting) were simply headed, gutted, and then salted whole for domestic use.

FRESH FISH

During the commercial fishing season, fresh fish was regularly eaten domestically, particularly as fish stew and as pan-fried fillets. The scrunchions mentioned below and elsewhere are the small crisp bits left after the fat has been rendered from salt fatback (page 121).

PAN-FRIED FISH FILLETS

serves 4

Most cooks had their own variations on the deceptively simple pan-fried fish, but they all agreed that if the fish was very fresh, as in straight out of the water, then the skin must be left on to prevent the fillet from falling apart in the pan. With the skin on, fry the fish skin-side up first, so that after being turned over, it will lift cleanly from the pan skin-side down.

4 medium fillets of fresh fish, skin on, size according to appetite
1 cup small cubes fatback pork
flour, salt, and pepper

Fry the fatback to make rendered fat and scrunchions. Dry the fillets and dust with flour, salt, and pepper. Fry them in the fat, about 5 or more minutes per side or until cooked through. Serve with 1 teaspoon scrunchions scattered over each portion.

Serve with potatoes and vegetables.

FISH STEW

serves 4 to 6

4 medium fillets of fresh fish, skin off
3 or 4 potatoes, chunked
½ cup small cubes fatback pork
salt and pepper

Fry the fatback to make rendered fat and scrunchions. Mix the potatoes with the fat and place in a medium saucepan. Add salt and pepper and enough water to just cover the potatoes. Bring to a boil, cover, and simmer about 15 minutes. Lay the fillets on top of the potatoes but do not add any extra water. Cover and simmer another 30 minutes.

Serve portions of fish, each with potatoes and cooking liquid, and a few scrunchions sprinkled on top. Eat with bread and butter or with vegetables on the side.

BOILED FISH

serves 4 to 6

For many, boiled fish was the best way to enjoy the taste of very fresh fish, unobstructed by any other flavours except salt, pepper, and butter. There is little point in making this unless the fish is straight from the water. Ideally, use only the loins of the fillet (the thicker end toward the head) because they are all about the same thickness and will all cook in about the same time. Keep the thinner tail-end pieces for pan frying. Leave the skin on the fillet to help keep it from falling apart as you lift it from the poaching water.

4 or more loin-ends of fillet, skin on
water
salt
butter

Half fill a wide pan with water and bring to a boil. Salt the water generously (more than you would for cooking vegetables). Place the fillets in the boiling water and turn down the heat so that the water is no longer boiling. Let them cook for 15 minutes or so, according to thickness.

Serve with butter on each portion.

SALT FISH

Salt fish was a reliable year-round mainstay of the Newfoundland kitchen, but particularly important in the winter months. It was always soaked before use, although some people claimed to like chewing on unsoaked salt fish—unspeakably salty for most. Soaking was typically done overnight, or a thicker piece of fish could be left for 24 hours. The water was changed several times. Then the cod was "boiled"—or, more accurately, simmered very gently, for 10 to 20 minutes, depending on its thickness.

An experienced cook knows at a glance how many people a particular piece of salt fish will serve, but a novice is totally baffled. As a rough guide, a whole, unsoaked salt fish or piece of a large one will yield about half its weight in cooked salt fish with bones, skin, and fins removed. More was usually cooked

Bay de Verde in the 1930s. *The Rooms Provincial Archives Division, VA 15a-14.1.*

than immediately needed because leftovers were useful for lunch or fishcakes, for example. Cooked salt fish was usually served plain with at most a little melted pork fat, with a sauce of some kind, or made into fishcakes.

Many salt fish dishes were called simply "salt fish and potatoes." The potatoes were not necessarily boiled; fried potatoes were widely enjoyed, as were fried onions. Scrunchions were popular, but some cooks preferred just a little melted fat to moisten the fish and potatoes.

PLAIN SALT FISH with pork fat

serves 4

1 or more pieces of salt fish (about 2 pounds unsoaked)
1 cup cubed fatback pork

Soak the salt fish overnight or for 24 hours if it is thick or a less salty fish is desired. Change the water several times. Fry the fatback to make rendered fat and scrunchions. Simmer the fish for about 15 minutes. Remove from the water, drain, and when just cool enough to handle, remove the fins, bones, and skin. Put a portion of the fish on each plate, and drizzle 1 tablespoon or more of the fat and scrunchions over it.

Serve with plain boiled potatoes.

SALT FISH with drawn butter

serves 4

1 or more pieces of salt fish (about 2 pounds unsoaked)
1 recipe of drawn butter (page 255)

Soak the salt fish overnight or for 24 hours if it is thick or a less salty fish is desired. Change the water several times. Make drawn butter and keep it warm. Boil the fish for about 15 minutes. Take it from the water, drain, then when just cool enough to handle, remove the fins, bones, and skin. Put a portion of the fish on each plate.

Serve with potatoes. Pour a little drawn butter over the fish, or over the fish and potatoes, according to preference.

SALT FISH with parsnips and egg sauce

serves 4

Many people have never heard of the combination of fish, egg sauce, and parsnips, but it has a respectable history. Mrs. Beeton, in her 1861 *Book of Household Management*, gave a recipe for salt fish served with egg sauce and parsnips, so in her honour I describe a similar dish from Newfoundland.

1 or more pieces of salt fish
(about 2 pounds unsoaked)
1 recipe of egg sauce (page 261)
8 to 10 parsnips, peeled

Soak the salt fish overnight or for 24 hours if it is thick or a less salty fish is desired. Change the water several times. Make the egg sauce and keep warm. Cook the parsnips and keep warm. Simmer the fish for about 15 minutes. Remove the fish from the water, drain, and when just cool enough to handle, pick out the fins, bones, and skin.

Pour a little egg sauce over portions of the fish and parsnips, and serve with potatoes.

FISHCAKES

makes 12

Fishcakes are patties of cooked, shredded salt fish mixed with cooked, mashed potato. Usually they were made from leftovers, although it is worthwhile cooking potatoes and salt fish just to make fishcakes.

The proportion of fish to potato varies by taste, a little more fish than potato is preferred by some, the reverse by others. People were also divided about the inclusion of onion—should it be in a fishcake or not, and if it should, was it best added raw or precooked? For me, fishcakes must incorporate onion, and I prefer it precooked. Add raw onion only if chopped very finely and if the fishcakes are cooked long enough to cook the onion.

In some places in Newfoundland, particularly on the eastern side, cooked parsnip was added. To try this variation, substitute 1 cup coarsely mashed parsnip for 1 cup potato in this recipe.

3 cups cooked, coarsely mashed salt fish
2 cups cooked, coarsely mashed potato
2 cups onion, finely chopped
salt
flour for dusting
3 tablespoons rendered pork fat

Fry the onion in a little pork fat on low heat until completely soft and starting to brown at the edges. Break up the cooked fish into small pieces with your fingers. If using leftover salt fish that has set quite hard, chop it with a knife. Mix the fish, potato, and onion. Taste and add salt if desired. Divide the mixture into 12 portions and form into round cakes. Dust with flour and fry briskly in hot fat until well browned on both sides.

SALT FISH HASH

serves 4 to 6

Salt fish hash was another tasty way of using up leftover cooked salt fish. It is essentially the same mixture as fishcakes but cooked loose in the pan. The proportions vary according to individual taste. It was also made with cooked, fresh fish.

3 cups cooked, coarsely mashed salt fish
3 or more cooked potatoes, in pieces
1 large onion, chopped
salt and pepper
4 tablespoons rendered pork fat

Fry the onion in the fat until it is soft and a bit brown. Add the potato and fry with the onion, breaking up the potato with a spoon. Add the fish and continue frying for another 5 minutes or so until it is all very hot. Sprinkle with salt and pepper to taste.

Serve as a main meal with vegetables and maybe extra potatoes.

ROAST SALT FISH

serves 4

Roast salt fish was a nice snack and a favourite way of eating leggies or small pieces of bigger salt fish. They were soaked in the usual fashion, but then cooked very quickly directly on hot coals. This recipe can be used to roast salt fish outdoors.

4 small pieces of salt fish or two leggies
a dozen sheets of newspaper

Soak the salt fish or leggies overnight. Let the fire die down until only embers remain. Drain the fish and wrap each piece in three or four sheets of newspaper. Soak each package for a few minutes in water until completely wet through. Put the packages directly on the embers. Leave for a few minutes until the paper has charred off the fish. Pull out and rinse off the ashes.

Serve with bread and butter.

SALT FISH (OR FRESH) AND HARD BREAD

Fish and brewis, and fishermen's (or fisherman's) brewis are two confusingly similar names, used in a confusingly interchangeable fashion. One opinion was that fishermen's brewis was cooked salt fish served mixed with brewis, whereas fish and brewis had the fish and the brewis placed separately on a serving platter or individual plates. Unfortunately, many people use the names exactly the other way around, or use them indiscriminately for either dish.

Yet another opinion was that fish and brewis was a salt fish dish, however presented, while fishermen's brewis was the same dish made with fresh fish. Other versions of this dish used chunks of stale, regular (i.e., leavened) bread instead of hard bread. Another variant involved pounding the hard bread into crumbs and cooking them in milk underneath the fish, and there was some consistency in calling this fisherman's brewis. All of these variants are called fish and brewis here.

Onion was frequently added to fish and brewis, in which case 2 chopped onions were fried in fat before adding the soaked bread. Any version was typically accompanied by either scrunchions or drawn butter or both. A little sweetness, such as molasses, was a positive addition. Some sprinkled 1 teaspoon of sugar on this dish, and relish or sweet pickle on the side was popular.

FISH and BREWIS

serves 4

4 cakes hard bread (about 10 ounces)
1 piece of salt fish (about 1½ pounds, unsoaked, on the bone)
1 cup fatback pork, cubed
salt
4 tablespoons molasses

Soak the salt fish overnight or for 24 hours if it is thick or a less salty fish is preferred. Change the water several times. Soak the hard bread in a separate bowl in plenty of water for about 12 hours.

Cover the fish with water and bring slowly to a boil. Simmer about 15 minutes, then carefully lift it out and leave until cool enough to handle. Carefully remove the skin, bones, and fins. Rub the large flakes of fish between your fingers to break them up. Drain the bread, cover with water, and bring to a boil. Turn off the heat and leave to soak for 10 minutes or until needed. Fry the fatback to make rendered fat and scrunchions. Drain the brewis and put in a large frying pan. Pour on the fat and fry on medium heat for 5 minutes or until well heated through. Break up the larger pieces with a spoon. Stir in the flaked fish and cook for another 5 minutes or so.

Spoon onto individual plates and drizzle with molasses. Serve with scrunchions.

FISH and BREWIS, stale bread instead of hard bread

serves 4

In the unlikely event that a loaf of bread went stale, frugality dictated using it in a dish like this one. After all, hard bread would keep, but an old loaf might go mouldy. Strictly speaking, this should not be called fish and brewis because it contains no brewis, but it always was.

½ loaf stale bread (about ¾ pound)
a piece of salt fish (about 1½ pounds unsoaked, on the bone)
1 cup fatback pork, in small cubes
salt as needed

Soak the salt fish overnight or for 24 hours if it is thick or a less salty fish is preferred. Change the water several times.

Cover the fish with fresh water and bring slowly to a boil. Simmer about 15 minutes, then lift it out. When cool enough to handle, remove all the skin, bones, and fins. Rub the larger flakes of fish between your fingers to break them into smaller flakes.

Cut the stale loaf into 2-inch chunks, including crusts. Cover with cold water and leave to soak for 5 minutes. Drain the bread, then pick up each chunk and gently squeeze out the excess water. Fry the fatback to make rendered fat and scrunchions. Put the bread in a large frying pan on a medium heat. Pour on the fat (including any salt that has sunk to the bottom), but reserve the scrunchions. Fry the bread on medium heat for 10 minutes until well heated through. Break up the chunks of bread with a spoon. Stale bread does not break up as easily as soaked hard bread, so cut it into 1-inch chunks with the edge of a spoon. Stir in the fish and cook for another 5 minutes or so.

Serve with scrunchions.

FISH and BREWIS made with fresh fish and hard bread crumbs

serves 4 to 6

To make this with salt fish, use 3 cups of soaked, cooked, flaked salt fish.

3 cakes hard bread
2 tablespoons dried savory
½ teaspoon salt
¼ teaspoon pepper
2 medium fillets of fresh fish
3 cups milk
2 tablespoons butter
extra salt and pepper

Put the cakes of hard bread in a pudding bag or wrap loosely in a clean cloth. Pound with a rolling pin or billet of wood to make crumbs. Do not use your best tea towel because the hard edges of the bread will damage the cloth.

Mix the dry crumbs with the savory, salt, and pepper. Spread this mixture evenly in a greased 8 by 10-inch baking pan. Lay the fillets on the crumbs, tucking the thin tails under if necessary to make them fit. Pour about 3 cups milk over the fillets and crumbs, or just enough to come to the top of the fillets. Cut the butter into small pieces and dot these over the fillets. Sprinkle with more salt and pepper. Bake uncovered at 350°F about 45 minutes.

PAN-FRIED COD HEADS

serves 4 to 6

"Cod heads" are not actually the complete head but rather the two sides of the head, each incorporating the cheek, half the tongue, and the operculum (the flap covering the gills). A typical method of cutting the head from the whole fish was to put a knife in the angle of the mouth, and cut backward (toward what would have been the tail end) and slightly upward to pass just through the base of the eye socket, then cut down and behind the operculum. Do this on each side so that the lower part of the head detaches from the upper. Cut any connection with the gills and remove. What remains is a butterfly-shaped piece; cut in two, leaving half the tongue on each.

5 large cod heads, or more smaller ones, halved
flour, salt, and pepper
4 tablespoons rendered pork fat
vinegar

Wash and dry the halved heads. Mix the salt and pepper with some flour, dust each half with this mixture, then fry in hot pork fat until browned and cooked through. Sprinkle each head with vinegar and serve with potatoes as a meal or with bread and butter and pickles as a snack or lunch.

PAN-FRIED COD CHEEKS

serves 4 to 6

Cod cheeks are the two muscle pads below the eyes, one on each side of the head, also known as faces or jowls. Some fishermen left the cheeks on the cod head, as described above, considering it an extravagance to remove the cheek and discard the rest; others did exactly that.

about 48 cod cheeks
flour, salt, and pepper
4 tablespoons rendered pork fat

Wash and dry the cheeks. Mix the flour, salt, and pepper, and dust the cheeks with this mixture. Fry the cheeks in the fat in a hot pan, about 5 or 10 minutes according to size, turning them over about halfway through the cooking time.

Serve with potatoes.

■ COD TONGUES

These really are the tongues, fleshy structures lying in the middle of the cod's lower jaws, each consisting of a gelatinous centre piece flanked by tubular muscles. Traditionally, tongues were a domestic delicacy, although there was a small market for salt cod tongues from the middle of the 19th century.

The best way to cook fresh cod tongues was simply pan-fried. They were also baked, either in a single layer or layered in a casserole, here called cod tongue pie. And they were stewed, typically with potatoes.

Salt cod tongues were widely popular, and some people preferred salt tongues to any other fish dish. Salt tongues were cooked in the same ways as fresh tongues; people who liked them a lot, or even preferred them to fresh, said that simply boiling them was one of the better ways of preparing them. A plain boiled cod tongue sounds dubious, but the process of salting and then freshening changes both taste and texture of the tongue (as it does the whole fish) and makes them far more palatable than expected.

Pan-fried cod tongues are simple food, but can be sublime—an elevated status achieved only if the tongues are very fresh, plump and firm, slightly translucent, and smelling faintly of the sea. Frozen cod tongues may be good but are never sublime. Rendered pork fat gives an authentic taste. For the novice eater, select small and medium tongues—larger tongues with their large gelatinous centres are an acquired taste. Salt tongues can also be pan-fried after soaking at least overnight.

PAN-FRIED COD TONGUES

serves 4

about 30 to 40 fresh cod tongues
about ¾ cup flour
salt and pepper
about ½ cup rendered pork fat

Season the flour generously with salt and pepper. Wash the tongues, lay on a clean cloth, and blot dry. Toss with the seasoned flour. Shake off any surplus flour and lay the tongues on a tray. Heat a large cast-iron frying pan over a medium-high heat. Put the fat in the hot pan, and when it is smoking hot, quickly lay the tongues in the pan, keeping them slightly apart. Fry in several batches if necessary. Fry briskly for about 3 to 5 minutes or until the underside is golden brown, then flip over and brown the other side. When cooked, spoon them out onto a plate, and fry the next batch.

Serve with potatoes and vegetables as a main meal or with bread, butter, and pickles as a light meal or a lunch.

BAKED COD TONGUES

serves 4

about 36 fresh or salt cod tongues
about ½ cup dry bread (or cracker) crumbs
salt and pepper
about ½ cup milk
about 4 tablespoons rendered pork fat (or butter)

If using salted tongues, soak them about 24 hours, changing the water several times. Drain well, lay them on a clean cloth, and blot dry.

Season the crumbs well with salt and pepper. Dip the tongues in the milk, let the excess milk drain off, then roll them in the seasoned crumbs. Lay them on a lightly greased baking sheet. Put a pea-sized amount of pork fat or butter on each tongue. Bake at 400°F for 20 to 30 minutes or until the crumbs are well browned and sizzling on the pan.

SALT COD TONGUE PIE

serves 4

Cod tongue pie was made with fresh or salt tongues, although the latter stand up much better to baking. This is only nominally a pie because there is no pastry involved, and might be better called a casserole.

about 36 salt cod tongues
3 cups bread crumbs from stale bread (or cracker crumbs)
1 medium onion, thinly sliced
4 tablespoons butter
salt and pepper
about 1 cup milk

Soak the tongues for about 24 hours, changing the water several times. Drain the tongues and lay about half of them in a single layer in a greased 8 by 8-inch pan. Spread about half the onion slices on the tongues. Sprinkle generously with salt and pepper. Pour in just enough milk to cover the tongues but not the onions. Layer on the remaining tongues, then the rest of the onion. Sprinkle with salt and pepper. Cut the butter into small pieces and mix with the crumbs. Pat the crumb mixture on top of the layers of tongues and onion. Bake at 350°F for about 1½ hours or until the crumbs are lightly browned.

BOILED SALT COD TONGUES

serves 4

36 salt cod tongues

Soak the tongues for about 24 hours, changing the water several times. Trim off any untidy pieces of skin. Bring a wide, shallow pan of salted water to a simmer. Place the trimmed tongues in the water, making sure they are all covered. Bring back just to a boil, then lower the heat so that the water barely simmers. Cook the tongues about 15 minutes. Lift them out and drain well.

Serve with butter.

COD TONGUE STEW

serves 4 to 6

- 24 to 36 cod tongues, more or fewer according to size, either fresh or salt
- 4 or 5 medium potatoes, peeled, in 1-inch chunks
- 1 medium onion, chopped
- ½ cup cubed fatback pork
- 1 tablespoon dried savory
- salt and pepper

If using salted tongues, soak them for 24 hours, changing the water several times. Fry the fatback in a large saucepan to make rendered fat and scrunchions. Remove and reserve the scrunchions. Fry the onion in the fat. Mix the potato with the onion in the pot. Add the savory, salt, and pepper. Barely cover with water, then lay the tongues on top. Bring to a boil and simmer about 30 minutes or until the potato is completely tender.

Serve with vegetables on the side and a few scrunchions sprinkled on each portion.

COD SOUNDS

The sound, or swim bladder, lies just under the sound bone, which is the part of the backbone lying above the body cavity. When fish were split, the sounds came out with the sound bones and were frequently discarded. Sometimes the sound was stripped from the bone and used either fresh or salted. From a large fish, the sound might be left on the sound bone, which could be 1 (or more) foot long, together with the strips of meat left on each side of the sound bone by the splitting knife. This was a favourite of those who liked fish on the bone. Although other fish species have sounds, they were not generally eaten.

Interestingly, in the 19th century a minor international market for salt cod sounds (off the bone) existed. Mrs. Beeton wrote that Newfoundland salt cod sounds were a great delicacy, but apart from saying they could be broiled, fried, or boiled, she gave only one recipe, a rather fanciful Cod Sounds en Poule, in which poached sounds were rolled around a forcemeat of oysters, eggs, anchovies, and bread crumbs. She says that sounds should be soaked in salt and water, but does not stress the need for a lengthy soaking in fresh water, so I wonder if she had simply borrowed this recipe without trying it.

Generally speaking, in Newfoundland fresh sounds were pan-fried, salt sounds were boiled, and either were used to make hash.

PAN-FRIED FRESH SOUNDS

serves 4 to 6

12 to 24 fresh sounds
salt and pepper
2 tablespoons or more rendered pork fat

Wash the sounds well and pat dry. Cut into pieces, and sprinkle with salt and pepper. Fry them in the fat in a hot pan for about 10 minutes, or until thoroughly cooked, turning occasionally.

BOILED SALT SOUNDS

serves 4 to 6

12 to 24 salted sounds, on or off the bone

Soak the sounds at least overnight, changing the water several times. Bring a pan of water to a boil. Put in the sounds and simmer about 15 minutes or until cooked. Drain them and cut in pieces as desired. Serve with butter.

Serve with potatoes and vegetables to make a main meal.

SOUND HASH
serves 4 to 6

12 cod sounds, fresh or salted
1 medium onion, chopped
4 medium potatoes, cooked
4 tablespoons rendered pork fat

If the sounds are salted, soak at least overnight. Cut the sounds into pieces. Fry the onion in the fat for a few minutes, just to soften it. Add the potato and sounds, and fry for about 10 minutes or until hot. Break up the potatoes with a spoon into bite-size pieces as you turn the mixture around in the pan.

■ COD BRITCHES

These are the roe of the fish, so-called because they look like a pair of very baggy trousers. Female roe were also called cod peas (or simply peas) because the eggs in a ripe ovary are like small peas. Britches were removed carefully from the fish, taking care to avoid rupturing the delicate membrane that contains them. They were also salted, in which case they would be soaked overnight (or 24 hours for large ones) before being boiled like fresh britches.

The cooking times for fresh britches depend on their size. My sources were vague about what constituted small or large britches, but as a rough guide, small is in the range of 3 to 5 inches long; large, longer than about 6 inches. And by careful observation, I can report that thick slices of poached britches were about ¾ inch thick.

FRESH BRITCHES
serves 4

4 large cod britches, or 8 or more small
2 tablespoons rendered pork fat
flour, salt, and pepper

Wash the britches and trim off any hanging strings, being careful not to puncture the enclosing membrane. Small britches should be fried whole in a little pork fat for 5 to 10 minutes. Larger britches are better boiled in salted water first, about 20 to 30 minutes. Let cool, slice thickly, dust with flour, salt, and pepper, and fry the slices for 2 or 3 minutes a side or until lightly browned and heated through.

COD HEARTS

For those who enjoyed the different taste and texture, the labour of salvaging the hearts when splitting fish was considered worthwhile.

COD HEARTS
serves 4 to 6

50 to 60 cod hearts
flour, salt, and pepper
4 tablespoons rendered pork fat

Wash the hearts well to remove any blood. Dry on a clean cloth and dust with flour, salt, and pepper. Fry in the fat, turning occasionally, until nicely browned.

COD LIVER

Cod livers were often saved for their oil, but sometimes were eaten fresh, dusted with flour, and fried whole in pork fat until well browned in the same fashion as cod hearts.

COD STOMACHS AND COD GILLS

These were both minority tastes, eaten fresh or salted. They were cleaned thoroughly, soaked overnight if salted, then fried in pork fat just like cod hearts.

Over: A blue-fin tuna being cut up on a wharf (unknown location, 1938). *The Rooms Provincial Archives Division, VA 2-26.*

Chapter 7

Fish other than Cod

Apart from the mainstay of cod, a spectrum of other fish was used in the traditional kitchen. At one end were species eaten occasionally, such as black-back flounder, yellow-tail flounder, grenadier, sculpin, eel pout, and wolf fish, which were usually simply filleted and fried (if they were eaten at all). At the other end were actively sought after prized fish, which are organized alphabetically in this chapter.

CAPELIN

Pronounced *kay-plin* in Newfoundland, and often spelled caplin, these small (8-inch-long) fish of the smelt family swim in vast shoals off the coasts of the island and come to shore in early summer to spawn on sand and gravel beaches. Traditionally, capelin were collected in bulk for fertilizer or bait and in lesser quantities for domestic consumption. They were eaten either fresh, or salted and dried. Opinions differ on cleaning capelin. Some people did not clean them at all, frying or salting them intact. Some cut off the heads and pulled out whatever was not attached; others cut off the heads and slit the belly to remove all the entrails.

As capelin straight from the water curl up as they are being cooked, many people preferred to wait at least overnight before frying them so they would lie flat in the pan.

Top: Capelin were netted from shallow water when they migrated to the beaches to spawn. **Bottom:** Filling a horse-drawn cart with capelin at Torbay, ca. 1920. **Right:** Capelin laid out to dry, unknown location, 1932. *The Rooms Provincial Archives Division, A 68-93., VA 20-16.3., VA 92-63.*

FRIED FRESH CAPELIN

serves 4 to 6

48 fresh capelin
flour, salt, and pepper
4 tablespoons rendered pork fat

Leave the capelin whole, or clean as desired. Dry with a cloth and dust with flour mixed with salt and pepper. Fry in the fat for 3 or 4 minutes each side, or until nicely browned. Serve with bread and butter and pickles.

SALT DRIED CAPELIN

Capelin were often preserved by salting, sometimes by packing them in coarse salt (like salt cod), or by putting them in a saturated salt solution for a limited time or in a medium-strength brine, as in this recipe.

2 gallons fresh capelin
1 gallon water
2½ cups coarse fishery salt

Mix the water and salt and set aside, stirring frequently. Cut open the bellies of the capelin and pull out the entrails but leave the head on. Wash the capelin thoroughly. When all the salt has dissolved in the water, submerge the capelin in the brine and leave for about 4 hours, or longer for a saltier capelin. Drain well and dry outdoors for 2 or 3 days. They can be hung on a line by their heads or laid on frames of chicken wire, but they should be protected from rain and brought indoors at night. When dried, store in a cool, dry place.

■ EELS

Eels are divisive: they might be completely ignored or viewed with disgust in one community and eaten with relish in the next. Eels are found in both salt and fresh water. They were sometimes accidentally caught in fresh water while angling for trout, or sought deliberately with a piece of fish as bait. Salt water was a more reliable place to find eels, and my sources outlined how best to catch them.

First, sharpen the tips of the tines of a large kitchen fork; ideally, reserve an old fork for this purpose. Choose a place to skin the eels, such as the corner-board of a shed, but any firmly fixed board at about head height is suitable. Slightly more elaborate is a thick board with a small hole in it. Nail both ends of a short length of stout twine to the back of the board, and push a loop of the twine through the hole to form a small noose. Nail the board to the shed with the noose facing out. Make a stout wooden cudgel to dispatch the eels. A bag or sack is needed to hold captured eels while you look for more. Finally, leave a small, very sharp knife close to the skinning location.

With sharpened fork in the hand and rubber boots on the feet, wade around the edges of rocky, seaweed-covered ledges at low tide, lifting up the seaweed to look for an eel. The low water of spring tides is ideal. A typical eel is about 30 inches long. When you see your prey, stab it through the head with the fork, drag it onto land, and bash its head several times with a cudgel or a beach rock. Place it in your bag—it may still be moving even though it is dead.

Either nail the head of an eel to a corner-board or slip the noose of twine around it just behind the head and pull down to ensure that the eel is fastened and will not slip out. Cut through the skin in a ring just behind the head and just below the loop of twine. Dig your fingernails under the edge of the skin and pull it back (or use a pair of pliers). Keep digging and peeling until you get a firm grip on the skin, then pull it off, like peeling off a finger of a glove. Cut off the head to release the body of the eel, slit along the belly, remove the entrails, and wash.

Now the eel is ready to be cooked. If eels were not plentiful, they were usually eaten fresh, either stewed or fried. When eels were plentiful, many people canned or bottled the surplus when the technology became available. One woman told me she always tucked away at least three cases (each containing 24 1-pound cans) of eel for the winter. She routinely fed a dozen or more hungry people, who could easily consume six or seven cans at a meal, so that's only about 10 meals. The canning process is described more fully in Chapter 21.

FRIED EEL

serves 6

2 skinned, washed eels, each about 18 to 24 inches to several feet long after trimming
4 tablespoons rendered pork fat
flour, salt, and pepper

Cut the eels into 3-inch lengths. Pat dry and roll in the seasoned flour. Fry in the fat in a large cast-iron frying pan on a medium heat for 15 minutes or more, turning occasionally until browned.

STEWED EEL

serves 6

2 skinned, washed eels, each about 18 to 24 inches to several feet long after trimming
2 tablespoons rendered pork fat
flour, salt, and pepper
2 onions, chopped

Cut the eels into 1½-inch lengths. Pat dry and roll in the seasoned flour. Fry on a medium-high heat in the fat in as many batches as necessary, turning each log as it cooks. Cook just until lightly browned, about 7 or 8 minutes. Remove from the pan.

Fry the onions in the same pan until soft but not brown. Put the eel and onion in a large saucepan, and add water to just below the top of the mixture. Bring to a boil and simmer gently for about 30 minutes, until meat and bone part easily. Turnip and carrot may be added to the stew. Serve with boiled potatoes and seasonal vegetables.

HERRING

Herring were typically caught in seines in both spring and fall, and many were sold for bait to schooners going to the Grand Banks. Salt herring was a major industry and great care was taken with the selection and preparation before they were packed with salt in barrels according to grade. The simplest method to gut herring, often called "ripped," was to cut off the head, rip open the belly, and remove the entrails. If the belly was full of roe, however, the fish were "Scotch packed": only the neck was cut, and as much of the entrails as possible pulled from the open end of the cavity, leaving the roe inside and the head attached. These commanded a better price and were kept only for home use if plentiful.

A cooper beside a herring barrel at the premises of Job Brothers & Company, St. John's, 1903. *Maritime History Archive, Memorial University, PF-315.156.*

FRIED FRESH HERRING

serves 6

6 fresh herring, scaled, gutted, headed
flour, salt, and pepper
4 tablespoons rendered pork fat

Put about ½ cup flour in a wide, shallow pan and mix in about ½ teaspoon of both salt and pepper. Wash and dry the gutted herring. Roll each in the seasoned flour, pick up by the tail, and tap sharply to knock off any surplus flour. Heat the pork fat in a large cast-iron frying pan, and lay 2 or 3 herring, or as many as fit without touching, in the pan. Fry on medium heat until browned on one side, about 5 minutes. Turn over, and fry the other side until browned. Repeat with the remaining herring.

Serve with bread and butter or boiled potatoes.

BOILED FRESH HERRING

serves 6

6 fresh herring, scaled, gutted, headed
salt

Bring a large saucepan of water, salted generously, to a boil. Put the herring into the water and return to a gentle simmer. Cover and simmer about 15 minutes.

Serve with bread and butter or boiled potatoes.

ROASTED FRESH HERRING

serves 6

Although usually called roasted, baked is a better description.

6 fresh herring, scaled, gutted, headed
4 tablespoons butter, melted
salt and pepper

Lay the herring on a greased baking sheet. Drizzle the butter over the herring. Sprinkle generously with salt and pepper. Bake at 350°F for about 30 minutes or until they are cooked.

Serve warm with potatoes and other vegetables or cold with pickles and bread and butter.

ROASTED CORNED HERRING

serves 6

Herring were also "corned," or lightly salted. Corning is a process in which herring, or any other fish, are put in salt for a short period—a few hours to overnight. After this brief salting, the fish need only to be thoroughly washed rather than soaked before cooking.

6 fresh herring, scaled, gutted, head left on
coarse salt to cover

Find a wide dish or baking pan that can hold the herring in one layer. Sprinkle a sparse layer of salt on the bottom of the pan and place the herring on top. Sprinkle more salt generously over them. They do not have to be completely immersed in salt but make sure that both sides of the herring are in contact with the salt. Leave for about 6 hours. Rinse off the surplus salt.

Push a thin branch or a length of twine through the

gills. Hang the herring in a cool place to dry overnight. Next day, cut the bodies from the heads, and lay the bodies in a single layer on an ungreased baking tray. Roast at 350°F for 30 to 40 minutes or until they are cooked through. Serve sprinkled with vinegar, and a little salt, with potatoes and vegetables.

VINEGARED HERRING

serves 6

Vinegared fresh herring were variously known as soused herring, spiced herring, or pickled herring (here *pickled* means herring cooked in vinegar, not pickled herring marinated cold for several days before eating). This method has a long recorded history. Hannah Glasse, the best known English cookery writer of the 18th century, has a recipe To Pickle or Bake Herrings in her 1747 book which differs only in detail from this Newfoundland recipe.

Enamelware was popular in the traditional kitchen, but for any recipes involving vinegar it is important to check for chips, as exposed metal will react with acid. For this recipe, any shallow, non-reactive pan will work, provided that it holds the number of herring being cooked.

Most stores carried a blend of dry pickling spices, typically a mixture of mustard seeds, black peppercorns, coriander seeds, whole cloves, dried chilies, small pieces of bay leaf, and a cinnamon stick. Failing that, any mixture of those spices could be used. A plainer version was made by leaving out the spices and onion. Traditionally, the vinegar was either store-bought or homemade using a vinegar plant (page 245).

6 fresh whole herring
3 cups vinegar
1 ½ cups water
1 tablespoon salt
2 tablespoons sugar
2 tablespoons pickling spices,
  or combination of spices to taste
1 onion, chopped

Head the herring, making sure to cut off the little fins near the head. Remove the entrails, but leave any roe inside the cavity. Rub off the scales if desired. Lay the herring head-to-tail in a covered baking dish; cut off the tails if it helps them fit better. Sprinkle the spices over the herring. Spread the onion on top. Mix the vinegar and water, and dissolve the salt and sugar in it; pour over the herring and onion. The liquid should almost cover the herring; if not, add more vinegar. Bake at 350°F for 45 minutes.

Serve hot or cold. As a main meal, serve with plain boiled potatoes, or as a snack simply with bread and butter.

PLAIN BOILED SALT HERRING

serves 6

A barrel of salt herring, sitting in a cool spot, was another reliable food for the winter. If Scotch packed herring with roe were available, some people preferred those with hard roe (female), often called "spawny" or "peas," while others liked those with soft roe (male), often called "milty" or "melts." While Scotch packed herring tasted better, and had the bonus of the roe, families were more likely to have ripped herring. Salt herring were eaten all over the Newfoundland, either home-cured or purchased.

6 salted herring

Soak the herring overnight (up to 24 hours), changing the water at least twice; place in a pot that holds them without crowding, cover with cold water, and bring to a boil. Simmer about 15 minutes, then turn off the heat.

Serve with boiled potatoes and thinly sliced raw onion.

NINE-HOUR SALT HERRING

serves 6

Long-cooked salt herring and salt herring cooked in vinegar were minority tastes. The nine hours of this recipe's title is only an approximation. Conveniently, the salt herring would be soaked overnight, put on the stove after breakfast, and eaten for supper. The long cooking renders the bones very soft, and the smaller ones disintegrate, which makes for easy eating.

6 salted herring

Soak the herring at least overnight, changing the water once or twice. Then put them in a pot that holds them without crowding, and cover with plenty of water—evaporation will occur during the long cooking. Bring to a boil, then turn down to the lowest possible heat so that it keeps very hot but does not actually boil for 6 to 9 hours (traditionally, the pot was simply pushed to the back of the cookstove).

Serve with potatoes, vegetables, thinly sliced raw onion, and hot mustard if desired.

ROLLED SALT HERRING IN VINEGAR

serves 4 to 6

This recipe can equally well be made with fresh herring fillets.

3 salted herring
2 teaspoons pickling spices
  or any mixed spices
1 onion, chopped
3 cups vinegar
1 cup water
¼ cup molasses
½ teaspoon salt

Soak the herring for about 24 hours with several changes of water. Fillet and remove any fins or ragged edges. Remove the skin by peeling it from the head end toward the tail. Roll up the skinned fillets starting at the tail end, and secure each with a skewer pushed through from side to side. Place in a covered baking dish that holds the rolled fillets in one layer with minimal space between them. Scatter the spices over the fillets, then scatter the onion on top. Mix the vinegar, water, molasses, and salt and stir until dissolved, and pour this over the fillets. Cover and bake at 350°F for about 1 hour.

Serve cold as a snack, with bread and butter and pickles.

LUMPFISH

Lumpfish live around the coast of Newfoundland. In late spring they migrate into shallow coastal water to spawn, usually on rocky substrates with sheltered areas and abundant seaweed, and back to deeper water in late summer and early fall. When lumpfish are inshore, the belly of the male turns red, so they are called red-lumps, as distinct from the blue-lumps, the slightly larger females. The blue-lump was not considered edible because her flesh was watery in the breeding season, so only red-lumps were eaten.

Red-lumps were caught by wading among seaweed-covered rocks at low tide, parting the seaweed, and occasionally spotting a red-lump clinging to a rock by its ventral sucker. It was grabbed, pulled off the rock, and stuffed into a bag. A meal for two people requires at least one red-lump—more if they are small—so four smaller fish would feed about six people.

FRIED LUMPFISH
serves 4

2 or 3 red lumpfish, according to size
flour, salt, and pepper
4 tablespoons rendered pork fat or butter

Head and fillet the lumpfish. Pull off the skin. Cut each fillet into 3 pieces. Dust each with flour, sprinkle with salt and pepper, and fry for 3 or 4 minutes in the fat on each side.

Serve with potatoes.

■ MACKEREL

Mackerel were popular, most often eaten fresh, either simply fried, stuffed, or vinegared. They were rarely salted or dried, but when the technology became available they were sometimes canned.

FRIED MACKEREL
serves 4 to 6

4 fresh mackerel
flour, salt, and pepper
4 tablespoons rendered pork fat or butter

Head, gut, and fillet the mackerel. Cut each fillet into 3 pieces. Roll in flour mixed with a little salt and pepper. Fry and serve as for lumpfish.

STUFFED MACKEREL
serves 4

4 mackerel
2 cups fresh bread crumbs
  (about 4 slices of bread)
1 tablespoon dried savory
½ teaspoon salt
¼ teaspoon pepper
1 egg, beaten
2 tablespoons rendered pork fat or butter

Fillet the mackerel, removing the fins and rib bones. If desired, the small bones may be pulled from the midline of the fillets. Lay 4 fillets skin-side down, alternating head and tail ends, in a shallow baking dish. For the stuffing, mix the crumbs, savory, salt, pepper, and egg. Spread stuffing over the fillets, and then lay the remaining 4 fillets on top, skin-side up, alternating the head and tail ends. Dot each fillet with pork fat or butter, and sprinkle with salt and pepper. Bake uncovered at 350°F for about 45 minutes.

Serve hot or cold. If left to get cold, this dish will set up very firm and can be sliced and served.

ROLLED, VINEGARED MACKEREL FILLETS

serves 4 to 6

Many 19th-century recipes offset the oily nature of mackerel with vinegar. For example, in 1861 Charles Francatelli, at one time chief cook to Queen Victoria, described a recipe very similar to this, pointing out that herring were amenable to the same treatment. Any of the recipes given here involving vinegar for either mackerel or herring are interchangeable.

Many recipes for whole or filleted mackerel (or herring) with vinegar in Newfoundland have different names such as soused, spiced, baked, and potted. That last name is misleading in this vinegary context, because it usually means something cooked and packed in butter—not what is involved here. Traditionally, wooden skewers, 2 or 3 inches long, were cut from kindling, and one pushed through each rolled-up fillet. A wooden toothpick or a small metal skewer can also be used to stop the fillets from unrolling. Be sure to use a non-reactive pan: glass, stainless steel, or glazed ceramic.

3 fresh mackerel
salt to sprinkle on the fillets
2 tablespoons butter
2 cups vinegar
2 cups water
¼ cup sugar
1 teaspoon salt

Fillet the mackerel and trim off the fins and bones. Lay skin-side down, sprinkle with salt, and spread each one with some of the butter. Roll up the fillets with the skin outside, starting from the thin end, and lay in a covered baking dish. Mix the water and vinegar, and stir in the sugar and salt until dissolved. Pour over the fillets. Cover and bake at 350°F for about 1 hour.

Serve hot with boiled potatoes, or cold with bread and pickles.

REDFISH

Traditionally called brim or bream (but they do not actually belong to the bream family), and since World War II rosefish or ocean perch, redfish were particularly popular on the south coast, where they were often caught in cod nets. Typically, redfish were roasted much like herring, after a light salting and drying.

■ SALMON

Where salmon were particularly plentiful, salt salmon were a commercial fish. Domestically, salmon were always a favourite, eaten both fresh and salted. Salmon peas (roe) were prized, and usually not salted because they were consumed fresh.

Fresh salmon were cooked whole or cut into steaks or fillets according to local custom and individual preference. In the recipe below either steaks or fillets can be used—depending on the size of the salmon and the largest available pot—with the time adjusted accordingly.

Leftover salmon was eaten cold as a snack or light supper or made into another substantial meal such as salmon loaf and salmon pie.

Salt salmon being sorted and weighed at the premises of Job Brothers & Company, St. John's, ca.1905. *Maritime History Archive, Memorial University, PF-315.013.*

BOILED FRESH SALMON

serves 4 to 6 with leftovers

1 fresh salmon, headed and gutted
2 tablespoons salt
1 recipe of egg sauce (page 260)

Cut the tail off the salmon. Put a plate upside down in the bottom of a stockpot to prevent the salmon from sticking to the bottom. Place the salmon in the pot whole or in two pieces, and just cover with water. Add salt and bring to a boil. Cook gently for about 30 minutes, or until the salmon is cooked through.

Serve with egg sauce and potatoes.

BOILED FRESH SALMON WITH SALT BEEF

serves 4 to 6

Some people cooked salmon with a little salt beef for additional flavour. This may have been required because of the traditional habit of cooking salmon too long in too much water—guaranteed to leach out flavour.

1 small piece of salt beef (½ pound or less)
1 tail piece of salmon (about 2 pounds)

Soak the salt beef in water overnight, changing the water several times. Put the beef in a saucepan, add enough water to cover it by about 2 inches, and bring to a boil. Boil for 2 or 3 hours. Then add the salmon and cook another 30 minutes or so.

Serve with potatoes and vegetables.

SALMON LOAF

serves 4

3 cups cooked salmon
1 cup bread crumbs
2 eggs
½ teaspoon salt
½ teaspoon pepper

Remove any skin and bones from the salmon, then mash coarsely. Beat the eggs with salt and pepper. Mix the salmon, eggs, and bread crumbs. Grease a loaf pan, put in the salmon mixture, and bake at 350°F for about 45 minutes or until the loaf is set completely.

Serve as a main meal with potatoes and vegetables.

Packing salt salmon in Cartwright, Labrador in 1914. *The Rooms Provincial Archives Division, VA 108-116.2.*

SALMON PIE

makes one 8 by 8-inch pie

4 cups cooked salmon
½ cup milk
2 eggs
2 cups mashed potato, from about 3 potatoes
salt and pepper
2 tablespoons butter

Remove any skin and bones from the salmon, then mash it coarsely with generous amounts of salt and pepper. Mash the potato with salt and pepper. Boil the eggs for 10 minutes, or until hard boiled, then peel and slice thickly. Put the salmon in an 8 by 8-inch baking dish. Lay the egg slices on top. Pour the milk over the salmon and eggs. Spread the potato over the salmon and eggs and roughly smooth it out. Dot with butter. Bake at 350°F for about 1 hour, or until the potato is lightly flecked with brown. Usually eaten as a supper with bread and butter.

SALT SALMON

serves 4 to 6

Those who preferred salt salmon to fresh selected bigger and fatter fish for salting. Some people split salmon like cod, along the ventral side and splayed out, while others cut down the dorsal side and opened them up. Either way, once salted they were kept in salt, rather than being air-dried like cod.

3 or 4 pounds salted salmon, skin on, bone in (either a whole fish or part of a larger one)
vinegar and mustard

Soak the salmon in plenty of fresh water for 12 hours or at least overnight, changing the water several times. Put the salmon into a pan and cover with fresh water. Bring to a boil and simmer about 15 minutes. Remove the salmon from the pot and remove all the bones and skin. Sprinkle vinegar on the salmon.

Serve with mustard on the side as a main meal with potatoes and drawn butter or with bread and butter as a snack or supper.

■ TROUT

Enjoyed across the island, mostly eaten fresh, either simply fried or baked with stuffing, trout would only be salted if abundant. Small trout were salted in the round (i.e., not split, but headed and gutted), but larger trout, of 3 pounds or more, would be split down the back, butterflied, salted, and then kept in salt. Salt trout were cooked and eaten like salt salmon.

Sea trout (unknown location, 1900). *Archives and Special Collections Division, Memorial University, 25 03 002.*

PAN-FRIED FRESH TROUT

serves 4

4 trout, about ¾ pound each, or more smaller ones
flour, salt, and pepper
4 tablespoons rendered pork fat

Head and gut the trout. Wash well and dry with a clean cloth. Heat the fat in a large frying pan over high heat until it starts to smoke. Mix a little flour with salt and pepper and dust the trout with it. Knock off any surplus flour and lay the trout in the hot frying pan. Cook in two or more batches as necessary. If the trout are large, cut each in half across the middle. Fry for about 5 minutes on each side or until they are crispy on the outside.

Serve with bread and butter as a snack or with potatoes and vegetables as a main meal.

BAKED, STUFFED FRESH TROUT

serves 4

2 cleaned trout, at least 1 pound each, or more smaller ones
1 recipe of thyme stuffing (page 159)

Grease the bottom of a baking pan large enough to hold the trout in one layer. Place the trout in the pan. If too long for the pan, cut off the heads and tails. Spoon about one-third of the stuffing into the cavity of each trout. Sprinkle the remaining stuffing over the trout. Bake at 350°F for 45 minutes. Smaller trout will take less time.

TUNA

This was the real thing: the big blue-fin tuna, about 4 to 6 feet long swimming in schools, although solitary individuals are much bigger. Around Newfoundland tuna are seen in bays with deep-water channels, and locally they are called horse mackerel (but elsewhere that name is applied to species of scad, which do not occur in Newfoundland waters, and are unrelated to the tuna). Tuna in the bay was cause for excitement and gathering of equipment. A small boat with men and gear on board was manoeuvred into the path of a school of tuna and an opportunity taken to harpoon one. The harpoon was attached to a long length of light rope, a 100-fathom coil for example, which had a small cask tied at the end as a float. That in turn was attached to another 100-fathom (or more) coil with another cask at the end. A harpooned tuna towed all that encumbrance as it fled, and quickly tired. It could then be pulled close to the boat, secured, towed to shore, and hauled up on a slipway. There it was cut up and handed out to the crowd that had gathered in anticipation.

All the meat on a tuna was enjoyed, but the fattier belly parts were particularly prized, as they are today. Tuna was primarily eaten fresh, although some people preferred it salted, and some would be pickled—kept in strong brine in barrels—rather than salted and dried as codfish were. If there was a glut, and the equipment was available, it was also canned.

Both fresh and salt tuna are equally good in this recipe. Salt tuna should be soaked in fresh water for about 24 hours or more, changing the water three or four times.

FRIED TUNA SLICES

serves 6

6 slices tuna (2 to 3 pounds total), about 1 inch thick
6 tablespoons rendered pork fat
salt and pepper

Heat the fat in a large skillet. Season the tuna slices on both sides and place in the pan. Fry on medium heat until browned and just cooked through.

Serve with potatoes and vegetables for dinner or with bread and butter for a light supper.

ROAST TUNA

serves 6

This can be made with fresh or salt tuna, but is better with the latter. If you use salt tuna, soak it in fresh water about 24 hours or more.

1 large piece of tuna (2 pounds or more)
4 slices fatback pork, or more to cover the tuna
salt and pepper

Trim the tuna and wipe dry. Season well with salt and pepper and place in a covered roasting pan. Lay the fatback on the tuna, using extra slices if necessary to more or less cover the top of the tuna. Cook at 350°F for about 1 hour, or until the tuna is cooked through. Serve with potatoes and vegetables.

TURBOT

This is not the same as the highly esteemed eastern Atlantic turbot, but a fish from an entirely different family, variously known as Greenland halibut, Greenland turbot, or, in Newfoundland, simply turbot. It was liked for both its excellent flavour and its slightly oily, gelatinous texture. It was eaten fresh, corned, and salted. Fresh turbot was simply filleted and fried, while salt turbot was boiled and eaten like salt fish, and can substitute in any salt fish recipe—it makes excellent fishcakes.

CORNED TURBOT

serves 4

2 medium turbot, about 2 pound each
coarse salt

Head and gut the turbot but otherwise leave them whole. Rinse well and place on a bed of coarse salt. Pour on more salt to cover, and leave for 2 or 3 hours. Rinse off the salt quickly. Hang them on a clothesline for several hours, just to dry the surface. Hang up a cloth or paper bag to dissuade flies if they are about.

Place some thin pieces of wood in a long pan to prevent the turbot from sticking to the bottom of the pan. Lay the turbot on the wood and bake at 350°F for about 30 minutes or until cooked through.

Right: Smoking fish, North West River, 1930. *The Rooms Provincial Archives Division, VA 110-16.2.* **Over:** An unidentified outport, late 19th century, with fenced gardens in the background. *Archives and Special Collections Division, Memorial University, 30 16 004.*

Chapter 8

Shellfish

Shellfish did not have a major presence on the traditional Newfoundland table because most species were never caught in Newfoundland waters. Shrimp, for example, were only caught after the commercial market brought with it the specialized gear to catch them well after World War II. Similarly, deep-water snow crabs were not commercially important until the 1980s, and had been discarded as a nuisance when they showed up in nets, although some people ate them like lobsters.

CLAMS

Clams of many species are found around Newfoundland, but those eaten were usually soft-shell clams, common in shallow, sandy-muddy areas at the edge of the sea. Before World War II, soft-shell clams were abundant and used as bait on lines of hooks set for cod, but also enjoyed in their own right. These days, much of their habitat has been destroyed or polluted, but they can still be found in out-of-the-way places.

Soft-shell clams were either cooked immediately after being dug or put in a bucket of sea water for a few hours with a handful or two of oatmeal thrown in. The clams ingested oatmeal particles from the water, which pushed whatever natural food was in the gut out the other end. Whether fresh from the sand or treated with oatmeal, clams were first opened by a brief boiling, sometimes followed by further cooking.

BOILED CLAMS

serves 4 to 6

2 gallons clams in the shell, freshly dug or kept in sea water with oatmeal

Use a pot which will be half filled by the clams. Cover the clams with salt water, or fresh water with a handful of salt (about 2 tablespoons of coarse salt for every quart of water). Bring to a boil, and cook for a few minutes until the clams have opened. Drain and remove the clams from their shells.

Serve plain, dressed with butter, or use in another recipe.

FRIED CLAMS

serves 4 to 6

1 quart cooked clams out of the shell
1 onion, chopped finely
4 tablespoons rendered pork fat or butter
salt and pepper
1 ½ cups bread crumbs
about ¾ cup water

Fry the onion gently in the fat until it is soft. Add the clams and bread crumbs and heat through. Add salt and pepper to taste. Add water to help the mixture bind together for ease of serving. Heat through.

Serve with potatoes and vegetables of your choice.

LOBSTERS

Lobsters were occasionally caught for domestic purposes, and several sources described gaffing, the low-technology method of catching them. I stress that this traditional practice is strictly illegal these days. To gaff a lobster, a large cod hook was lashed on the end of a long pole, at least 6 feet (or more) long. The fisherman went out in a small boat in water about 3 or 4 feet deep on a calm day so that the bottom is visible. Bait such as pieces of fish was thrown down by rocky ledges, where lobsters tend to hide. Any emerging lobster was gaffed and slung aboard the boat.

Canning technology for lobsters arrived in Newfoundland in the 1880s (see Chapter 21) and brought with it the lobster pot to catch enough to meet the demands of the new commercial market. Lobsters became an important cash crop, too valuable for most to eat at home. The canning process did not use the lobster bodies, which were eaten by those that liked them.

Whole lobsters were usually boiled but also roasted and fried. A favourite way of boiling lobsters was over a fire on the beach on a warm evening. Apart from the pleasures of outdoor eating, this avoided the smell of boiling lobsters in the house. Opinions were divided about whether boiled lobsters should be eaten with a sauce such as drawn butter. Surplus boiled lobster meat was often chopped and fried in the same fashion as clams.

BOILED LOBSTER

serves 4 to 6

6 medium live lobsters (about 1 ½ pounds each)

Bring about 3 gallons sea water to a boil in a 4- or 5-gallon pot. When the water is at a full boil, put in the lobsters and return to a boil. Boil for about 20 minutes.

ROASTED LOBSTER

serves 6

Another method best outdoors on a beach fire.

6 medium live lobsters (about 1 ½ pounds each)

Let the beach fire die down to no more than a bed of embers covered in ash. Lay the lobsters on the embers and roast for about 20 minutes. As they will curl up while cooking, turn them around so that all sides are exposed to the embers.

■ MUSSELS

Mussels are abundant around the coasts of Newfoundland, except where their shallow-water habitat is scoured by ice. As for lobster, many people did not like the smell of boiling mussels and whenever possible preferred to cook them outdoors. Mussels were always first boiled, then either eaten immediately straight from the shell or used in another recipe. They could be fried—the recipe for fried clams above can be used, substituting an equal volume of cooked mussels. Mussels were also made into pies, recipe as below, or occasionally bottled (Chapter 21).

BOILED MUSSELS

serves 4 to 6

Surplus mussels could be fried like clams or periwinkles, and either of those recipes can substitute cooked mussels.

2 gallons fresh mussels in the shell

Wash the mussels well to eliminate any sand and weed, and pull off the beards. Put 1 cup water in a 4-gallon pot. Add the mussels and bring to a boil. Boil for about 15 minutes, stirring several times. Serve in the shells, discarding any that did not open.

MUSSEL PIE

makes one 9-inch pie

Although Newfoundlanders were normally heavy-handed with a salt shaker, in this case no extra salt was added because the cooking liquid from the mussels was already salty enough.

3 quarts fresh mussels in the shell
1 cup mussel-cooking liquid
3 tablespoons flour
1 recipe of lard pastry (page 198)

Put the mussels in a large pot with ½ cup water and bring to a boil. Boil about 5 minutes, stirring occasionally, or until the shells are all fully open and the meat has firmed up. Scoop the mussels from the pot, reserving the cooking liquid. Remove the mussels from their shells. Bring 1 cup reserved liquid to a boil. Add about 6 tablespoons water to the flour in a small bottle and shake vigorously. Pour this into the liquid and stir until it thickens. Mix the thickened sauce with the cooked mussels.

Divide the pastry dough. Roll one half into a circle to fit a 9-inch pie plate, including the rim. Lay this pastry onto the pie plate. Spread the mussel and sauce mixture over this. Roll out the second piece of pastry into a 9-inch circle. Wet the rims of the pastry and lay the top layer over the filling. Press the edges together and crimp firmly with a fork. Bake at 350°F for about 1 hour. Serve with vegetables.

OYSTERS

Oysters do not live around Newfoundland, only reaching as far north as Nova Scotia and Prince Edward Island, but they were imported from eastern Canada and the northeastern US to feed a brisk retail, wholesale, and restaurant trade. Tinned oysters were also a busy trade.

It is not clear where this love for oysters came from, but since oysters were abundant along the south coast of England, from where so many settlers originated, it is possible they brought the taste with them. Oysters were not always expensive delicacies for the wealthy but were a food for all classes of society. Oysters on the south coast of England are a different species from that of the western Atlantic, but for the settlers they were all oysters.

Oysters were not widely available outside of towns, and in St. John's I have met no one who cooked them, and only one man who learned how to open oysters before World War II. His advice on how to open oysters is timeless.

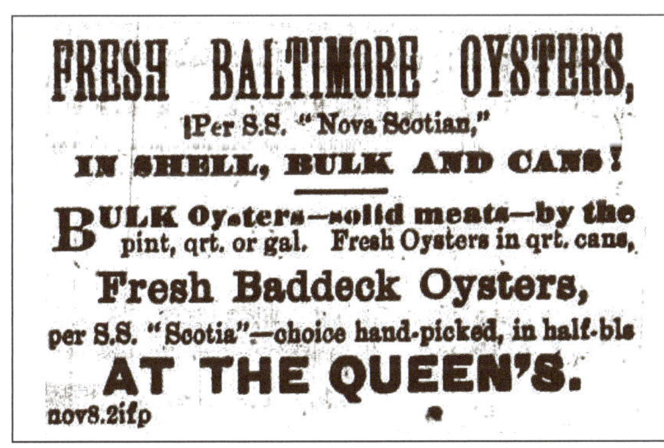

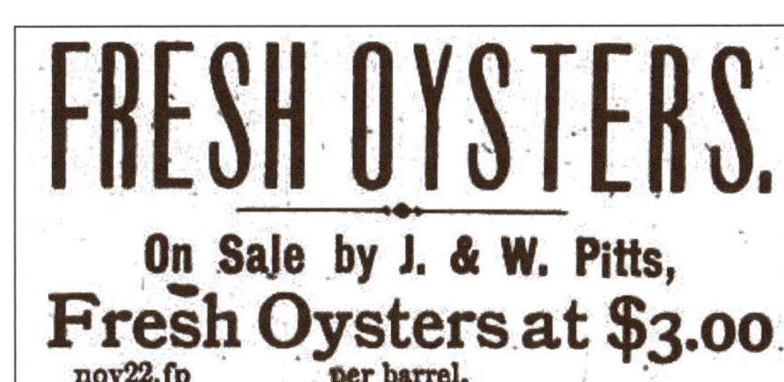

FRESH OYSTERS on the half shell

serves 6

A thick coarse cloth and an oyster knife are essential for cleaning oysters. The best oyster knife has a slightly curved blade that can be slipped under the top shell without messing up the meat.

6 dozen fresh oysters

Scrub the oysters in cold water, paying attention to the grooves at the beak end. Hold an oyster flat-side up in the cloth in one hand. Probe with the tip of the oyster knife at the beak end, looking for a spot to lever against, so that the shells can be twisted apart. Do not try to push the knife hard into the oyster—that is when hands get gashed—but just enough to feel resistance when you twist. Sometimes the shells pop apart at the first attempt, but if not, carefully push the knife a little deeper and try again. Occasionally wipe the knife on the cloth as it picks up dirt from the shells. Once the two shells have popped apart, press the blade to the underside of the flat, top shell, and slide it along to sever the muscle that connects the shells. Flick off the top shell, then slide the knife under the meat and cut the attachment of the muscle to the bottom shell. The oyster is now ready to be eaten.

CREAMED OYSTERS on toast

serves 6

The 1905 and 1928 cookbooks had two oyster recipes in common—if these were worth printing 23 years apart, they must have enjoyed some local popularity. The first of these is creamed oysters on toast, and the recipes in the two books are very similar.

The lavish use of cream and egg yolks speaks to a relatively affluent audience. The number of oysters required depends on their size: about 36 small (3-inch-long) oysters will yield the required 1½ cups of meat and juice. The amount of salt is tricky because the saltiness of the oyster liquid varies, so taste and add accordingly.

1½ cups oysters out of the shell in their juice (from about 36 medium oysters)
¾ cup cream
6 egg yolks
salt and pepper
6 slices buttered toast, kept warm

Open the oysters, saving all the juice. Bring the oysters and juice to a simmer to barely cook them. Strain and reserve the juice. Chop the oysters coarsely. Whisk the juice with the yolks and cream. Add salt and pepper to taste. Heat the liquid gently until it thickens lightly, then add the oysters and warm through. Divide between the slices of toast.

OYSTER CROQUETTES

serves 4

This is an adaptation of the 1905 recipe for oyster croquettes (the 1928 version differs significantly). It contains both oysters and beef, clearly a survivor from the 18th and 19th centuries when oysters were widely used as fillers and to add flavour to meat dishes. The traditional English pork pie, for example, contained oysters for this reason, and even today some recipes for English meat pies use anchovies to provide a background savoury note.

- 2 cups oysters, out of the shell
- 2 cups finely chopped or ground cooked beef
- 6 tablespoons bread crumbs
- 3 eggs
- 1 cup cracker crumbs
- 2 tablespoons melted butter

Drain and finely chop the oysters; reserve some of the juice. Mix the bread crumbs with just enough of the juice to make a stiff paste. Beat 2 eggs, and mix with the oysters, beef, and soaked crumbs. Gently squeeze the mixture together and form into 8 croquettes. Beat the third egg. Roll each croquette in the beaten egg and then in the cracker crumbs, pressing them onto the surface. Fry in the butter until well browned.

PERIWINKLES

Periwinkles were introduced to eastern Canadian waters in the middle of the 19th century. They are now abundant around Newfoundland, easily gathered from the intertidal zone, and are called wrinkles in many places. Small ones are more trouble than the yield of meat is worth, so traditionally a little extra time was spent looking for large ones, ¾ inch (or more) high. Periwinkles were eaten both as part of a family boil-up on the beach and as a main meal indoors.

BOILED WRINKLES on the beach

Build a fire on the beach and let it die down to a bed of embers. Half fill a large cooking pot with sea water and put it on the embers to boil. Set the children to gathering large wrinkles: about 1 quart per person, more or less according to taste. When the water is boiling, add the wrinkles and boil for about 15 minutes. Tip them out onto a clean-looking area of the beach, with only small pebbles, so that you don't lose the wrinkles between bigger rocks. Everyone picks up a few wrinkles and digs them out of their shells, often using a sliver split from a piece of driftwood.

This recipe is from the days when ladies not only wore hats to picnics but used hatpins to keep them in place. The ladies would pull out their hatpins and either dip them in the boiling water or pass them briefly through a flame of the fire and use them to delicately winkle the wrinkles from their shells.

When extracting the meat from the shell, be sure to remove the operculum, the little hard plate that seals the opening to the shell when the wrinkle withdraws, although some will fall off by themselves during cooking.

WRINKLES as a main meal
serves 4 to 6

1 gallon wrinkles in the shell
2 tablespoons butter
salt and pepper
water
flour to thicken

Set a large pot half full of water to boil and add a little salt. When the water is boiling, add the wrinkles. Boil about 15 minutes, then scoop them out and hook out the meat with a toothpick or needle. Make sure you remove the opercula. Fry the wrinkles in the butter for a few minutes and add salt and pepper. Add enough water to come about halfway up the wrinkles. Mix some flour with a little water. Spoon this into the pot and cook until the liquid thickens.

Serve with potatoes as a main meal.

SQUID

Squid were abundant in season, and schooners came from far and wide to catch them for bait, which may be why squid were not generally thought fit to eat. But there is an intriguing entry in the 1928 cookbook of two recipes using tinned sepia. Sepia, properly speaking, is the cuttlefish (or in other contexts the colour of its ink), which is an eastern Atlantic species not seen in Newfoundland waters. This raises the question: was this genuine cuttlefish imported in tins from Europe, or was it the local squid tinned and given the more sophisticated name of sepia? My money is on the latter. This recipe is derived from Fillet of Sepia and Macaroni from the 1928 cookbook.

Macaroni came in lengths that were broken up before boiling, or chopped afterwards. Pre-cut elbow-shaped macaroni may be used in this recipe. Tinned squid may be hard to find, so substitute 1 pound of prepared, fresh squid that has been simmered gently in water for 1 hour.

FILLET of SEPIA and MACARONI
serves 4

1 1-pound tin sepia
¾ cup macaroni pieces
salt and pepper
flour
¼ cup butter
¼ cup buttered bread crumbs
¼ cup grated cheese

Cook the macaroni in boiling salted water until soft, then drain and rinse in cold water. Put a layer of macaroni in the bottom of a small buttered dish, and cover with half the sepia. Sprinkle with the flour, salt, and pepper and dot with half the butter. Repeat with another layer. Top with the bread crumbs and cheese. Bake 20 minutes at 400°F.

WHELKS

Whelks on the west coast of the island are also called coo-coo or cuckoos, a name derived from a French dialect word. They are common around the island, and although primarily a sub-tidal species, can be gathered at very low tide. They were also frequently found on lobster pots or other gear deployed in the water. Not universally popular, whelks were nevertheless eaten by many families. They were treated like large periwinkles, eaten simply boiled (for about 20 minutes) or boiled first and then fried. As for periwinkles, the operculum should be removed before eating the meat.

Over: Four free-range goats near the United Church, Carmanville, 1939. *The Rooms Provincial Archives Division, VA 14-218.*

Chapter 9

Domestic Meat

Cattle, pigs, sheep, and goats were raised all across Newfoundland, but usually only farmers had all four. Local geography determined which animals were popular in any given community. Lots of pasture land meant cows and sheep, but many coastal communities were wedged between beach and cliffs, unsuitable for cows, but perfect for goats and pigs. Many animals were free-range and gardens were fenced to keep them out. Some animals returned home voluntarily in the evenings, but others stayed away for extended periods, and ear-notching was widely used to establish ownership.

There were two general approaches to keeping livestock. Either breeding stock was kept alive over the winter in sheltered quarters and then bred in the spring, or young animals were bought in the spring and fattened up over the summer. The latter method was more widespread because of the cost of keeping animals over the winter. Young animals were bought from neighbours or neighbouring communities, or imported from elsewhere—families on the south coast of Newfoundland, for example, often brought young livestock in from Prince Edward Island or Nova Scotia.

Either way, some animals were killed in early winter, typically December. The meat was eaten fresh, put in salt in barrels, or simply hung in a shed, where it would keep in the cold weather. In many communities it was *de rigueur* to share fresh meat, with widely recognized customs about who shared what with whom. Typically, you shared with your immediate neighbours, even those you knew would or could not reciprocate, and with extended family members wherever they lived.

CATTLE

If at all possible, a cow was kept for milk, and if there was sufficient pastureland, other cattle were kept for meat or as draft animals. If a community kept breeding stock, one family kept a bull and breeding cows were taken to the bull in season.

Female calves were reared to become milking and breeding animals, while males were castrated and reared for meat or to become draft oxen. Families became attached to an animal they had reared from calf to adult, so it was often sold and the cash used to buy meat from an animal they hadn't raised. Older draft animals were killed as a cash crop after five or six years and replaced by a younger animal. Domestic butchery was basic, with axe, saw, and sharp knife the principal tools. Only larger communities had professional butchers.

In addition to the recipes below, beef was frequently salted (see Chapter 10), and sometimes bottled or canned when the technology became available (see Chapter 21).

ROAST BEEF

serves 4 to 6

Roast beef was popular everywhere, usually as braised beef or a pot roast, cooked in a covered pan in the oven. This made perfect sense because the animal was often of uncertain age, potentially rather old and tough, and the homespun style of butchery often yielded anonymous cuts of meat with no differentiation according to cooking time. Long, slow cooking in a covered pan would work for any cut. Only occasionally, where professional butchers could offer defined cuts of a known age, was beef roasted in an open pan and eaten rare. The general roasting process was much the same for beef, mutton, and pork.

Those people who had pumpkin in the garden often put peeled chunks of it to cook around the roasting beef as well as (or instead of) the onion.

1 piece of beef (about 4 pounds on the bone)
2 onions, in chunks
6 slices fatback pork
6 tablespoons flour
salt and pepper

Place the onion around the beef in a roasting pan. Lay the fatback on the beef. Add a little water, no more than about ½ inch, to the pan. Cover and place in a 350°F oven for 2 or 3 hours or until the beef is cooked. Remove the beef and keep it warm. Make gravy in the roasting pan: shake the flour with about twice as much water in a jar, then stir into the fat and juices in the pan. Bring to a boil and simmer, adding salt and pepper to taste. Add a little more water or flour to make the gravy thinner or thicker according to taste.

An ox with a cart-load of dried salt cod at Port au Choix, ca. 1913–1915. *Archives and Special Collections Division, Memorial University, 1.01.147.*

BEEF STEW

serves 4 to 6

Beef stew was another sure way of dealing with anonymous cuts of uncertain age, and less meat could be stretched over more appetites by adding extra vegetables Some people cooked the potatoes separately from the stew and served them boiled or mashed.

- 5 cups cubed beef (about 2 pounds)
- 4 tablespoons rendered beef or pork fat
- 2 onions, chopped
- 2 carrots, chopped
- ½ turnip, chopped
- 4 potatoes, chopped
- 2 small parsnips, chopped (optional)

Trim off the fat and remove any sinews and gristle. Render some of the trimmed beef fat; if the beef did not have enough fat, use pork fat, and fry the beef in it until brown. Put the beef cubes in a pot and just cover with boiling water. Add the onion and simmer for about 2 hours, or until the beef is tender. Add the vegetables. Simmer another 30 minutes or more until the vegetables are tender.

Serve hot, with extra vegetables if desired.

BEEF and VEGETABLE PIE

makes one 9-inch pie

Beef pies, sometimes made with just pastry on top, but more often with pastry both under and over, were another good way of stretching a limited amount of meat. They had a wide range of vegetable content, from just a little onion to a full complement of vegetables.

1 pound beef, in 1-inch cubes
2 tablespoons rendered pork fat
2½ cups water
1 cup chopped turnip
1 cup chopped carrot
1 cup chopped onion
½ cup chopped parsnip
2 cups potato cubes
½ teaspoon salt
3 tablespoons flour mixed with
about 2 tablespoons water
1 recipe of lard pastry (page 198)

Fry the beef in the fat in a hot pan until browned. Add about 2½ cups water, or enough to completely cover the beef. Bring to a boil and simmer 1 hour or until the beef is just getting tender. Add the vegetables and some salt and simmer another 45 minutes or until everything is tender. Pour off all the cooking liquid into a small pot. Mash the flour to a smooth paste with a little water, stir into the liquid and bring to a boil, stirring continuously until thickened. Add salt and pepper to taste and pour over the meat and vegetables. Set aside to cool.

A few hours before you want to eat the pie, make the pastry. Divide the dough into halves and roll out one to fit a 9-inch pie plate, making sure it will cover the rim. Fit it into the pie plate. Spread the cooled beef and vegetable mixture evenly over the pastry. Roll out the remaining pastry, brush the rim of the pastry in the dish with water, and lay the second circle on top. Press down well to seal and crimp the two layers together. Cut a slit in the centre of the pastry to let steam escape. Bake at 350°F for 75 to 90 minutes, until the pastry is nicely browned.

FRIED BEEF KIDNEY

serves 4

Beef kidneys were either prized or given away. Those fond of kidney often had a meal of it simply cut into cubes and fried, but it was more often used in a beef and kidney pudding or pie. In any case, the kidney had to be carefully trimmed.

1 beef kidney
4 tablespoons rendered pork fat
salt and pepper

If you are lucky, the thick layer of fat encasing the kidney is still attached. Pull this off and reserve it to make suet. Peel off any membranes around the kidney. Cut the kidney open and chop into large chunks following the natural lobes. Cut the white interior fat from each chunk and discard. Cut the larger chunks so that all pieces are about the same size. Melt the fat over medium to high heat and fry the kidney pieces. Stir frequently, turning them over, until nicely browned.

Serve as a main meal with potatoes and vegetables or as a snack or lunch with bread and butter and pickles.

BEEF and KIDNEY PUDDING

serves 4 to 6

½ beef kidney (about ½ pound), trimmed, in 1-inch cubes
1 pound beef, trimmed, in 1-inch cubes
2 tablespoons flour
¼ teaspoon salt
¼ teaspoon pepper
about 6 tablespoons water
1 recipe of lard pastry from 3 cups of flour with baking powder (page 198)

Reserve about one-quarter of the pastry to make a lid; roll the rest into a circle about ⅛ inch thick, a little thicker than for a fruit pie. Lay this circle into a 6-cup pudding basin and gently push it in to fit, making sure there is a small rim of pastry overhanging the top.

Mix the flour with the salt and pepper. Roll the beef and kidney cubes in the flour mixture and put them into the pastry-lined basin. Sprinkle any surplus flour mixture over the top. Fill the basin with enough water to just cover the pieces. Roll out the reserved pastry to make a lid. Wet the edge of the pastry in the basin, lay on the pastry lid, and press the two layers firmly together to seal. Trim off any surplus pastry. Steam over simmering water for about 4 hours. Check occasionally to ensure that the water has not all evaporated, and add more boiling water as necessary.

BEEF and KIDNEY PIE

makes one 9-inch pie

½ beef kidney (about ½ pound), trimmed, in 1-inch cubes
1 pound beef, in 1-inch cubes
1 onion, chopped
½ teaspoon salt
¼ teaspoon pepper
2½ cups water, or to just cover the meat
3 tablespoons flour
1 batch of lard pastry from 3 cups of flour with baking powder (page 198)

Mix the beef, kidney, salt, and pepper. Add enough water to just cover the pieces. Bring to a boil and simmer about 1 hour or until tender. Pour off the cooking liquid and reserve. Mix the flour with a little water, being careful to avoid making any lumps. Mix this with the cooking liquid and return to a boil to thicken.

Pour the thickened gravy over the meat and leave to cool. Divide the pastry dough in half. Roll one half into a circle big enough to fit the pie plate and its rim. Lay the pastry on the pie plate and gently push it into the plate. When the filling is cool, spoon it into the pastry-lined pie plate. Roll out the remaining pastry to make a lid. Wet the pastry on the rim of the pie plate and lay the pastry lid on top. Press the two layers firmly together and crimp to seal. Make several cuts in the top pastry to release steam while it is baking. Bake at 350°F for 60 to 75 minutes, or until the pastry is browned.

MINCED BEEF STEW or PIE

serves 4 to 6

Whenever an animal was butchered, a little lean meat could be gleaned from surplus bones. Bones were boiled for soup, and the scraps were chopped finely to make a meal. Generally speaking, such chopped meat was called *minced* in British terminology and *ground* in the American; Newfoundland inherited both terms and used them interchangeably. The meat chopping was originally by hand, but by the end of the 19th century small hand-cranked meat mincers that clamped to the edge of the kitchen table were available. In 1920, Ruth Cameron, in her column "Side Talks" in the *Evening Telegram*, claimed that 90 per cent of Newfoundland households possessed a meat grinder—perhaps more of a guess than an accurate survey, but indicative of the gadget's widespread use.

- 2 cups finely chopped or ground beef (about 1 pound)
- 1 onion, chopped
- 2 tablespoons lard or rendered pork fat
- 2 cups water
- 1 cup chopped turnip
- 1 cup chopped carrot
- 1 teaspoon salt
- ¼ teaspoon pepper
- 3 tablespoons flour
- 6 tablespoons cold water
- 1 recipe of lard or suet pastry for a double-crust pie if desired (page 198)

Fry the onion with the beef in the lard until the onions are soft. Mash the beef with a spoon as it cooks to break it apart. Add the water, turnip, carrot, salt, and pepper. Bring to a boil and simmer about 30 minutes or until the vegetables are cooked through. Shake the flour with cold water in a small jar. Stir the flour mixture into the stew, and simmer 10 minutes or more, stirring occasionally.

Serve immediately as a stew, with boiled potatoes and extra vegetables if desired. Or set the stew aside to cool, and then make into a pie using a 9-inch pie plate and enough pastry for a double crust.

OX TONGUE

serves 4 to 6

Ox tongues are beef tongues, the pair of terms an interesting survivor of the class distinctions that followed the Norman conquest of England in 1066. The common folk kept the Saxon term *ox* for the bits they usually ate, the (supposedly) less desirable ox tongue, oxtail, and ox cheek. The nobility picked up the French *boeuf* to describe choicer pieces like ribs and loins which were on their tables. In Newfoundland, the store occasionally had a barrel of ox tongues in pickle, and some people preferred them to fresh. But when a steer was killed, the tongue was usually eaten fresh because it really wasn't worth salting only one.

1 ox tongue (about 2 to 4 pounds)
2 onions, chopped

If the tongue has been salted, soak it in several changes of fresh water for about 2 days. Wash the tongue well. Put it in a saucepan and cover generously with water. Add the onion and bring to a boil. Simmer for 2 to 4 hours according to size, until the tongue is tender and easily pierced with a small knife. Drain, reserving the cooking water to bolster a gravy or stew another time. Trim the tongue while it is still warm. Remove the fat and gristle from the base, together with any small bones. Slit the skin and peel off.

Serve the tongue warm as a main meal with potatoes and carrots or cold as a supper or lunch with mustard and bread and butter.

STUFFED BEEF HEART

serves 6 or more

Whenever a cow or steer was killed, the heart was prized by some and disliked by as many. Beef hearts, also called ox hearts, are typically 3 to 5 pounds each, depending on the size of the animal. Even a smaller one provided a substantial meal for a family.

Unless you raise the animal yourself, it is often difficult to find an intact heart. Those in supermarkets have usually been sliced open, making them difficult to stuff. It can be done by pressing handfuls of stuffing onto the exposed interior surfaces, wrapping the heart around it, and tying it with twine to hold it all together. As it's messy, it's much better to find a local butcher who kills his own cattle and will sell the intact heart.

1 beef heart (about 3 to 5 pounds)
1 recipe of stuffing for beef heart (page 160)
2 or 3 carrots
2 or 3 onions
½ teaspoon salt

Trim off the bigger slabs of fat from the surface of the heart and the flaps of tissue and the tubes at the thick end to expose the openings of the heart cavities. Push the stuffing into the cavities. Do not fill right to the top as the stuffing will expand while cooking. Add any surplus stuffing to the cooking pot. Tie cotton twine around the heart several times lengthways to hold the open (thick) end of the heart together.

Slice half an onion into the bottom of a covered pot that will just comfortably hold the stuffed heart. Add the carrots and onions, cut to fit around the heart. Add water to come almost to the top of the heart. Add salt. Bake at 300°F for about 4 hours. Remove the cooked heart from the pot, cut off the strings, and serve thick slices moistened with the cooking liquid. Any leftovers, or the whole heart, can be left to cool and then sliced to eat with bread and pickles.

FRIED BEEF LIVER with onions

serves 4 to 6

Beef liver, also called ox liver by many, was another occasional delicacy whenever a steer was killed. This was invariably sliced and then fried or baked.

4 or more thick slices of liver
(about 2 pounds total)
2 onions, chopped
flour
salt and pepper
2 tablespoons rendered pork fat

Fry the onions in the fat until cooked through and browning at the edges. Remove and reserve the onions. Cut out the major tubes from the liver and remove the thin skin. Dust the trimmed slices with a little flour, then sprinkle generously with salt and pepper. Fry in the same pan until well browned and cooked to taste, about 10 or more minutes. When the liver is about done, return the onions to the pan to heat through.

This dish is good with a few slices of bacon fried before the onions, also reheated at the last minute.

BAKED BEEF LIVER

serves 4 to 6

If the oven was hot, it was convenient to bake the slices of liver.

4 or more thick slices of liver
(about 2 pounds total)
flour, salt, and pepper
2 tablespoons rendered pork fat

Cut out the major tubes from the liver and remove the thin skin. Dust the slices with flour, salt, and pepper, and lay in a shallow pan. Melt a little fat and drizzle about half of it over the slices, then turn them over and drizzle the other half on the other side. Bake at 350°F for 15 to 20 minutes.

FRIED VEAL

serves 4 to 6

If there was a surplus of young cattle, one or two might be reared for several months and eaten as veal; this was rare because selling them or rearing them further usually made more economic sense. If circumstances delivered such an animal, it was consumed with relish. Larger cuts of veal—a big piece of the leg, a shoulder, or a loin—were roasted (more accurately braised) in the same manner as roast beef or roast pork. Smaller, choice steaks, cut from the leg or loin, were considered a delicacy and fried with some ceremony.

Have all the vegetables for the meal cooked ahead of time, because veal doesn't take very long to cook.

4 larger or 6 smaller steaks cut from the leg or loin
flour, salt, and pepper
4 tablespoons rendered pork fat

Dust the veal with flour, salt, and pepper. Fry quickly in a hot pan for a few minutes on each side, depending on the thickness.

PORK

Pig-keeping was widespread. In some communities pigs were scarce, while in others almost every family kept one or two. With exceptions, pigs were not usually free-range but were provided with a sty, usually with a fenced enclosure. Most families who raised pigs bought piglets in the spring to fatten over the summer and fall. If there was a pig-farmer with breeding stock nearby to supply piglets, so much the better, otherwise they were brought in from somewhere else on the island or from Canada.

Pigs were fattened up on vegetable scraps from the kitchen, surplus vegetables, and wild vegetation. It was remarkable how often my sources remembered the food preferences of individual pigs: this one relished potato peelings, that one had a penchant for carrots but disliked turnips, another was fond of wild chickweed, gathered in armfuls by the children. After fattening for six to eight months, pigs were typically killed in December, when they averaged around 200 pounds dressed weight. The liver, kidneys, and heart were always eaten fresh, as were the choicer parts of the carcass. The cold weather at pig-killing time meant that portions of fresh meat kept for long periods hung up in the shed, semi-frozen if there was a cold snap.

Because salt pork was readily available to purchase, many ate home-raised pork fresh. But if there was a surplus of fresh pork, or for the more frugally minded, some pork was put up in salt in barrels. Which parts were salted depended on individual taste. Some salted only the flanks and parts of the shoulder, the cuts usually sold in commercially salted barrels of pork, but some also salted one or both of the back legs, to eventually become ham. Pork was also made into brawn and puddings.

In rural areas, fresh pork was only enjoyed in the weeks following the demise of the pig, but towns had imported fresh pork available year-round. Several different cuts of fresh pork were roasted, such as half a leg, a loin, or part of the shoulder. Pork was roasted like beef, although many people liked to use an open pan with no lid so that the fat and skin would crisp up. Roast pork was usually served with mashed potatoes, accompanied by vegetables and applesauce.

Pork tongues were eaten fresh or salted. A single tongue was only a meal for two, so fresh tongues were often traded so that, for example, one family would end up with six kidneys, another with three tongues. Salt tongues were popular all year, and many preferred them to fresh. Both fresh and salt tongues were cooked and eaten as ox tongues were. Pork heart, kidney, and liver were cooked like the corresponding organs of lamb or sheep.

Ham was available year-round in larger centres, and the press was full of advertisements for Irish, Canadian, and American hams. If you had killed your own pig, you could make your own ham, and in communities where ham was a traditional Easter meal, people salted at least one back leg and kept it until that season the following year.

TO MAKE A LARGE HAM

serves several families

1 salted back leg of a pig

Soak the salted leg in fresh water for 3 or 4 days, changing the water several times each day. Build a low platform of flat stones in a convenient sheltered location. Make the platform 1 foot or so wider all around than the diameter of the barrel that will be used. The height of the platform is not critical; it can be a few inches to a foot or more off the ground. Knock the ends out of a 200-pound barrel and stand it on the stone platform. Put a layer of dry sawdust at the bottom of the barrel, about 6 inches deep. Push a metal rod long enough to rest across the top of the barrel behind the big tendon at the end of the soaked leg and suspend it in the barrel.

Put two lengths of heavy iron chain, each about 2 or 3 feet long, in the firebox of your cookstove and leave there until fully red-hot. If you don't have an old-fashioned cookstove, keep a small fire burning close by to heat the chains. Seize one of these chains with tongs and drop it on the sawdust at the bottom of the barrel. Cover the top of the barrel and the pork leg with a piece of canvas or other cloth to contain the smoke, but you want a few wisps of smoke leaking out at the top to let you know that the sawdust is still smouldering. If the sawdust stops smouldering, lift the chain from the sawdust, put it back in the firebox, and take the other red-hot chain and drop it on the sawdust. Repeat this as necessary. Smoke the leg about 3 days, adding a little more sawdust as necessary and letting the fire go out at night.

SHEEP: LAMB AND MUTTON

Many families kept a few sheep, for both wool and meat. If pasture land was available, so much the better, but sheep could forage for themselves if let roam free. They were often kept over the winter to provide a steady source of wool or to get mature animals. Sheep kept over the winter needed a shed, usually with a small attached fenced area. Some people bought young animals in the spring, just as for piglets, and fattened them up. Then, like other animals, they were killed in the late fall in the cold weather. It was a bonus if it was cold enough to keep the meat semi-frozen for months, to be eaten fresh, because, in general, lamb and mutton were not salted.

Lamb and mutton were not widely popular in Newfoundland, perhaps partly because of the smell when mutton in particular was roasted in a kitchen with little ventilation. But roast lamb and mutton were enjoyed by some, and the favourite cuts for this were the leg, loin, and ribs. The rib portions were roasted whole. All were roasted in covered roasting pans. Mint sauce (page 259) was a usual accompaniment. Stew, made like beef stew, was also enjoyed, and any part of the animal was used, although meat from the forequarter was favoured.

STUFFED LAMB HEARTS

serves 4

Lamb hearts were never wasted but traded with those who prized them.

- 4 lamb hearts (about 4 to 5 ounces each)
- 1 recipe of stuffing for lamb hearts (page 160)
- 2 carrots
- 2 onions
- ½ teaspoon salt

Trim any excess fat from the tops (where the cavities open) of the hearts. Trim off surplus flaps of tissue to expose the openings of the cavities. Drop the cleaned hearts into boiling water and simmer about 5 minutes. This stiffens up the meat and makes the hearts much easier to stuff. Push the stuffing into the cavities. Start in the centre cavities and fill them nearly full, then fill the outer. Do not fill the cavities to the top as the stuffing expands as it cooks.

Stand the hearts upright in a covered pot which holds them without squeezing them together. Wedge them with quarters of onion and lengths of carrot. Add water almost to the top of the heart. Add salt. Add any surplus stuffing to the pot. Bake at 350°F for about 3½ hours. Remove the hearts, strain and reserve the juice, and keep warm.

Serve sliced hearts warm with vegetables and a little of the reserved juice. Or leave the hearts cool and serve sliced as a substantial supper or lunch with bread and butter and pickles.

FRIED LAMB KIDNEYS

serves 4

8 to 12 lamb kidneys
flour, salt, and pepper
4 tablespoons rendered pork fat, lard, or butter

Peel off the thin skin covering each kidney. Lay each kidney on a flat surface and cut it horizontally in half. Cut out the white fat from the middle of each half. Cut each half in two, giving four quarters from each kidney. Toss the kidney pieces with a little flour, salt, and pepper. Fry briskly in the fat.

GOAT

Goats are hardy creatures which thrive in places impossible for other animals and with their notoriously broad diet they were ideal for a free-range existence. A shed or barn was usually provided for the goats, particularly if breeding females were kept for milk. Females usually produced kids in the spring and then gave milk until it dried up in late fall. Lactating females, although they spent their days roaming and foraging, would return to their shed to be milked in the evening. Not everyone kept a male goat because of their infamous smell and because one billy could service many females.

Goat's milk was primarily used as fresh milk, but was sometimes plentiful enough to make a batch of goat's milk butter, which was made in the same fashion as cow's butter (page 165). Goat's milk butter is very pale and prized for its flavour.

Some goats were kept for meat, which was invariably eaten fresh. It was prepared and cooked in the same ways as lamb or mutton.

Goats are notoriously clever at getting through fences, so free-range goats were often equipped with yokes (ca. 1934–1938), to prevent them from getting into the gardens. *The Rooms Provincial Archives Division, VA 7-25.*

BRAWN, BLACK PUDDINGS, AND WHITE PUDDINGS

Brawn, also called head cheese or potted head-meat, was another way of using every scrap of a butchered animal. Basically, brawn is the meat on a head, which is rather difficult to get at, stewed so that the meat easily comes off the bone. Then it is chopped up with flavourings and set in its own jelly.

Brawn is not common in popular anthologies of local recipes, I suspect, because there is simply too much anatomy involved for squeamish modern cooks and also because heads are difficult to obtain. But for previous generations, much closer to the hard realities of life, it would have been unthinkable to discard such a rich source of meat as the head of a pig or cow.

Brawn can be made from the head of any large animal, domestic or wild, such as cow, pig, sheep, or moose. When made from a cow's head, sometimes a small amount of fresh pork was added to improve the flavour, or a sheep's head and a pig's head were combined for the same purpose.

BRAWN

serves 10 to 12

1 cow's head, a large pig's head, or 2 sheep's heads, skinned and cleaned
4 onions, finely chopped
1 cup finely chopped lean salt beef or salt pork
1 cup finely chopped fresh pork meat (optional)
1 tablespoon salt
2 teaspoons pepper

Trim the head thoroughly. Remove the skin, including the ears. Remove the eyeballs and cut off the nostrils. Wash the trimmed head thoroughly. The tongue can be removed and cooked as a separate dish or left in. Put the head in a pot big enough to hold it and just cover with water. Bring to a boil and simmer for 5 or 6 hours or until the meat is falling off the bone, replenishing the water as necessary with boiling water.

Take the pot off the heat and leave it until the head is cool enough to handle. Some people skimmed off the fat from the liquid, but very often there is so little fat on a head that it's hardly worth it. Split the skull to remove the brains and reserve them to eat separately. Pick all the meat off the bone and chop it coarsely, including the tongue. Put the chopped meat back in the pot with the cooking liquid. Add the onion, salt meat, salt, pepper, and fresh pork, if using. Bring to a boil and simmer for another 4 or 5 hours with the lid off. Let the liquid evaporate but don't let the pot go totally dry; there should be plenty of liquid in between the pieces of meat. Toward the end of the cooking time, taste it and add more salt and pepper if desired. Spoon the brawn into one or more shallow pans and leave to set.

Serve sliced with pickles as a light meal or with hot cooked vegetables as a main meal.

Black puddings, also called blood puddings, have a long history. When animals were killed in the fall, and highly perishable blood was suddenly in plentiful supply, people soon figured out how to mix it with fillings and flavourings and stuff it into a stomach or length of intestine. The Romans made blood puddings, and their popularity in modern Italy, Spain, Portugal, France, Germany, and Britain is supposedly a relic of that empire. But their popularity elsewhere, in Iceland and Finland for example, doesn't fit this story; the distribution of blood puddings likely reflects more the history of animal husbandry than of empire.

Whatever their history, blood puddings are treasured wherever they are made. They are the focus of many local food fairs and festivals in the north of Britain, and the French

Confrérie des Chevaliers du Goûte-Boudin was founded to promote blood puddings and holds an annual competition.

In Newfoundland, black puddings were made almost exclusively from the blood of cows, sheep, or pigs, according to what animal was being killed. The blood of different animals was never mixed, and my sources were vague about why not ("that's just the way we did it"). A likely explanation is because different animals were killed at different times, and because blood was so perishable, it could not be kept but had to be processed immediately.

BLACK PUDDINGS

made from 1 gallon of blood

Because blood puddings were eaten for any meal of the day, they were always consumed within a few days and never kept for very long. This recipe is very much in the French tradition of using onion as a filler. It was described to me by a woman from the west side of the Northern Peninsula, part of the old Newfoundland French Shore, so I suspect there was a connection. Puddings made in the British tradition were more likely to have a cereal of some sort as a filler, typically oatmeal in Ireland and England, or sometimes barley in Scotland.

1 cup milk
1 tablespoon salt
1 teaspoon pepper
4½ cups fatback pork, in ¼-inch cubes (about 1 pound)
1 cup sugar
2 tablespoons mixed pickling spices
8 cups onion, chopped small (about 2½ pounds)

Clean and thoroughly scrub a 2-gallon bucket for each average-sized sheep or pig. A cow will require about four 2-gallon buckets and correspondingly more of all the other ingredients. Put about 1 cup milk in the bottom of the bucket. Hoist the animal by its back legs as soon as it has been killed and bleed it directly into the prepared bucket until you have about 1 gallon of blood. Stir in the salt, pepper, spices, fatback, and onion.

Cut the small intestine from the just-killed animal. Clean the outside of the intestine carefully using a strong brine solution, then turn it inside out and scrape and scrub the inside until thoroughly clean. Rinse well and reserve to use as pudding casings. Fill the casing through a funnel with the prepared mixture, pushing it down with the handle of a wooden spoon. Tie off the casing with twine about every 10 inches, leaving 1 inch empty at both ends of each length so you are only filling about 8 inches in every 10. This leaves room for the filling to expand.

Have a large pot of boiling water ready. To prevent the puddings from sticking to the bottom of the pot, put a stick across the top and suspend the puddings on a string so that they are submerged but not touching the bottom. Boil for 10 or 15 minutes, or until no blood oozes out when a needle is stuck into the middle of a pudding. Do not test them by piercing with a knife because they are likely to split open.

Serve either fresh from the boiling water or allow to cool. Cooled puddings can be eaten cold as a supper or snack with pickles and bread and butter, reheated in simmering water and eaten with vegetables as a main course, or sliced and fried for breakfast or a main meal.

WHITE PUDDINGS

serves 4 to 6

White puddings are sometimes called oatmeal puddings because of the usual principal ingredient. These come directly from the Irish and British traditions, and Newfoundland is one of the few places outside the British Isles where they can be found. They were made in homes across the island and are still being produced by a few local butchers.

White puddings are essentially sausages made from suet and oatmeal, often with some pale pork meat included, with onion and seasonings. They were stuffed into a casing just like black puddings, and for this a leftover length of intestine was kept in salt to preserve it until needed, and then soaked and rinsed. White puddings were also poached in a cloth pudding bag.

1 cup finely chopped onion
1 cup finely chopped lean pork
4 cups suet
3 cups oatmeal
2 teaspoons salt
1 teaspoon pepper

Chop the suet by hand, grate it coarsely, or put it through a meat grinder. Mix with the onion, pork, oatmeal, salt, and pepper. Then proceed as for black puddings, if using casing. If using a pudding bag, fill the bag, leaving some space, and simmer for about 30 minutes.

White puddings can be served hot as a main meal or cooled and then fried in slices for breakfast or lunch.

Over: T. J. Malone's grocery store at 185 New Gower Street, St. John's, 1916–1927. The people to the left are likely Mr. and Mrs. Malone (with six young children), while the four women to the right are likely shop assistants. *City of St. John's Archives, 01-76-008.*

ALONE
GROCERIES T.J.MALONE
CHOICE BEEF TABLE BUTTER
CHOICE FAMILY MESS PORK PORK LOINS
SWEET GRAPES 17 LB
HAM BACON
BEST FLOUR 55

Chapter 10

Salt Meats: Pork, Fatback, and Beef

Salting and brining are long-standing techniques for preserving meat after animals are slaughtered in the fall. The heavy salting required for long-term preservation is very different from the brief, light salting fashionable in the early 21st century. Salt meats packed in barrels of brine were essential ship's provisions, particularly salt beef, often called salt horse, no doubt in part an irreverent sailor's description, but also perhaps because it sometimes really was.

Salt meats were an essential part of the settlement of Newfoundland. While supplies of fresh meat were intermittent or absent, a barrel of salt meat sat in the shed all year, to be dipped into when needed. Despite the easy availability of fresh meats in recent decades, salt meat is still popular for its taste and texture. Salt meats can be bought across Newfoundland, in supermarkets and rural general stores. In the latter, salt meat is still often displayed in large, open-topped tubs (plastic rather than the wooden barrels of years past), with a metal hook so that customers can fish around for their preferred piece. Supermarkets usually carry salt meats in small individual

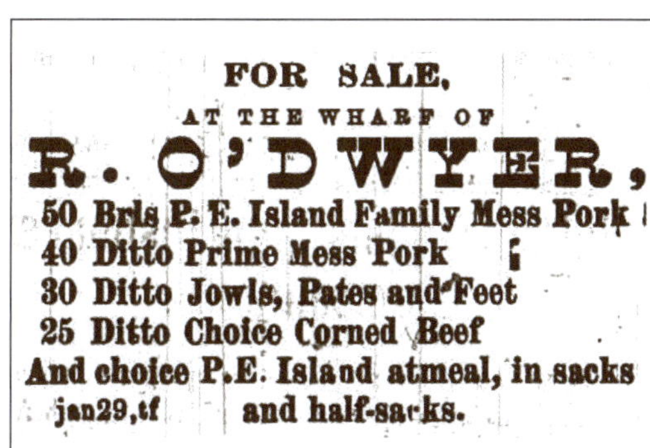
FOR SALE,
AT THE WHARF OF
R. O'DWYER,
50 Brls P. E. Island Family Mess Pork
40 Ditto Prime Mess Pork
30 Ditto Jowls, Pates and Feet
25 Ditto Choice Corned Beef
And choice P.E. Island atmeal, in sacks
jan29,tf and half-sacks.

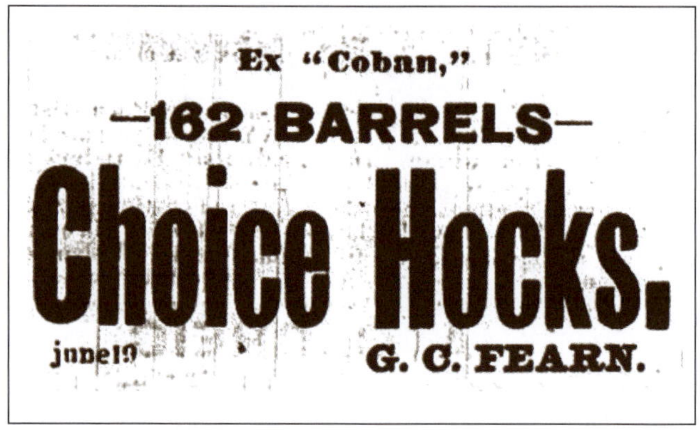

plastic tubs, with lids and a handle for easy carrying. When empty, these tubs are popularly reused—they have become, for example, the berry bucket of choice.

Domestically, an extensive variety of meats and poultry was salted, but commercially it was all pork or beef, with the occasional exception like sheep tongues.

SALT PORK

In the 21st century, salt pork is largely limited to a choice between ribs, riblets, or tongues, but in the 19th century and the first decades of the 20th century, newspaper advertisements show an extensive range of salt pork products: pork tongues, spare ribs, jowls (sometimes spelled or perhaps misspelled *joles*), pork hocks, pork heads, pork briskets, pork bellies, fatback, short cut clear pork, ham butt pork, mess pork, clear mess pork, heavy mess pork, prime mess pork, and family mess pork. Judging by the advertisements, the various types of mess pork were the most popular.

Most of those terms have fallen out of use, but they were simply trade descriptions of what was in the barrel. For example, mess pork was 6- or 7-inch-wide strips from the sides of the thickest and fattest hogs cut back to belly, whereas prime mess pork was 4-pound pieces cut from the sides of lighter hogs and included the shoulder. Nominally, each barrel contained 200 pounds of pork, but in reality between 190 and 196 pounds were packed to allow for their slight increase in weight after some time in brine in the barrel.

Like all salt meats, salt pork was soaked at least overnight but often for 24 hours or more before being simmered for a time appropriate to its size. Salt pork could be the focus of a main meal with vegetable accompaniments, or simmered in a soup as background flavour, particularly in pea soup (page 46). A piece of salt pork was often substituted for salt beef in the traditional boiled dinner.

SALT FATBACK PORK

Fatback is the thick layer of fat between the skin and the meat on top of the backbone of a pig. In Newfoundland fatback meant the salted fat—the unsalted version was called fresh fatback or similar. The fat was cut into slabs, salted, and shipped to market in barrels topped up with brine. Fatback was a mainstay of the Newfoundland kitchen, because a barrel of fatback in brine was a reliable resource; other fats like butter or margarine were either unavailable or difficult to store properly. Fatback was a source of rendered fat, and the scrunchions—crispy remains after rendering—accompanied many other foods.

Small cubes of fatback, either uncooked or as scrunchions, were incorporated into savoury dishes such as potato cakes (page 157), steamed puddings (chapter 16), small buns (page 156), and breads. Although margarine became widely popular when it arrived late in the 19th century, it never completely usurped fatback in the Newfoundland kitchen.

RENDERED FATBACK

makes 1 ¼ cups fat and 1 cup scrunchions

Rendering fatback for both liquid fat and the scrunchions was a simple process. The rendered fat was used for frying and in cakes and buns, and the scrunchions served with salt fish or added to buns or cakes.

3 cups (about 1 pound) small cubes salt fatback

Place the fatback in a frying pan and heat very gently with the lid on. The fatback will first release water and then start to render. After about 15 minutes remove the lid and continue frying on a low heat until the cubes have shrunk and are pale golden. Do not cook them until they are dark brown, or they will burn. Drain the rendered fat into a small jar and keep in a cool place. Reserve the scrunchions separately.

SALT BEEF

A cautionary word about terminology. Salt beef was so ubiquitous that it was (and still is) often simply called salt meat, whereas salt pork was specified as such. For clarity, however, the type of meat will be specified in these recipes. In the early 21st century, shoppers are limited to one or two choices of salt beef cuts, but in the 19th and early 20th centuries, options included ox tongue, packet beef, plate beef, medium family beef, choice family beef, naval beef, and navel beef among others. As for pork, the names were trade descriptions of the contents of the barrel. Both *naval* and *navel* beef appeared in advertisements in the *Evening Telegram*, St. John's, in 1911, and both spellings persist to this day. But were they indeed different cuts of beef with different names or was one a misspelling of the other?

Salt beef was eaten in a limited number of ways. Small pieces were usually put in pea soup or any other hearty vegetable soup. A piece was often cooked as a flavour enhancer with the vegetables that accompanied any main meal—and always a crucial part of a boiled dinner, one of the more important meals in the Newfoundland kitchen.

BOILED DINNER

A boiled dinner had many names in Newfoundland. It was called Sunday dinner, because many people only had it on that day. It was called simply a cooked dinner, but of course most other foods were cooked but never referred to as such. It was called a salt meat dinner, or corned (salted) beef and cabbage, even though the cabbage was only one of several vegetables involved. It was also called Jiggs' dinner, more frequently in towns than elsewhere. The etymology of Jiggs' dinner is not clear. The most likely explanation is that it was the favourite corned beef and cabbage meal of Jiggs, the central character in George McManus's long-running cartoon strip which started in 1913. A far less believable explanation is that Jiggs is short for jiggers, the men who jigged for cod, who relished a boiled dinner after a day's jigging. And although considered a typical Newfoundland meal, it is essentially the same as the New England boiled dinner, and similar dishes are found in the peasant traditions of most of western Europe.

A boiled dinner was a meal of salt beef and vegetables, typically turnip, carrot, cabbage, potato, and sometimes parsnip, cooked in one pot, along with a pease pudding and often dumplings. What follows is a typical, basic recipe that could have been (and still can be) found anywhere across the island.

BOILED DINNER

serves 8 to 10

3 pounds salt beef
1 cup split yellow peas
12 carrots
1 turnip
6 parsnips
12 potatoes
1 cabbage
1 gallon turnip greens, in season
1 recipe of dumpling dough, with or without fat (page 49)

Put the salt beef in water to soak about 12 hours before cooking it, and change the water several times. In a separate bowl, soak the split peas overnight; there is no need to change the water.

About 5 hours before meal time, rinse the soaked beef. Put it, and about 5 quarts water, in a 12- to 16-quart stockpot and bring to a boil. Drain the peas, put them in a pudding bag, and tie off the neck of the bag, leaving room for expansion—at least one-quarter of the bag should be empty. Place the bag in the pot with the beef. Leave to simmer.

Peel and trim the carrots and parsnips, and if they are more than about 1 inch thick, halve lengthways. Peel the turnip and cut into 1-inch slices or wedges. Trim the cabbage and cut into wedges. Peel the potatoes and cut them in half, then place in a bowl and cover with cold water until needed.

About 1 hour and 15 minutes before meal time, add the turnip and carrot to the pot. About 15 minutes later, add the potato and parsnip, and finally, after about 30 minutes, add the cabbage. Make the dumpling dough and form it into balls. After the cabbage has cooked for about 30 minutes (i.e., at least 60 minutes after the first vegetables went in), add the dumplings and simmer another 10 minutes, or longer for large dumplings.

Remove the dumplings and vegetables and keep them warm. Lift out the pease pudding and let it drain. Remove the beef, cut it in pieces, and keep warm. Let the pudding bag drain in a sieve set over the stockpot, untie the string, invert the bag into a bowl, and roll it up to leave the peas behind, scraping the sides of the bag with a spoon as necessary. If desired, thin the pudding by mixing in a little pot liquor (the liquid the food was cooked in). Moisten the reserved vegetables and beef with pot liquor. When serving this dinner, moisten each plateful with a few more spoonfuls of the pot liquor.

If turnip greens are in season, cook 1 gallon or more in a separate pot in salted water for about 20 to 30 minutes, drain, and serve. They can be cooked in the pot along with everything else, but then they have to be retrieved by skimming them off the top, which gets messy.

Serve with pickles and bread and butter.

If you want to cook this iconic Newfoundland dish but are unfamiliar with the style and ingredients, a little more explanation will be useful. This was a one-pot meal easily expanded for more mouths or bigger appetites, not something to be cooked for two people. The cook was always generous with quantities because all the components had many uses as leftovers. The first requirement was a large pot—a 3- or 4-gallon vessel would hold enough for eight or more people, but for Sunday dinner for an extended family, several large pots were needed. One nearly 90-year-old woman I talked to cooked a boiled dinner for her entire extended family every Sunday, seeing it as a matriarchal obligation. She used three 5-gallon pots and did all the preparation to feed 30 or more people herself, although she did allow the youngsters—anyone under the age of 65—to clean up afterwards.

To cater to 21st-century tastes, vacuum-packed pieces of very lean salt beef are available, and can be good—but remember that salt beef needs some fat on it. Not everyone will eat it, but it must be present to flavour the cooking liquid and vegetables. Although the salt beef is absolutely essential to this meal, it was not the primary ingredient: the small portion any one person eats is more of a relish to complement the vegetables.

How much salt beef is needed is difficult to specify, but about ⅓ to ½ pound per person is a good estimate, assuming it is roughly 50 per cent fat. Then you must soak it to get rid of most of the salt. There's nothing elaborate about this—no need to get up in the middle of the night—simply rinse it well, soak in excess fresh water for about 12 hours, and change the water several times when convenient.

The vegetables were always prepared well ahead of time. Most people staggered the cooking times as described, but some cooks put all the vegetables in at once. In general, cooking times seem long by today's standards. The heat of a wood stove could not be cranked up at the turn of a knob, so cooking times were necessarily longer to give pots time to return to a boil each time cold ingredients were added. The quantities of vegetables given above are even more approximate than usual. If you are used to these ingredients, you can look at a turnip or a cabbage and know how many it will feed. If in doubt, the guidelines above will do for a start.

Over: Caribou were killed for both food and sport. This dead caribou is at an unknown location in Newfoundland, pre-1912.
Archives and Special Collections Division, Memorial University, 25 02 003.

Chapter 11

Wild Meat from Land and Sea

LAND ANIMALS

Beaver, muskrat, and black bear are grouped together here because they were only occasionally found in Newfoundland kitchens—eaten when opportunity presented, but usually only hunted by professional hunters or trappers. I met a few people who had eaten these animals, and only one or two who had cooked them. Their advice was to cook them like beef, so the recipes in Chapter 9 can be followed. For further information, I suggest Eleanor Ellis's 1999 *Northern Cookbook*.

Caribou, native to Newfoundland, were quite plentiful in the 19th century before their precipitous decline in the 20th century. When sold as food in Newfoundland, caribou meat was usually called venison, and advertisements for it were numerous in the late 19th and early 20th centuries, when it was shipped from the west and north of the island to St. John's. Caribou meat was prepared and cooked much like beef, mutton, or pork, and recipes for them were easily adapted to caribou.

Moose were first successfully introduced to Newfoundland at Howley (central Newfoundland) in 1904. By 1935 they had reached most of the island except the Avalon Peninsula, where they were first seen in 1941. The first official hunting season was in 1935, when 80 licences were issued. Moose may seem a traditional Newfoundland food, but it only became so after World War II and therefore outside the scope of this book. I suspect that many were shot and eaten well before moose hunting was regulated, and recipes for beef were easily adapted to this new meat.

The snowshoe hare was introduced to Newfoundland in the 1860s and 1870s. It spread rapidly across the island and quickly became a popular and important item in the Newfoundland kitchen. The native Arctic hare is at the southern edge of its range in Newfoundland, restricted to a limited number of Arctic-like upland areas, and has never been an important source of food. I am following local custom by calling hares "rabbits."

Rabbit-hunting season has always been roughly from mid-October through the following four or five months. Most rabbits were eaten fresh, although, if they were plentiful, they were bottled or canned once the technologies were available (see Chapter 21). Rarely, rabbit was pickled in a saturated brine solution, but this was not popular because pickled rabbit was said not to keep well in warmer weather.

Fresh rabbit was fried, stewed, and made into pies and soup. A rabbit was typically cut into six portions: four legs and two halves of the loin (with kidneys left attached). The rib cage (often called the lantern) was sometimes put in a stew but more often reserved for soup. The heart and liver were cleaned and added to a fry, stew, or pie. The head was enjoyed in a stew, pie, or soup. One of my early introductions to Newfoundland was being served rabbit stew with one of the heads put on my plate as a special treat. There it was, semi-floating in a bowl of stew, with a chunk of carrot wedged by chance between its bared teeth, in a grim parody of the roast suckling pig and its apple. I didn't know what to do, and I hope my reluctance more amused than offended my hosts. A quick demonstration enlightened me: first pick out and eat the tongue, then the meaty bits on the cheeks, and finally suck out the brains—not for the faint-hearted.

Fried rabbit is best with a younger, smaller, and more tender animal. Larger, older rabbits are best kept for stew, pie, or soup.

FRIED RABBIT

serves 4

2 rabbits, skinned and cleaned
flour, salt, and pepper
2 tablespoons rendered pork fat

Cut off the rabbit heads and rib cages and reserve for making soup. Cut off the legs. Split each loin into halves, leaving a kidney attached to each. Mix the flour, salt, and pepper. Pat the pieces, including hearts and livers, dry with a clean cloth, and dust with the seasoned flour. Fry in a hot pan in the fat for 5 to 10 minutes a side, or until cooked through and nicely browned.

Serve with bread and butter and pickles as a snack or light supper or with vegetables as a main meal.

RABBIT STEW

serves 4 to 6

A popular alternative to thickening a rabbit stew with flour was to cook rice with the vegetables. To do so, use about ¼ cup uncooked rice in the recipe below.

2 rabbits, skinned and cleaned
salt and pepper
2 tablespoons rendered pork fat
1 onion, chopped
2 or 3 carrots, chopped
4 tablespoons flour
½ cup cold water
1 recipe of dumplings (page 49, optional)

Cut off the rabbit heads and legs. Cut off the rib cages and reserve for soup. Split each loin into halves, leaving a kidney attached to each. Lightly brown the pieces, including the heads, livers, and hearts, in the fat in a hot pan. Put the browned rabbit in a saucepan that will be half filled by the pieces. Add the onion and enough water to cover. Add a little salt and pepper, bring to a boil, and simmer gently for 1 hour or until the rabbit is just tender. Add the carrot and simmer another 30 minutes. Shake the flour with the water and use spoonfuls to thicken the stew. Dumplings can be added to the stew for the last 10 minutes or so, depending on their size.

Serve as a main meal with boiled potatoes, turnip, and parsnip.

RABBIT PIE

serves 4 to 6

Rabbit pie, essentially a stew with pastry, was an excellent way of stretching a limited amount of rabbit. This recipe is similar to the stew above but illustrates how a single rabbit could serve the same number of people by adding more vegetables and pastry.

- 1 rabbit, skinned and cleaned
- 2 tablespoons rendered pork fat
- 1 onion, chopped
- 2 carrots, chopped
- 1 parsnip, chopped
- ¼ turnip, chopped
- 4 tablespoons flour
- ½ cup cold water
- 1 recipe of pastry (page 198)

Cut off the rib cage and reserve for making soup. Keep the head, heart, and liver and clean them well. Cut off the legs. Split each loin into halves, leaving a kidney attached to each. Lightly brown the pieces, including the head, liver, and heart, in the fat in a hot pan. Put the rabbit in a saucepan that will be about half filled by the pieces. Add the onion and enough water to cover. Add a little salt and pepper, bring to a boil, and simmer gently for 1 hour or more until the rabbit is just tender. Add the carrot, turnip, and parsnip, and simmer another 30 minutes. Shake the flour with the water and use spoonfuls of this to thicken the stew. Leave to cool if possible.

Make the pastry and roll it out into two circles. Line a 9-inch pie plate with one circle, and spoon in the cooled stew. Moisten the rim of the bottom pastry, lay the other circle of pastry on top, and press the two together. Crimp the pastry edges firmly together to seal. Cut several small slits in the top, and bake at 350°F for 1 hour or until the pastry is well browned. Serve with potatoes as a main meal.

SEA ANIMALS

Every fall a huge herd of harp seals migrates south from the Arctic and in mid-December arrives at the top of the Northern Peninsula, where it splits into two groups. The larger group travels down the east side of the island, while the smaller group goes down the west side into the Gulf of St. Lawrence. In late February to early March of the following year, females give birth on the pack ice, and the herds slowly move north again on the retreating ice. For the first inhabitants of Newfoundland, the Archaic Indians and particularly the Paleoeskimos, this annual glut of seals was a vital resource that sustained their way of life. From the 19th century to the 1970s, the eastern seal herd was the focus of an industrial-scale commercial hunt.

The commercial seal fishery was primarily for pelts, seen here being cleaned on the St. John's harbourfront, 1892–1917. *The Rooms Provincial Archives Division, B 1-103.*

The seal fishery, as it was called, was primarily for pelts, although some of the meat was brought back to be sold or taken home by sealers. This fishery was prosecuted by ordinary fishermen from large ships which went out to the retreating ice front. This annual sealing voyage, called "going to the Front," was an important source of cash in the seasonal cycle of mixed economic activities. It was also a rite of passage for many young men, but it was a dirty and dangerous business, and Newfoundlanders are well aware of the tragedies that were all too common.

In the earliest days of European settlement, a domestic seal harvest focused on meat rather than blubber or pelts. This was carried out from the land (hence the term "landsman harvest"). Nets were employed to catch the seals, or men in small boats ventured out to shoot them, or "fish" for them with baited hooks—a typical arrangement was a line with a series of 2½-inch-long hooks, each baited with a whole herring or other fish. Sometimes seals were taken right off the beach when a fortunate wind drove them onshore. Other species of seal, such as the harbour seal, were hunted, but none was as important or as abundant as the harp seal, which in season could provide more meat than any one family could use.

Depending on local custom, and sometimes on the elasticity of the conscience of the local Roman Catholic priest, seal was considered either meat or fish, or sometimes both. If fish, then it could be eaten on a Friday, but if meat, it could not. And if meat, it might be considered fresh meat, and suitable for a Sunday dinner. But the reverse was also true—that it was not proper fresh meat, such as beef or rabbit, and so unsuitable for a proper Sunday dinner.

Newfoundlanders in general distinguished only three cuts of seal meat: head, flippers, and the rest of the body simply called carcass. The liver was used by some. The head was often discarded, but sometimes kept to be eaten. The flippers (front limbs) were cut off and reserved. The rest of the body was typically split down the backbone into two sides, each then divided into portions.

The bulk of seal meat was eaten fresh in season. It was not common practice to salt seal because the conventional wisdom was that lighter salting suited seal best but such salting would not preserve the meat through warm weather. Where the technology was available, some seal was canned.

Seal fat is infamous for its strong, fishy flavour, which is why many recipes contain stern warnings about trimming off every scrap of fat. Maybe. But I suspect the length of time since the seal was killed was a major factor in fat fishiness. Many Newfoundlanders never ate seal brought back from the industrial hunt because it had been dead too long and the fat was half rancid. They would only eat locally caught seal which, they claimed, had quite fragrant fat because it was fresh. When trying any of the recipes below with a freshly killed seal, remove only the obvious lumps of fat. If the seal is of unknown freshness, try to remove all visible fat. Soaking the meat in a solution of baking soda (about 1 teaspoon or more dissolved in 1 quart of water) for about 1 hour turns the fat an opaque white which makes it easier to see and remove.

Seal flippers were widely considered the choicest body part. If possible, buy ready-trimmed flippers. These will be skinned with the hand cut off at the wrist, leaving the flattish stubs of the radius and ulna visible at one end of the flipper. To work with untrimmed flippers, cut off all the skin and fur and remove any fat. Cut off the hand and fingers at the wrist by grasping the middle of the flipper with one hand (i.e., grasp the upper arm and forearm simultaneously) and the hand of the seal firmly in your other hand. Wiggle one against the other. A point of articulation between seal hand and forearm will be obvious. Cut down at that point to sever the wrist, and discard the hand and fingers. What is left is the forearm, upper arm, and shoulder blade with all the attached muscles. Flippers do not have much fat on them, so if the flippers are fresh it can be left on, otherwise see the note above about seal fat. A typical trimmed flipper is about 12 ounces but can be less than ½ pound or more than 1 pound. They can be prepared in any of the ways used for carcass pieces or used in the three recipes below, and in flipper pie.

FRIED SEAL FLIPPERS

serves 4

Only make this recipe with small flippers, no more than about 12 ounces each, from young seals. After the initial browning, keep the heat low so that the meat does not burn on the outside before it is cooked through. To my mind this is not the best way to cook flippers—moist heat is better, which allows longer cooking and ensures tenderness without drying out the meat.

2 seal flippers (about 8 to 12 ounces each), washed well
2 tablespoons rendered pork fat
salt and pepper

Melt the fat in a frying pan (which has a cover) just big enough to hold the flippers. Sprinkle them with salt and pepper, then brown on both sides, about 3 to 4 minutes per side on a medium heat. Cover the pan and continue to fry on a very low heat, for 20 minutes each side or until the meat is tender.

Serve with potatoes and vegetables.

SEAL FLIPPERS with MUSTARD

serves 4

The mustard used here was usually a loose paste made from dry, powdered mustard, equivalent in strength to an average Dijon. Occasionally strong English mustard was specified, for this and other recipes. Far less prepared English mustard would be required, no more than about ¼ teaspoon on each side of two flippers.

This method works well with flipper or a piece of carcass. If the flippers are more than 1 pound each (likely from an older animal), stew about 1 hour on the first side, then another hour plus however long is necessary on the second side to allow a small knife to penetrate the meat easily.

2 seal flippers (about 1 pound each), washed well
2 tablespoons rendered pork fat
salt and pepper
4 teaspoons prepared mustard
water

Melt the fat in a frying pan (with a cover) which can hold the flippers side by side. Sprinkle them with salt and pepper, then brown on both sides, about 3 to 4 minutes per side on medium heat. Brush one side of both flippers with half of the mustard, add about ¼ inch of water to the pan, cover and stew very gently for about 45 minutes. Turn the flippers over, and brush with the remaining mustard. Add a little more water to replace any lost to evaporation. Cover and stew very gently for 45 minutes or longer, until the meat is very tender and starting to fall off the bone.

SEAL FLIPPERS with VINEGAR

serves 4

2 flippers (about 1 pound each), washed well
½ cup white vinegar, or more to taste
2 tablespoons rendered pork fat
salt and pepper

Place the flippers in a large saucepan, cover them with lightly salted water, and bring to a boil. Simmer about 1½ hours, or until the meat can be pierced with the point of a small knife but is not falling off the bone. Remove the partly cooked flippers, drain well, and place in a wide frying pan (with a cover) that just holds them. Add the fat and vinegar, cover the pan, and fry them on a low heat for about 1 hour, turning once or twice and basting with the vinegary pan juices. Add salt and pepper. At the end of the cooking time, most of the vinegar should have evaporated. If there is any quantity left, simmer uncovered until much of the liquid has evaporated. If a stronger vinegar taste is preferred, use more vinegar.

Serve hot with potatoes and vegetables, or cold with bread and butter and pickles.

SEAL FLIPPER PIE with dumpling-paste topping

serves 4 to 6

Flipper pies were (and are) a favourite dish, the only way many people ate seal. Such popularity inevitably spawned a contentious range of opinions on how best to make them. Pastry top and bottom, or just on top? If just on top, biscuit-style topping or pastry proper? Should the filling be rather dry, mostly meat, with the vegetables cooked separately and served alongside? Or should it be rich with gravy and vegetables cooked with the meat? This recipe falls on the dry side of the spectrum, with a dumpling-paste topping; the next recipe is richer and topped with pastry. If well made, flipper pie can be a delicacy, surprisingly so for the uninitiated.

This is a basic flipper pie. I have called the topping dumpling paste for clarity, but it was traditionally always called pastry.

2 flippers (each about ¾ pound), washed well
6 strips fatback
1 large onion, chopped
salt and pepper
1 ½ cups water, approximately
1 recipe of dumpling-paste topping (page 199)

Soak the flippers in cold water overnight. Next day, put them in a covered baking pan that will hold them in one layer, or slightly overlapping. Add the onion and then water to come about halfway up the flippers. Sprinkle with salt and pepper, and lay the fatback on top. Cover and bake at 350°F. After about 2 hours, check the tenderness of the meat; if it is not tender, bake for another 30 minutes or more. Make sure there is enough liquid left in the pan, and if necessary add boiling water to come about halfway up the flippers. Make the dumpling-paste topping and roll it out to fit the pan. Lay on the flippers and bake 30 to 40 minutes or more (uncovered), until the topping is lightly browned.

Serve with vegetables and potatoes.

SEAL FLIPPER PIE with pastry on top

serves 4 to 6

There were many modifications of this recipe. Parsnips were a favourite addition, and frequently potatoes were added to the vegetable mixture in the pie rather than being cooked and served separately. Sometimes a slug or two of dark rum was added; the rum complements and stands up to the strong taste of the seal meat.

2 seal flippers (about 1 ½ to 2 pounds total)
10 strips fatback
1 large onion, chopped
salt and pepper
2 cups water
4 cups vegetable cubes, mixed carrot, turnip, and parsnip
2 tablespoons flour
1 recipe of butter pastry for a single crust (page 198)

Wash the flippers well and pat dry. Place in a covered baking pan that holds them comfortably, without too much surplus space. Scatter the onion around and between the flippers, sprinkle with salt and pepper, and lay the fatback on the flippers. Add water to almost cover the flippers, cover, and bake at 325°F for about 2½ hours. Add the vegetables, pushing the cubes down between and around the flippers, and if necessary add more boiling water to almost cover the vegetables. Cover and bake another 1 to 1 ½ hours. Pour off most of the liquid; you will get about 1 ½ to 2 cups. Thicken with about 2 tablespoons flour, or more for a thicker gravy. Pour this gravy over the flippers and vegetables. Make the pastry and roll it out into a rough circle a little larger than the pan. Trim the edges. Lay it on the flippers, vegetables, and gravy, and bake another 45 minutes or until it is lightly browned.

Serve with potatoes.

FRIED SEAL CARCASS

serves 6

Seal carcass encompassed anything which was neither head nor flipper, which meant it was part of the shoulder, ribs, or loin. The ribs were usually cut off and discarded or used for soup (page 48). Most traditional cooking methods for carcass were stews or oven braises, in which potentially tough old meat could be coaxed into an edible tenderness.

This recipe is similar to that for fried flipper, and the same cautions apply: use meat from a young animal only, keep the heat low to avoid burning, and choose methods which keep the meat moist so that it can be cooked for a longer time.

2 or 3 pieces of seal loin
(about 4 pounds total, on the bone),
washed well
4 tablespoons rendered pork fat

Heat the fat in a wide, covered frying pan on a low to medium heat. Add the seal, cover, and fry for about 30 minutes, turning the pieces over once. Uncover and fry for another 15 to 30 minutes, turning pieces as necessary, until they are nicely browned all over.

Serve as a dinner with vegetables or as a supper with bread and butter.

ROAST SEAL CARCASS

serves 6

Beware the words *roast*, *braised*, and *baked* in traditional Newfoundland meat cookery because there is little difference between them. Roast tends to refer to drier preparations, with little or no water added to the pot, but plenty of recipes for roast include liquid. Baked and braised, usually indistinguishable, always have added liquid. But my sources insisted on the different terms, so I give an example of each, even though they differ only in detail.

2 pieces of seal loin, bone in
(about 2 pounds each), or an
equivalent amount of shoulder
3 onions, quartered
6 thin slices fatback

Lay the seal in a single layer in a covered roasting pan. Lay the onions between and beside the seal. Lay the fatback on the seal. Cover and bake at 350°F for about 2 hours, or longer if needed to make the meat completely tender.

Serve with potatoes and vegetables.

BRAISED SEAL

serves 4 to 6

1 piece of seal shoulder, or 4 flippers (about 4 pounds)
2 medium onions, chopped
12 strips fatback
2 cups water
4 tablespoons flour mixed with ½ cup water
salt and pepper

Wash the seal well and cut off any obvious fat. Lay the onions in a roasting pan. Put the seal on the onions and the fatback on the seal. Add about 2 cups water, and sprinkle salt and pepper on top. Cover and bake at 350°F for 2 to 2½ hours. Check after 1 hour and add ½ cup water if it looks dry. While the seal is roasting, mix ½ cup water into the flour, incorporating any lumps to make a smooth mixture. When the meat is tender and starting to fall off the bone, remove it from the pan and keep warm. Put the pan on the stove to heat the liquid left in it. Stir about half the flour mixture into the liquid to thicken it, adding more as needed to make it as thick as desired.

Lay the meat on the gravy and serve at once or put back in the oven to heat through if required. Serve with potatoes and vegetables.

BAKED SEAL CARCASS with mustard

serves 6

4 pounds seal carcass, in one or more pieces, bone in
4 tablespoons rendered pork fat
salt and pepper
6 tablespoons dry mustard
water

Wash the seal well and soak in water overnight. Drain and pat dry. Fry on a medium heat, turning until both sides are browned. Spread about half the mustard over one side of the seal. Add water to about one-third of the way up the seal, season with salt and pepper, cover, and bake at 350°F for about 1 hour. Turn over the seal, brush the other side with the remaining mustard, add water to bring the level back up, cover, and bake for another hour or until the meat is tender and the liquid reduced. Serve with potatoes and vegetables.

SEAL HEAD

serves 4

Seal heads were highly appreciated by some. Typically, the tongue was left in the head during cooking. The brains were particularly enjoyed, sometimes eaten with the head, but often separately. I am assured that the large muscles behind the eye (but not the eyeball itself) were a delicacy, but I have no personal knowledge of this.

2 seal heads
½ cup salt pork cubes
4 onions, quartered

Remove the skin and the eyeballs. Remove the snout by cutting down in a scooping motion to the bone. Wash the heads well, then place in a large saucepan which just holds the heads without too much spare space. Add the salt pork, onions, and water to barely cover. Bring to a boil and simmer at least 2 hours or until the meat is falling off the bone.

If preferred—or if appetites are small—do not eat the brains at the same time as the meat on the head, but reserve the skulls intact in a cool place. Next day, split the skull open with a small hatchet or by placing a large knife along the centre of the skull and tapping the knife blade with a hammer. Lever the skull open and carefully lift out the brains. Eat the cold brains, sliced, with bread and butter and pickles.

FRIED SEAL LIVER
serves 6

Seal liver was loved or hated, but I am unable to pass comment because this is one of the few recipes in this book I have not prepared. My sources reported that seal liver has a milder flavour than the meat and can be enjoyed by those who find the taste of seal meat a little strong.

2 to 3 pounds seal liver
flour, salt, and pepper
4 tablespoons rendered pork fat

Trim the liver well to remove the fat, larger tubes, and connective tissue. Rinse well and pat dry. Cut into approximately ½-inch-thick slices. Combine flour with a little salt and pepper. Turn the liver in the seasoned flour and shake off the surplus. Fry in the fat on a medium-high heat, turning once, until well browned on both sides and cooked through.

Serve with potatoes and vegetables.

■ WHALE

In the 16th century, Basques hunted whales on an industrial scale at several places in what is now the province of Newfoundland and Labrador. But apart from that, for the first 300 years of the European settlement of Newfoundland whales were only an intermittent supply of meat when they beached themselves—not something to be relied on. The arrival of the explosive harpoon (a harpoon with an explosive charge in the head that detonated when it pierced the whale) in the late 19th century made whale hunting an economically feasible enterprise, with its heyday in the early 20th century. As late as 1969 whaling was still practiced on a small scale, mainly to provide cheap protein for mink farms. As a sideline, whale meat was sold for human consumption, and many people can remember whale meat tidily packaged on the supermarket shelf under the label "Arctic Steak." Those packaged whale steaks were from minke whales, and the butchery was rather haphazard. The whale was delivered to supermarkets in frozen blocks, where it was sawed, still frozen, into ½-inch-thick slabs. Then it was trimmed into portions to fit the plastic trays on which it was sold. In the 1960s in St. John's it was cheap meat, and I quite liked it. It was rich, dark, and finely textured, not really like the beef it is usually compared with.

Typically whale was fried like steak, maybe with onions on the side. It was also made into a stew or pie with extra vegetables, and recipes for beef can be used.

PAN-FRIED WHALE STEAK

serves 4

Whale meat is not good rare, so there is no point having steaks any thicker than ¾ inch thick for pan frying. Although it looks very lean, whale meat contains fat which renders out in the pan and leaves greasy, fatty smells. I would never attempt this again without a good extractor fan over my stove.

4 whale steaks, each about ¾ inch thick
3 tablespoons rendered pork fat
salt and pepper

Sprinkle the steaks with salt and pepper and fry in the fat on a medium heat for about 10 minutes or more per side.

Serve with potatoes and vegetables.

Over: Free range domestic ducks and ducklings, at an unknown location in Newfoundland 1934–1938. *The Rooms Provincial Archives Division, VA 7-2.*

Chapter 12

Domestic Poultry, Eggs, and Wild Birds

CHICKENS

Keeping chickens was common across Newfoundland, primarily for eggs but also for the meat. As laying hens were often eaten at around two years old before they got too tough and stringy, each year new chicks were hatched to replace those killed. If there was a surplus of young chicks, a few might be reared for three or four months to eating size. Those who did not have a cockerel got young chicks from someone who did. Chicks were bought from the merchant as a last resort.

My sources were vague about which breeds were kept, simply calling them brown, speckled brown, all-white, and so forth. The named breeds advertised for sale before 1900 were primarily light brahma, Plymouth Rock, white leghorn, and wynadottes, with the occasional mention of Spanish, Cochin, and Houdan. The brahmas and Plymouth Rock were particularly popular because they were large,

On SATURDAY next, at 1 oclock,

BY JAMES HYNES,

(At his Rooms, opposite JOB BROTHERS & Co.)

A Lot of Light Brahma FOWL,

ap30 OF SUPERIOR QUALITY.

These free-range hens at an unknown location in Newfoundland in 1934–1937 were fitted with yokes to prevent them getting into the gardens. *The Rooms Provincial Archives Division, VA 7-34.*

cold-hardy birds which would lay a few eggs through the winter and make a meal for a family. In the first quarter of the 20th century many more breeds were mentioned in advertisements: white, buff, and black Orpingtons; white, Columbian, silver laced, gold laced, and partridge wynadottes; brown leghorn; Indian game; single comb Minorca; ancona; black langsham; campine; Polish; blue Andalusian; Rhode Island red; white rock, and barred Plymouth Rock, among others. Many of those records were from the St. John's poultry show, held between 1912 and 1924, and some of these breeds may have been ornamental rather than egg- and meat-producers.

A family of six or seven likely had eight or 10 hens plus a rooster. The birds always had a hen house, with roosts and nesting boxes. Some had an enclosed pen attached, but many hens free ranged during the day and returned to the hen house in the evening. It was usually the woman's job to both feed the chickens and collect the eggs, although these tasks were often delegated to the children. Chickens were fed vegetable peelings, vegetables not fit for the table, tea leaves, and other kitchen waste. Grain was rarely bought because of the expense, although some people did buy cracked corn or other feed to supplement the household scraps. Hens were never fed fish scraps because the eggs would taste fishy.

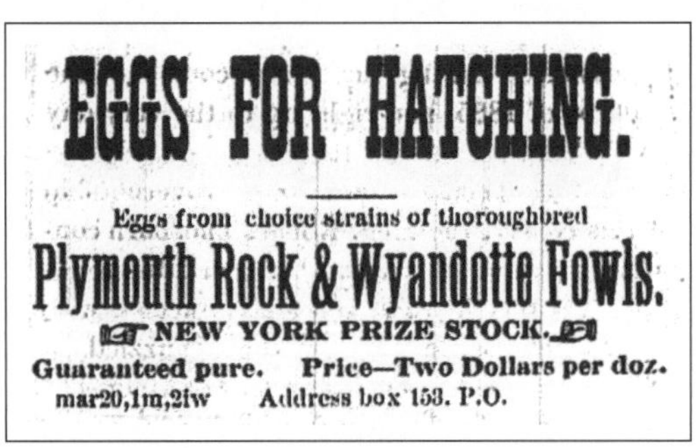

EGGS FOR HATCHING.

Eggs from choice strains of thoroughbred

Plymouth Rock & Wyandotte Fowls.

NEW YORK PRIZE STOCK.

Guaranteed pure. Price—Two Dollars per doz.

mar20,1m,2iw Address box 153. P.O.

Chickens for the table were either older layers or younger ones reared just for eating. Either could be roasted, but older birds were usually stewed, which tenderized meat that could be tough. Older chickens were sometimes bottled (see Chapter 21).

CHICKEN STEW

serves 4 to 6

Putting vegetables in a stew as in this recipe was common practice. However, for chicken stew in particular, it was also common to cook the vegetables separately, putting none in the stew pot except the onion.

1 large, old chicken
1 onion, chopped
4 carrots, cut in 1-inch pieces
1 small turnip, cut in 1-inch pieces
salt and pepper

Pluck the chicken. Cut off the head and feet. Clean out the cavity and wash it well. Cut the chicken into at least 8 or 10 pieces, according to its size, and put them in a large saucepan. Add the onion, carrot, and turnip, pushing them down between the chicken. Sprinkle generously with salt and pepper. Add enough water to come almost to the top of the pieces. Bring to a boil and simmer for several hours, or until the chicken is tender.

Serve with potatoes.

ROAST CHICKEN

serves 6

Younger chickens were usually roasted (braised is a better description) with stuffing.

2 small chickens
1 recipe of stuffing (page 159)
fatback strips

Fill the chicken cavities with stuffing. Put the chickens in a covered roasting pan and lay the fatback on the breasts. Cover and roast at 350°F for about 1 hour; uncover and roast another 30 minutes or more until cooked.

EGGS

"Eggs" were chicken eggs. From any other bird they were specified: duck eggs or gull eggs, for example. But eggs of any species, domestic or wild, were eaten in the same ways. They were widely eaten for breakfast, fried, boiled, and scrambled. They were also used for cakes and other baked goods, and a sweet egg custard was a popular dessert. A surplus of eggs was easily kept for the short term by packing them two or three layers deep in sawdust in a shallow crate and putting them in the root cellar.

Eggs! High-class Eggs!

WE OFFER FROM THOROUGH bred fowls, of the following kinds, (Eggs for setting of 13):

Plymouth Rock.
White Wyandotes.
Spanish—at $1.00 per clutch.

And for sale—A Cock and Five Hens, Black Spanish—mated for breeding.

mar28,2fp

A. D. RANKIN.

Longer-term storage, in the days before refrigeration, was more of a problem, and many people wanted to keep eggs over the winter because most hens stopped laying as days shortened in the fall. Eggs could be preserved in one of two ways: in salt or in waterglass (a solution of sodium silicate). The latter was widely used in rural US and Canada until World War II but was not common in Newfoundland, presumably because it was a needless expense when everyone had access to abundant coarse salt.

TO PRESERVE EGGS in WATERGLASS

to preserve about 8 dozen eggs

A 9-inch-diameter crock will hold about 8 dozen eggs in about 6 layers, which will need 6 quarts or more waterglass solution.

8 dozen eggs
4½ cups waterglass powder
6 quarts water

Dissolve the waterglass in the water. Gently lay the eggs in the crock and pour the solution over them, making sure they are well covered.

TO PRESERVE EGGS in SALT

to preserve about 5 dozen eggs

Preserving eggs in salt was by far the more usual custom in Newfoundland. Very few eggs were lost this way—often less than one in two dozen—but eggs that had been kept in salt were always broken individually into a small bowl for fear they had gone bad, and were used primarily for baking. In this fashion the eggs kept many months, and many families kept a few through to the following Easter for the cakes of that season.

Use a 1-foot-square box, about 6 inches high (or 8 inches if you are going to have three layers), to store the eggs.

5 dozen eggs
7 or 8 quarts coarse salt

Spread 1 quart coarse salt on the bottom of the box. Lay about 30 eggs on the salt, leaving a little space between them, and pushing them down gently into it. Pour more salt between the eggs to just cover them. Then put another layer of about 30 eggs on top, and cover with more salt. Two layers are safe, but three layers are possible. Put the eggs in a cool place until needed.

PICKLED EGGS

Some people liked pickled eggs and would preserve a small number to eat as a relish with suppers, snacks, or lunches.

12 eggs
2 cups vinegar
4 teaspoons sugar
1 teaspoon salt

Hard-boil the eggs for about 15 minutes and then place in cold water. Carefully remove the shells. Put the peeled eggs in a 1-quart jar. Dissolve the sugar and salt in the vinegar, and cover the eggs with this solution. Cover the jar and leave for a few days.

Serve as a snack at any time of day or as part of a packed meal.

DOMESTIC DUCKS

Ducks, never as popular as chickens, were widely kept. None of my sources seemed to know what breeds they had, simply calling them dark brown, multicoloured, or at least not totally white; the breeds mentioned in newspaper advertisements were Indian runner, Rouen, Aylesbury, and white Pekin. Fertilized duck eggs were usually put under a broody hen to hatch, eventually returning the ducklings to their rightful mother. I'm not sure if this was done out of distrust of the duck's mothering instincts or as a way of keeping the eggs safe from predators if the mother had made a nest outdoors. The ducks usually returned to their duck house after roaming free range or in an attached enclosure during the day. If a small pond was nearby, the

ducks would use that, or if a sheltered beach was handy, they would splash about in the shallow salt water.

Typically three or four ducks were kept for a family's use, while some raised larger flocks because ducks were a cash crop. Duck eggs were only eaten fresh, usually boiled. They were not usually preserved because there were never enough to bother with. For eating, ducks were treated much like chickens. Younger ones, killed in the fall after fattening over the summer, were roasted. Because a roast duck rendered copious fat, it was carefully poured off during cooking and kept for other uses. Older ducks were stewed or braised for a longer time.

DOMESTIC GEESE

Geese were less common than ducks, but often several families in a community kept one or two at least over the summer. It was common practice to buy goslings in the spring, fatten them up, and kill them in late fall. This depended on buying them from someone who specialized in geese, or as a last resort from the merchant. The only breeds I have heard of in Newfoundland were the Emden and the Toulouse. Geese were eaten like chicken or duck.

WILD BIRDS

Virtually any wild bird was potential meat for the table, but small fry like warblers and robins were not worth the expense and effort of shooting them, not to mention the trouble of cleaning them. On the other hand, many larger species were not sufficiently abundant to be worth pursuing. I have met people who had shot and eaten unlikely birds such as owls, but only opportunistically—they never went looking for these species. In practice, the only birds hunted were alcids (such as turrs and dovekies), ducks, geese, gulls, and a few others. Many of these were hunted near the shore, where hunters built hiding places called gazes—semicircles of beach rocks piled up where a concealed hunter could wait.

Preparing wild birds for the table was much like preparing domestic birds: feathers were plucked, head and feet cut off, and the cavity emptied. After the major feathers had been removed, the mass of small, downy feathers close to the skin were often singed off by passing the bird through the flames of the wood stove. All birds were either stewed on top of the stove, or oven-roasted / baked. The recipe for chicken stew (page 143) can be applied to any wild bird. Roasting wild birds was a standard process across the island, with many but slight variations; the recipe for roast turr can be applied to any wild bird.

ALCIDS

Several alcids were traditionally hunted and eaten. Turrs (elsewhere called murres) were favourites and hunted in the fall and winter. The two closely related species, the common turr and the thick-billed turr, were rarely differentiated and were treated the same in the kitchen. The smaller but fatter bull-bird was also popular, and near their colonies puffins were enjoyed. I was told repeatedly to eat puffins very fresh because they spoiled easily (but these were older people talking about the past; puffins are strictly protected now).

ROAST TURR

serves 4 to 6

2 or 3 turrs, cleaned and washed
salt and pepper
flour
1 recipe of stuffing (page 159)

Prick the turrs all over with a sharp fork to help the fat render out. Make the stuffing and stuff the turrs.

Place in a roasting pan and roast uncovered at 350°F for about 2 hours, pouring off any rendered fat at least once. When the meat is tender and falling off the bone, remove the turrs and keep them warm. Add 2 cups water to the drippings in the pan, stir, then thicken with a little flour to make a gravy.

Serve with potatoes and vegetables.

GULLS

Their scavenging habits and social gatherings around sewage outlets have produced a modern revulsion at the idea of eating gulls, so I had assumed gulls were starvation fodder, turned to only out of necessity. I found the opposite more generally true because many people saw them simply as part of the seasonal cycle of wild food. And gulls were certainly seasonal, because in spring and early summer they were too thin from the rigours of nesting and brood rearing. But in the fall, when they had recovered their plump fatness, they were in their prime, and were both shot and caught on hooks baited with pieces of fish. The herring gull and the greater black-backed gull (locally called the saddle-back) were the two most often eaten because they were both common and large. Although smaller, kittiwakes were often eaten; their meat is said to be particularly sweet and makes a delicious soup. Other species were eaten less frequently, but as opportunity arose any species of gull might be on the table. Gulls were cooked as for turr and their eggs gathered when possible.

WILD GEESE AND DUCKS

Many vagrant species of goose are found in Newfoundland, but a wild goose was usually a Canada goose. Similarly, many species of duck were visitors to the island, but only a few were hunted regularly. Salt-water ducks, particularly the common eider and the shell-bird that hang around shallow inlets of the sea, were deservedly popular in coastal communities. On fresh water, the mallard, American black duck, and pintail were common targets. But again, opportunistically any species could end up on the table. Wild duck eggs were eaten when found. Wild ducks and geese were cooked like their domestic counterparts, or as for turr.

OTHER SPECIES

Loons were hunted and eaten but were reputed to be notoriously tough with an unpleasant flavour. Partridge (elsewhere ptarmigan) were a popular quarry; the more common willow partridge was hunted across the island, but the Arctic species only where there was mountainous country. They were roasted as for turr.

Over: Sir William Whiteway (second from left) and guests at tea, pre-1908. Canon Cartwright far left. Others Methodist Sunday School Picnic, Carbonear, August 1919. James Rorke driving one of the cars. *Courtesy of the Maritime History Archive, PF-314.01.299.*

Chapter 13
Miscellaneous Savoury Dishes

This chapter is a miscellany of savoury dishes with little in common except that none was considered a full dinner by itself. Most of these recipes could be a supper or a lunch before bed—for example, toasted cheese—while others were quick, convenient foods, as when children home from school were clamouring for a snack. Then handfuls of bread dough quickly became damper bread—a slather of jam, and the youngsters were back out the door. From all accounts, children were always hungry, and appetites quite sharp, with snacks in constant demand, no doubt the result of physical activity. The recipes are organized alphabetically.

CORNISH PASTIES

serves 4 to 5

Cornish pasties are specifically associated with the English county of Cornwall, but in a more general sense they are turnovers, which can be found all over Britain and in many parts of America. Since the Newfoundland pasties I have seen were indistinguishable from a Cornish pasty, I will group them under that name. Cornwall played only a small part in the settlement of Newfoundland, but wherever Cornish people went, their pasties went with them.

Cornish pasties, mostly vegetables with a little meat in a pastry envelope, evolved in a frugal agrarian society. They were a natural fit for Newfoundland because available resources resembled those in Cornwall: flour and a little fat to make a pastry, basic root vegetables, and a scrap of meat or bacon to give a savoury edge. With judicious seasoning pasties are simplicity itself—but good enough to have survived for centuries.

The vegetable mixture can be varied but should be approximately the same volume so that the pasties are neither under- nor over-filled. The meat is equally flexible: bacon, cooked salt meat, or chopped fresh meat of any kind can be used.

1 recipe of lard pastry made with 3 cups flour (page 198)
2 cups diced potato
1 cup diced carrot
1 cup diced turnip
½ cup diced onion
½ cup diced bacon
¾ teaspoon salt
¼ teaspoon pepper

Mix the chopped vegetables, bacon, salt, and pepper well. Roll out the pastry thinly and cut out 4 circles, each about 8 inches in diameter, then re-roll the scraps to make a fifth. Divide the filling between the pastry circles, about 1 cup on each, putting it in the centre of the circle and keeping it away from the edges. Wet the rim of the pastry circles with water, then fold the pastry circles over the filling to make half-moons, making sure not to trap any filling at the edges. Press the edges firmly together and crimp with a fork. Cut a slash in the top of each to let the steam escape. Bake at 350°F for about 1 hour.

DAMPER BREAD

serves 4

Damper bread and toutons are made from the same dough. Damper bread was a quick and substantial snack made from raw bread dough. They were also called damper cakes or damper dogs among other names. Newfoundland damper bread is not the same as Australian damper bread, which is dough cooked in the hot ashes of a camp fire, nor is it the same as the strips of dough wound around sticks and toasted over camp fires by Boy Scouts. *Damper* is a Newfoundland dialect for the flat iron plate covering each of the holes in the top of a traditional freestanding cast-iron cookstove. Lumps of bread dough were cooked directly on the hot damper.

2 cups basic white bread dough (about 1 pound, page 29)
a small piece of fatback

Divide the dough into about 8 equal pieces and flatten each to a small cake about ½ inch thick. Wipe several dampers on the hot stove clean with a damp cloth and rub with a piece of fatback to very lightly grease the surfaces. Press the dough cakes onto these greased surfaces and let cook until well browned, then turn over and press the other side to the damper and cook until browned. Serve with butter or molasses or whatever you fancy.

HASH AND COLCANNON

These come from two different traditions. Colcannon is Irish, the name from the Gaelic, and originally (and still so in Ireland) referred specifically to a mixture of cooked potato and cabbage, chopped and fried together. It spread to England in the 18th century and evolved into what is now called bubble and squeak. Colcannon was particularly associated with Halloween, and this association persisted in Newfoundland, where October 31 was often called colcannon night. Hash is from the US, originally a combination of meat and vegetables chopped up and fried together, although now it also refers to just cooked vegetables chopped and fried. Some people still make a distinction between the two, insisting that colcannon is only potato and cabbage, whereas hash is a mixture of any vegetables, including potato and cabbage. The two terms are often used interchangeably in Newfoundland to mean mixtures of cooked vegetables reheated with fat of some kind. Hash is by far the more common term.

At heart, hash was a way for frugal cooks to create another meal from leftover vegetables. While meat was usually in a finite quantity, more vegetables than strictly needed were usually cooked.

One approach to hash was a free-for-all, where any combination of cooked vegetables was chopped up and fried together. Alternatively, one or two vegetables were the principal components and the hash named accordingly: cabbage hash or turnip and potato hash. Onion was sometimes added. Or cooked vegetables might be mashed together with the fat and reheated in the oven. Occasionally, any of the above styles was made with freshly cooked vegetables. Cabbage was frequently part of a hash, but leftover salt cabbage was never used. Hashes were also made with leftover cooked fish and potatoes.

HASH using mixed, cooked vegetables

serves 4

3 tablespoons rendered pork fat
¾ cup carrot, cooked, coarsely chopped
¾ cup turnip, cooked, coarsely chopped
½ cup parsnip, cooked, coarsely chopped
2 cups cabbage, cooked, coarsely chopped
2 cups potato, cooked, coarsely chopped

Fry the vegetable mixture on a low heat with the fat, turning frequently, until hot and browning at the edges.

Serve at once with butter and salt and pepper.

TURNIP and POTATO HASH

serves 4

1 onion, chopped
about 4 cups turnip, cooked, coarsely chopped
about 2 cups potato, cooked, coarsely chopped
2 tablespoons rendered pork fat

Fry the onion in the fat on a medium heat until soft. Add the turnip and potato. Fry together, stirring frequently, until heated through and starting to brown at the edges.

CARROT and PARSNIP HASH

serves 4

4 tablespoons butter
3 cups cooked carrot
3 cups cooked parsnip

Mash together equal quantities of cooked carrot and parsnip. Mash in 2 or 3 tablespoons butter. Add salt and pepper generously. Spread in a shallow pan (about 8 x 10 inches) and dot with the remaining butter. Bake at 350°F until very hot and starting to brown at the edges, about 30 to 45 minutes, but the time is flexible.

MUSHROOMS on TOAST

serves 4

I warn elsewhere (page 45) about the traditional but potentially fatal belief that if a wild mushroom peeled easily it was safe. For those that gathered them, fried mushrooms on toast, with or without a little bacon, were a favourite supper.

½ cup chopped bacon
1 quart mushrooms, sliced
2 tablespoons butter
2 tablespoons cream
salt and pepper
4 slices bread, toasted and buttered

Gently fry the bacon until any fat starts to render. Add the butter and mushrooms. Cover the pan and fry gently until all the water comes out of the mushrooms, then remove the lid and let all the surplus water evaporate. Add the cream, and salt and pepper to taste. Heat gently until warmed through. Divide between 4 slices of hot, buttered toast.

English-style PANCAKES

makes about 18

Pancakes in Newfoundland came from both the British and the American traditions. English pancakes are unleavened, thin, and wide, much like a French crepe. American pancakes are substantial, leavened, thick, and smaller in diameter. The British style was traditionally more popular, particularly on Pancake Day, and usually eaten with molasses or jam, although some followed the English habit of a squeeze of lemon juice and a sprinkle of sugar.

2 eggs
½ teaspoon salt
2 cups flour
½ cup milk, plus extra to thin the batter
3 tablespoons butter or rendered pork fat

Whisk the eggs and salt together. Whisk in about ½ cup flour to make a loose paste. Whisk in about ¼ cup milk. Repeat until all the flour has been incorporated. Do not add all the flour or all the milk at once because it will either be too stiff to stir or so loose that lumps will form. The batter can be used at once, but better if left to stand for 1 hour or more.

Lightly grease an 8-inch frying pan with butter and put on a medium-high heat. Re-grease the pan every five or six pancakes or more often if they stick a bit. Pour in about ¼ cup batter and swirl it around to cover the bottom of the pan. Cook until the underside is nicely browned in patches, then flip over and briefly cook the other side. Reserve in a warm place while cooking the rest of the batter, or simply serve as the pancakes are done—by the time the last person is served the first will be ready for another. Stir the batter occasionally: it should always be thin enough to just cover the bottom of an 8-inch pan as it is tilted from side to side. If the batter is a bit thick, stir in a little extra milk.

To serve, spread a little jam or molasses onto each pancake and roll it up.

American-style PANCAKES

makes about 12

2 cups flour
½ teaspoon salt
1 tablespoon sugar
1 tablespoon baking powder
1 ½ cups milk, plus extra to thin the batter
1 egg
2 tablespoons melted butter
3 or 4 tablespoons butter or
rendered pork fat

Mix the dry ingredients. Beat the egg with the milk, then continue beating while adding both the melted butter and the dry mixture. Thin with extra tablespoons of milk as required to make a thick batter that will still pour. Grease a heavy frying pan with butter or rendered pork fat. Drop 3 or 4 tablespoons of batter onto the hot pan, enough that will slowly spread itself into a 3- or 4-inch-diameter pancake. Fry for several minutes until lightly browned underneath, then flip over and fry another minute or so until browned on the other side. Add more butter to the pan as needed. Repeat with the rest of the batter. Keep cooked pancakes warm.

Serve with butter and jam, or molasses.

PASTA

Macaroni, often called Naples macaroni, arrived in Newfoundland in the 1890s and until around 1918 came as long tubes that had to be snapped into pieces or chopped into short lengths after cooking. Although pre-cut macaroni arrived at the end of World War I, the long tube-style macaroni was still available between the wars. Other forms of pasta such as spaghetti and vermicelli were advertised from around 1918 onwards but seem to have made little impact on the Newfoundland kitchen until after World War II. Macaroni was either boiled and served with butter instead of potatoes as a starchy accompaniment to other foods or made into macaroni cheese (page 170).

PORK BUNS with raw fatback

makes 12

Pork buns were either yeast-risen buns, essentially bread rolls with diced fatback, or small cakes leavened with baking powder, a sort of savoury tea bun incorporating raw or fried fatback.

2 cups flour
4 teaspoons baking powder
¼ teaspoon salt
¼ cup butter
½ cup fatback, ⅛-inch cubes
¾ cup water

Mix the flour, salt, and baking powder. Rub the butter into this mixture. Mix in the fatback. Stir in the water to make a stiff paste. Turn out onto a lightly floured surface and roll to about ¾ inch thick. Cut out circles about 2½ inches in diameter. Re-roll the scraps and cut more circles, about 12 total. Lay the circles on a lightly greased baking sheet. Bake at 350°F for 45 minutes or until lightly browned.

PORK BUNS with fried fatback
makes 12

2 cups flour
4 teaspoons baking powder
¼ teaspoon salt
2 tablespoons molasses
1 ¼ cups fatback, ⅛-inch cubes
¾ cup water

On a very low heat, fry the fatback until some fat has rendered and the cubes have shrunk slightly. Drain off the fat and let it cool a few minutes. Mix the flour, salt, baking powder, and molasses. Mix in the cooled liquid fat, then the cooked fatback. Stir in the water to make a stiff paste. Roll out about ¾ inch thick and cut out circles about 2½ inches wide. Re-roll the scraps and cut more circles, about 12 total. Lay the circles on a greased baking sheet. Bake at 350°F for 45 minutes or until lightly browned.

■ POTATO CAKES

Potato cakes were a great way of using up leftover potatoes. Recipes for sweet potato cakes are in Chapter 19, savoury potato cakes here. The proportions of flour and potato were flexible, so usually whatever was on hand could be turned into a filling accompaniment for other things. Less flour resulted in a very soft, flexible potato cake; more flour, and the cakes become increasingly stiff and doughy.

Variations on the theme of savoury potato cakes were legion, but were often eaten with a drizzle of molasses.

PLAIN POTATO CAKES

serves 4 to 6

about 3 cups mashed potato
¼ cup butter
½ teaspoon salt
2 teaspoons baking powder
½ cup flour, or more to taste

Start with about 3 cups leftover potato, mashed. Cook extra if needed. Stir in the butter, salt, and baking powder and mix well. Add the flour in small amounts, starting with less than ½ cup, and adding more as needed to make a stiff paste that won't stick to your fingers. Divide into 12 portions, flatten each into a cake about ¾ inch thick, and place on a greased baking sheet. Bake at 350°F for 40 minutes or until the tops are lightly browned.

POTATO CAKES with FATBACK

serves 4 to 6

The amount of fatback pork can be adjusted according to taste. Fry it gently—the idea is to just take the raw edge off the fatback and render a little fat, not to make scrunchions.

3 cups mashed potato
1 cup fatback pork, in small cubes
2 teaspoons baking powder
1 cup flour
½ teaspoon salt
½ teaspoon black pepper

Soak the fatback in water for 10 to 15 minutes to eliminate excess salt, then gently fry on a very low heat until it just starts to sizzle and release fat. Do not brown it or render out all the fat. Combine the mashed potato, baking powder, flour, salt, pepper, fried fatback, and any rendered fat. Divide the dough into 8 to 12 small cakes, each about ¾ inch thick. Place on a greased baking sheet and bake at 350°F for 45 minutes or until lightly browned on top.

SAVOURY RICE PUDDING

serves 4 to 6

Nineteenth-century advertisements often referred to Rangoon rice, and this terminology persisted up to around 1920. After about 1900 Patna rice and Japan rice were offered. Rice was used in both sweet rice puddings (page 230) and in savoury rice puddings served instead of pease pudding with any main course.

2 cups raw rice

Wash the rice well in several changes of water and put it into a pudding bag. Leave a lot of space above the rice in the bag. Tie off the bag, and cook alone in boiling water or in a pot with a boiled dinner, just like a pease pudding, for about 30 minutes.

STUFFING (DRESSING)

These words are treated as synonyms here. Stuffing was widely employed to fill birds, fish, or parts of animals like hearts. The recipes were remarkably uniform, and those given here illustrate both their essential similarity and some minor differences.

A major variant was the amount of savory used—between 1 teaspoon and several tablespoons. Although savory was the default herb for stuffing in Newfoundland, some cooks did use thyme or sage. The last made what is known elsewhere as sage and onion stuffing, often used in poultry, particularly ducks and geese. Some cooks used the onion raw, others fried it a little first. The amount of butter varied, and sometimes rendered pork fat was used instead.

STUFFING general purpose, for birds or fish

2 cups bread crumbs
½ teaspoon salt
1 medium onion, chopped fine
1 tablespoon dry savory
pepper
6 tablespoons butter, melted

Mix the crumbs, salt, onion, and savory well. Add pepper to taste. Drizzle the butter into this mixture as you stir.

STUFFING general purpose, with thyme

2 tablespoons butter
½ cup finely chopped onion
1 cup fresh bread crumbs
1½ teaspoons dry thyme
¼ teaspoon salt

Fry the onion in the butter on a low heat until soft. Mix in the bread crumbs, thyme, salt, and pepper.

STUFFING for beef, lamb, or other animal heart

1 cup fresh bread crumbs
1 onion, chopped small
2 tablespoons dried savory
⅓ cup finely diced bacon, fatback pork, or salt pork meat
½ teaspoon salt
¼ teaspoon black pepper
1 egg, beaten

Mix all the ingredients well.

TOUTONS

serves 4

Also spelled *toutins* and other less common variants, these were another snack made from raw bread dough. Sometimes diced fatback was added to the dough, which was then essentially the same mixture as pork buns (page 156) but distinguished by being fried rather than baked.

Toutons were typically breakfast food. In cooler weather, when bread dough had been set to rise the previous night, portions were simply cut off in the morning and fried. In warmer weather, when dough was risen and baked all in one day, chunks of dough were set aside in a cool place to be used for breakfast.

If toutons accompanied other breakfast foods such as salt fish, they were usually eaten plain or with butter. But if served by themselves, they were augmented with jam, butter, or a drizzle of molasses. They were also eaten as a dessert with a sweet sauce, or in any fashion as a late-evening lunch. If bacon was also on the breakfast menu, it would be fried, and the toutons cooked in the bacon fat.

When well made, these are delicious, substantial morsels. The trick is to fry the toutons quickly enough in pork or bacon fat to nicely brown the outsides, and slowly enough so that they puff slightly and are cooked through. These are good instead of fried potatoes with bacon or eggs, for example.

2 cups raw white bread dough (about 1 pound, page 29)
3 tablespoons rendered pork fat

Divide the dough into 8 roughly equal pieces. With lightly floured hands, press each piece into a little cake about 2½ inches in diameter and about ½ inch thick. Fry in the fat on a medium heat for 3 or 4 minutes or until nicely browned, then turn over and fry the other side.

Serve warm with molasses, butter, or jam.

Methodist Sunday School Picnic, Carbonear, August 1919. James Rorke driving one of the cars. *Maritime History Archive, Memorial University, PF-314.01.299*

Over: Free-range cows (a few sheep are also visible) at Cappahayden, in 1945. *The Rooms Provincial Archives Division, VA 15b-11.10.*

Chapter 14

Dairy: Milk, Butter, and Cheese (and Margarine)

MILK

Except near towns where sufficient population made it worthwhile, there was little in the way of dairy farming on the island. Many small communities had no access to fresh milk; in others, cows were kept by individual families, and milking was typically a woman's work. Goat's milk, available in some communities, was treated much the same as cow's milk. Both were drunk fresh and used in cooking, and sometimes the cream was taken off the top for desserts or to make butter if milk was plentiful. Keeping milk fresh was a perennial problem in hot weather, and lowering it down a well or carrying it to a root cellar to keep it cool were yet more labour. Sour milk was put to good use in breads and buns as the acidic ingredient to activate baking soda.

The arrival of tinned milk late in the 19th century was a boon. Any small community, with or without a cow or goat, now had a relatively cheap, safe, and year-round source of milk, and cooks quickly learned how to substitute it for fresh milk. Reindeer brand tinned milk was first advertised in Newfoundland in 1885, and many other brands were soon available. Carnation tinned milk, still the brand of choice in Newfoundland, was put on the local market in 1899 and was soon available in all parts of the island. For many people, fresh milk is still second choice for putting in tea.

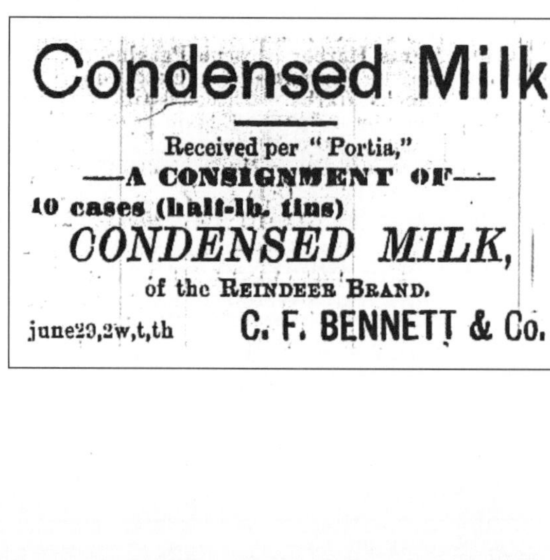

BUTTER

Both Irish and English settlers came from dairy-rich homelands and brought their taste for butter with them. The domestic supply, when it existed at all, could never match demand, so very large quantities were imported, initially from England or Ireland. Because of the distances involved, butter was both heavily salted and immersed in pickle or brine (both are strong salt solutions). In the second half of the 19th century the Canadian dairy industry expanded and its butter dominated the Newfoundland market, although Irish butter was advertised until the 1920s.

Those who had a milk cow would occasionally have more milk than required for daily purposes—so why buy butter when you could make it? The amount would depend on how much spare milk was available. The following is a traditional way of making small quantities of butter. You will need about 1 quart of scalded cream, from milk accumulated over several days.

Each day, for up to about a week, scald any surplus milk. Heat it on the stove until it is frothing around the edges but not at a full boil. Cool the milk and skim off the thick cream, leaving the skimmed milk behind. Reserve the skimmed milk for drinking or use in another recipe. Keep the scalded cream as cool as possible, and add to it each day, until there is at least a quart. The cooler it is, the easier it will be to make butter. Beat the accumulated scalded cream with a big spoon or with your hand. If beating by hand, use a rhythmic side-to-side flapping motion of the hand and fingers in the bowl. Beat until the scalded cream starts separating into butter and buttermilk. This will take at least 1 hour, and longer in warmer weather. Pour off the buttermilk and reserve for another recipe. Wash the butter two or three times in cold, fresh water. Then knead in salt to taste. Pat the butter into an earthenware crock or enamel pan and keep in a cool place.

Making the scalded cream in small batches each day extended its life; before going sour it passed through a mature stage where it acquired a pleasant tang (rather like crème fraîche) and was considered perfect for making butter. Making butter by hand in the above fashion was only for small quantities, so if you had 1 gallon or more of scalded cream, a separator, a small tabletop churn for making butter, was required. The skimmed milk was enjoyed as a drink with a snack and used in bread or buns. Some liked buttermilk as a drink, and buttermilk tea buns were prized.

Surplus goat's milk was made into goat's-milk butter as above. This was considered a tasty butter, although it was paler in colour than that made from cow's milk.

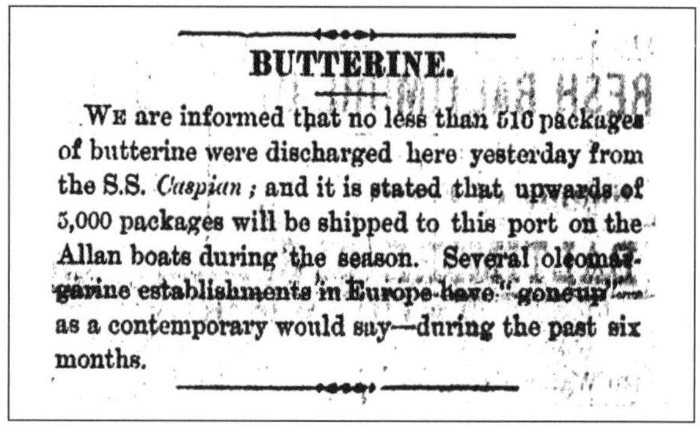
BUTTERINE.

We are informed that no less than 516 packages of butterine were discharged here yesterday from the S.S. *Caspian*; and it is stated that upwards of 5,000 packages will be shipped to this port on the Allan boats during the season. Several oleomargarine establishments in Europe have "gone up"—as a contemporary would say—during the past six months.

There are technical differences, but for this book oleomargarine and butterine are considered the same, and these two butter substitutes were in commercial production in Europe and America by around 1880. It is not clear when margarine first reached Newfoundland, but it was sufficiently novel in May 1881 to warrant this editorial comment in the *Evening Telegram*: "We are informed that no less than 516 packages of butterine were discharged here yesterday from the S.S. *Caspian*; and it is stated that upwards of 5,000 packages will be shipped to this port on the Allan boats during the season." In June 1882, Clift, Wood and Co. of St. John's advertised American oleomargarine and butterine for sale, and from 1885 on oleomargarine was regularly advertised in the *Evening Telegram*; the name was eventually shortened to "margarine" or more misleading terms like "cooking butter."

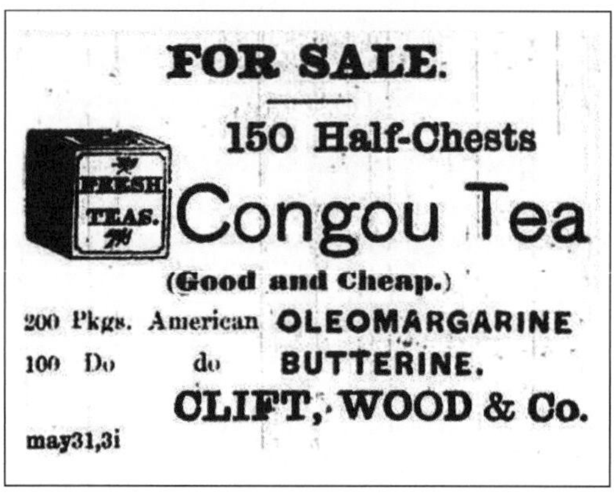

Local entrepreneurs saw the opportunity, and by 1883 Harvey's in St. John's was manufacturing butterine based on seal and fish oil (even back then, everyone was looking for alternative uses for seal products). In 1894 another margarine factory opened, and a third in 1925. Margarine was made in St. John's until 2003, when Unilever Canada closed its St. John's plant which had made the Good Luck brand famous across the island.

But the use of butter persisted alongside the new, cheaper, convenient margarine and the name butter applied to both. Some people distinguished "table butter" (real butter) from simply "butter" (margarine), but this was not hard and fast. Broadly speaking the two are interchangeable in all the recipes in this book, although many cooks were very clear that although they might have used margarine for expediency, they would save homemade butter for a cake for a special occasion.

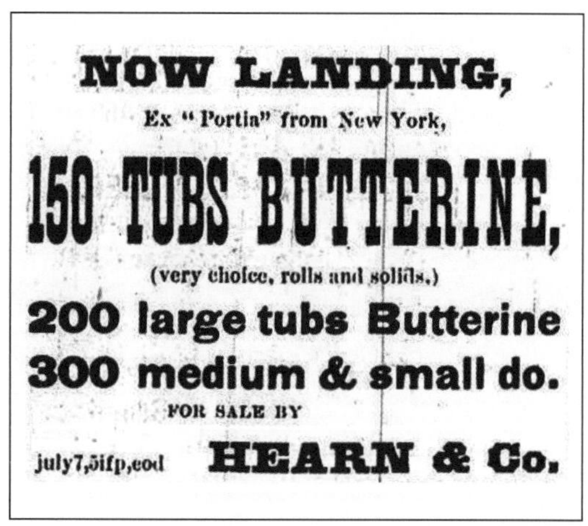

CHEESE

Cheese-making was virtually unknown in Newfoundland until the late 20th century, which is no surprise given that the coastal communities of Newfoundland were built around fishing, not dairy farming. But Irish and English settlers brought their love of cheese, so it was imported, mostly from England and Ireland, until the middle of the 19th century. It was no doubt mature, hard cheese—nothing else could have withstood the rigours of transportation—but the types were rarely named. One ledger entry from the first half of the 19th century lists "21 baskets Ches Cheese," which is likely Cheshire cheese, made in Cheshire and the northeast counties of Wales, all close to the port of Liverpool for export to Newfoundland; another mentions "25 best Double Gloster Cheeses." This cheese (properly Gloucester) was made in Gloucestershire, with easy access down the River Severn to the port of Bristol.

In the second half of the 19th century, local merchants turned almost exclusively to Canada for bulk supplies of cheese. The size of cheeses was rarely specified, but from first-hand accounts of the Newfoundland general store in the earlier years of the 20th century a typical Canadian cheese was a 20- to 40-pound wheel or a large rectangular block of similar weight. That cheese, a yellow-orange, generic cheddar-style, was a fixture in general stores across the island. It was an undistinguished cheese, marginally improved by toasting. The early 19th-century Cheshire and Gloucester raw-milk cheeses must have been tastier.

A slice of cheese might be cut for a snack at any time or put on a plate with bread and butter and pickles for what is now known as a ploughman's lunch. Cheese sandwiches were favourites, particularly when eaten while on a boating trip or berry-picking. But to make a hot dish from cheese, it was toasted or baked in some fashion.

TOASTED CHEESE

serves 4

Toasted cheese has been relished wherever hard cheese was made. As Ben Gunn of *Treasure Island* remarked after three years without cheese, "Many's the long night I've dreamed of cheese—toasted mostly." The original toasted cheese was held in front of an open fire on a toasting fork to melt the cheese on the bread, but when cookstoves with enclosed fireboxes arrived, it was toasted in the oven.

4 cups grated hard cheese
4 slices bread
butter

Toast the bread and lightly butter one side of each slice. Place the cheese on the buttered sides. Cover to the edges of the toast so that they do not burn while the cheese is melting. Bake at 400°F until the cheese is melted and bubbling.

Serve as is or with pickles or a dab of mustard.

WELSH RABBIT simple version

serves 4

Simple toasted cheese was sometimes called Welsh rabbit, but while the distinction was never absolute, most cooks reckoned that Welsh rabbit involved making the cheese into a sauce before putting it on the bread. Just to confuse the issue, the names Welsh rabbit and Welsh rarebit were used interchangeably in Newfoundland and elsewhere. Rarebit, presumably meaning a choice morsel of food, seems to be the later and supposedly more genteel name—likely why the Presbyterian Ladies' Aid Society used it in their 1928 cookbook. By either name, this was a favourite supper dish. A simple version had cheese melted directly in milk or beer; a more complex version involved a cheese sauce thickened with flour, eggs, or both.

The favourite seasoning for Welsh rabbit was mustard; the amounts in these recipes are for dry mustard powder. Hot English mustard powder has better flavour, but only use about one-quarter of the amount specified.

3 cups grated hard cheese
¼ cup milk or beer
3 tablespoons butter
1 teaspoon dry mustard
4 slices bread, toasted

Gently heat the cheese, milk, and butter together until they form a smooth cream. Stir in the mustard. Lay the toasted bread on an ungreased baking sheet. Carefully spoon the cheese sauce over the bread and bake at 400°F until the cheese mixture starts to brown.

WELSH RABBIT cheese sauce thickened with flour

serves 4

2 tablespoons butter
4 teaspoons flour
1 teaspoon dry mustard
¼ teaspoon salt
1 cup milk
1 cup grated hard cheese
4 slices bread, toasted and buttered

Mix the flour, mustard, and salt. Melt the butter and mix into the flour mixture. Stir in the milk and heat gently until it has thickened, stir in the cheese, and continue to heat until it has all melted. Divide the cheese mixture between the slices of toast, spreading it out evenly. Place the toast on an ungreased baking sheet and bake at 350°F until the tops are lightly browned.

WELSH RABBIT cheese sauce thickened with egg

serves 4

Most Welsh rabbit was baked to brown the top, but if you were craving this dish and the oven was cold, cheese sauce was simply spooned over toast (but can also be baked).

2 cups grated hard cheese
2 teaspoons mustard powder
¼ teaspoon pepper
2 eggs
4 tablespoons milk
4 slices bread, toasted and buttered

Mix the cheese, mustard, pepper, and milk in a small saucepan, and heat gently to just melt the cheese. Beat the eggs and stir in; continue to heat gently until the mixture has thickened. Divide between the buttered toast.

CHEESE FINGERS

makes 20 to 24

Cheese fingers have been made wherever hard cheese was eaten, usually a variation of a pastry dough mixed with grated cheese, rolled out and cut in strips, and baked. They were eaten as a snack or served with soup instead of bread.

¾ cup flour, plus extra for rolling
2 tablespoons butter
3 cups grated hard cheese
½ cup milk

Rub the butter into the flour. Stir in the cheese. Add the milk and mix together to make a sticky dough. Turn out onto a well-floured surface and press into a circle. Use extra flour to prevent the dough from sticking. Roll out about ¼ inch thick and cut out disks, about 2½ inches in diameter, or fingers about 3 by ¾ inches. Lay on a lightly greased baking sheet. Bake at 350°F for 20 minutes or until the fingers or disks are flecked with brown.

MACARONI CHEESE with plain cheese sauce

serves 4 to 6

Macaroni cheese was a more popular name than macaroni *and* cheese. Methods of making it varied, from using a plain cheese sauce to mixing cooked macaroni with a white sauce, eggs, and cheese.

My first attempts at these macaroni dishes turned out disappointingly dry. Then I realized that I had cooked my macaroni as I was used to doing, about 9 or 10 minutes, and this slightly under-done pasta absorbed a great deal of liquid from the sauce as it baked. I tried cooking the macaroni for nearly 20 minutes as one source had mentioned, far too long by modern standards, and the result was fine. For more details on pasta see Chapter 13.

2 cups macaroni
2 recipes of cheese sauce (page 258)
1 cup grated hard cheese

Break the macaroni into ½-inch lengths if required. Cook in salted water until soft, about 18 or 20 minutes, then drain. Mix the macaroni with the cheese sauce and spread in a 9 by 9-inch pan. Sprinkle the cheese evenly over the top. Bake at 350°F for 1 hour, or until the cheese on top has melted and browned.

MACARONI CHEESE set with eggs

serves 4 to 6

2 cups broken-up macaroni
4 tablespoons butter
6 tablespoons flour
4 cups milk
1½ teaspoons salt
½ teaspoon black pepper
4 eggs
2 cups grated cheese
1 cup cracker crumbs

Make a basic white sauce: melt the butter and stir in the flour until well combined, mix in the milk and stir until thickened, add salt and pepper, and set aside. Cook the macaroni in salted water until soft. Drain well. Mix the eggs and cheese into the white sauce, then with the macaroni. Put this mixture into a 9 by 9-inch dish, and sprinkle with cracker crumbs. Bake at 350°F for 1 hour, or until the crumbs have browned lightly and the filling is set.

Over: A fenced garden in Badger's Quay, 1939, with capelin spread on the beds as fertilizer. Note the necessary method of working around large and immovable boulders. *The Rooms Provincial Archives Division, VA 14-106.*

Chapter 15
Vegetables

Vegetables were usually cooked by boiling them in salted water until done, and typically served plain with salt and pepper, often with a knob of butter, sometimes with a spoonful of pot liquor over them, and occasionally with a sauce. Only when the cooking method departed from this general scheme has it been included in this chapter. Cooked vegetables mixed together as hash are covered elsewhere (page 153).

BEANS (DRY)

Small, pale beans, usually called white beans, but also navy beans, presumably because of their history as a mainstay of ship's supplies, and occasionally haricot beans (elsewhere this can refer to other beans such as cannellini), were stocked by virtually every store on the island. In the 20th century dry lima beans were advertised, but these did not seem to be regularly cooked until after World War II.

Between 1885 and 1913, calavance beans were advertised. These are of uncertain identity (see Appendix 1), but the name survived in St. John's at least until the 1950s; people who grew up in that decade report that their mothers called the regular white bean calavances. In any case, these beans never seem to have become mainstream, so perhaps Amelia Simmons, author of the first American cookbook, was right in 1796 when she summarily dismissed them: "Calivanse … are tough and tasteless, and little worth in cookery ..." These days they are remembered mainly from a line in Johnny Burke's early 20th-century ballad "The Kelligrews Soiree," in which he uses an alternative spelling:

There was birch rind, tar twine, cherry wine and turpentine,
Jowls and cavalances, ginger beer and tea;
Pig's feet, cat's meat, dumplings boiled up in a sheet,
Dandelion and crackie's teeth at the Kelligrews Soiree.

White beans were always soaked overnight in fresh water. They could then be boiled until tender and used as a vegetable side dish. But the primary use was for baked beans, when they were simmered only briefly and then baked with flavourings at 250°F for several hours or overnight. In this typical, simple example, the salt pork is mainly for flavour; pick off any meaty bits and serve them with the beans. Beans were a favourite breakfast food, but also eaten for supper, when there was a tradition of eating them with fried potatoes.

BAKED BEANS

serves 8

- 2½ cups white beans, soaked overnight
- 2 quarts water
- 1 onion, chopped
- 1 cup molasses
- 2 teaspoons salt
- 1 tablespoon hot English mustard
- 1 quart bean-cooking liquid
- 1 piece of salt pork riblets (12 to 16 ounces), soaked overnight with two or three changes of water

Drain the beans, rinse well, and bring to a boil in about 2 quarts water. Simmer about 10 minutes, just to start them cooking. Drain and save the cooking water. Put the drained beans in a pot or crock with a lid—the beans should about half fill or at most three-quarters fill it. Mix the onion with the beans. Mix the salt, molasses, and mustard with 1 quart bean-cooking liquid and pour over the beans and onion. Lay the soaked salt pork riblets on top. Cover and put in a 250°F oven for about 6 hours, or overnight. If possible, check the liquid level after about 4 hours. If it looks a little dry, add more of the liquid or water. If it looks too liquid, leave the cover off for an hour or two.

BEANS (FRESH)

Fresh beans were an occasional garden crop, usually called green beans to distinguish them from the dry version.

BEETS

Beets were a dual-purpose vegetable. Beet greens (or beet tops) were eaten in spring and early summer as a green vegetable, and the roots (simply called beets) were harvested in the fall for immediate consumption, pickling, and storing in a root cellar. Beet greens can be cooked just like turnip greens. Beetroots were usually simply boiled in their skins, or if the oven was on for another purpose they could be baked.

BAKED BEETS

beets as needed to fill a shallow pan with a lid

Trim the leaf stalks and the root off the beets, but do not peel. Pack into a shallow pan. Cover and bake until tender. These are best cooked at 250°F and can take 3 to 4 hours depending on size. When fully cooked, trim a sliver off each end of the beets to remove the bases of the stalk and root. The rest of the skin will slip off easily.

Fresh beets were eaten as a vegetable accompaniment to many main meals, often with a sprinkle of vinegar. Some were pickled (page 244) and were a standard item in the root cellar.

CABBAGE

Cabbage was grown all over the island. It was eaten fresh, cut in quarters or smaller and cooked in the standard fashion. Leftover cooked cabbage was popular in hash, often simply called cabbage hash even though other vegetables were included (page 153). Salted cabbage, also called brined or pickled cabbage, was never made into hash. It was popular, however, and often preferred to the fresh vegetable.

SALTED CABBAGE
serves 4 to 6

4 large quarters of salted cabbage
3 or 4 tablespoons butter

Soak the cabbage in plenty of water for about 24 hours; overnight is not long enough. Boil the cabbage for about 20 to 30 minutes in fresh water with the butter. Eat with salt and pepper and more butter.

CARROTS

Carrots were another primary garden crop grown all over the island. They were eaten primarily with meat-based meals and were less popular with fish. They also formed part of other dishes such as Jiggs' dinner, soup, or hash.

DANDELIONS

This introduced European plant is found all over the island. There are records of it being made into soup and salads, but its general use was as a green vegetable. Many residents looked forward to them eagerly as the first greens of the year, a welcome addition to the stodgy winter diet. Only the tender new leaves were picked, ideally no more than 3 or 4 inches long, as soon as they sprouted in the spring. They were primarily eaten alongside the main course of a meal, a boiled dinner for example, and were cooked like turnip greens. Dandelion leaves were also used to make dandelion beer and the flowers for dandelion wine (page 272).

DOCK

Dock, sometimes called curly dock or curled dock, is another introduced species found all over the island. Only the young, tender leaves were picked. If dock leaves were scarce, they would be kept for Sunday dinner, but if plentiful would be eaten through the season as an accompaniment to main meals. They were considered a tough and unmanageable vegetable, and I was advised to boil them for up to 1 hour.

HOPS

The tender growing tips of hops were cut off three or four leaves down from the tip and widely used as a vegetable. They were boiled, but only for about 5 minutes or less, then eaten with any main meal.

LETTUCE

Lettuce was grown as a salad green, and the leaves were eaten sprinkled with vinegar as a side dish to a main meal, or with a slice of bread and butter as a snack or a lunch.

ONIONS

Onions were popular but not as ubiquitous as potatoes, carrot, turnip, and cabbage. They were eaten as a boiled vegetable to accompany any kind of main meal, often dressed with a white sauce, and were frequently part of another dish such as hash or soup. They might be eaten raw, particularly with oily fish such as herring or mackerel. Small onions were pickled in vinegar with spices in a similar fashion to beet (page 242).

PARSNIPS

Parsnips were widely grown and eaten as a vegetable with a main meal, as part of a stew or soup, and for many people were an essential part of a boiled dinner (page 123). They were also relished with a meal of salt fish, and this association is an old one. Mrs. Beeton's recipe for salt fish and parsnips has already been mentioned (page 58), and Charles Francatelli, one-time chief cook to Queen Victoria, only mentioned salt fish once, but said it should be accompanied by boiled parsnips. They also made a popular wine (page 271).

PEAS (DRIED)

Dried peas were a mainstay and widely cooked in a limited number of ways. Cooked, whole, dry peas were served as a vegetable accompaniment to a main meal, simply dressed with salt and pepper, and butter melting on top.

PEAS (FRESH)

Fresh peas, grown by some families, were taken out of the pods and cooked and eaten in the standard fashion.

POTATOES

They were usually peeled before use, the exceptions being baked potatoes, and small new potatoes which were simply washed and boiled in their skins, often with a handful of fresh mint in the water. Boiled potatoes were sometimes cooked separately from other ingredients and served alongside them on the plate, or at other times cooked in the pot with other food, as in a boiled dinner (page 123). They were also mashed, roasted, and oven-baked. Baked potatoes were popular, but a frugal cook waited until the oven was hot for some other purpose before slipping in a few potatoes to bake.

Smothered potatoes (also known as scalloped potatoes) were a welcome change from other ways of cooking potatoes. They were used, for example, to accompany leftover meat that had already been served with boiled potatoes, so this would make a welcome difference.

SMOTHERED POTATOES

serves 4 to 6

- about 12 to 16 potatoes (about 4 pounds), peeled and thinly sliced
- 1 small onion, chopped finely
- 1 ½ teaspoons flour
- 3 tablespoons butter, plus extra for greasing the dish
- about 3 cups milk
- salt and pepper

Grease a deep 8 by 8-inch or similar sized dish. Layer the potatoes in the dish. After every layer, three times in all, sprinkle salt and pepper, about one-third of the chopped onion, and about ½ teaspoon flour over the potatoes. Do not flour the top layer. Slice the butter thinly and lay on top. Pour in enough milk to come just below the top layer of potatoes. Bake uncovered at 350°F for about 2 hours or until most of the milk has evaporated and only a little thick liquid is seen when the pan is tipped at an angle.

If milk was scarce, this still made a tasty dish with plain water. If water was used it was important to make sure that almost all the surplus water had been absorbed or evaporated before eating the potatoes.

PUMPKINS, SQUASH, AND VEGETABLE MARROWS

These three were rarities in gardens around the island. Where they were grown, they were boiled as other vegetables, or sliced and roasted in the pan with the meat. Pumpkins and marrows were also made into pickles, relishes, jams, and sweet pies. Pies were made either with slices of the fresh vegetable or from the jam.

SHALLOTS

Where they were grown, shallots were appreciated for both flavour and keeping qualities. They were boiled, fried, or baked wherever onions would be used and as part of all types of soups, stews, and other composite dishes such as fishcakes. Shallots were seldom eaten raw, unlike onions, because their taste was considered too pungent. They were also pickled like onions in vinegar.

TURNIPS

The vegetables Newfoundlanders call turnips are Swedish turnips (swedes for short), grown primarily as cattle fodder across northern Europe. That produced a popular prejudice against them in Europe, and Charles Francatelli summed it up in 1861: "Swedish turnips are mostly given as food to cattle; true, but there is no good reason why they should not be considered as excellent food for Christians, for they are sweeter, and yield more substance than the ordinary turnips; let them be peeled, boiled in plenty of water, and when done, mashed with a little milk, butter, pepper and salt." Newfoundlanders adopted them with enthusiasm, and they became one of the most important garden vegetables—the young leaves in the spring were much relished as a boiled green vegetable, and then later in the year the bulbous root was eaten, cooked in chunks, mashed, or as part of a hash.

The basic mashed turnip recommended by Francatelli is hard to beat and was used with variations throughout Newfoundland. Here is a typical version.

MASHED TURNIP

serves 4 as a side

2 medium turnips, peeled and chunked
4 to 6 tablespoons butter
salt and pepper
a little milk, if needed

Boil the turnip in lightly salted water. When completely tender, drain and return to the pot. Mash with generous amounts of butter, salt, and pepper. If they are dry, add enough milk to make them easy to eat, although very often turnips are moist enough as they are.

TURNIP GREENS

The young leaves of turnip plants are among the first greens available in the spring. Bags of turnip greens are still one of the iconic Newfoundland foods to be found on both roadside stalls and supermarket shelves. Indeed, they are so popular that some people planted turnip seed repeatedly to ensure a supply of these greens for several months. Traditionally, greens were simply boiled with a little fat, and a few scraps of bacon or cooked salt meat were a favourite addition.

TURNIP GREENS

serves 4 to 6 as a side

A small piece of salt meat may be simmered for 3 or 4 hours before the greens are added, and then the meat can be chopped up and mixed with the cooked greens, or saved for another meal. Or, simmer a piece of bacon before adding the greens, or even just a piece of fatback. The addition of a salty and fatty element improves the greens, and they are perhaps at their best when mixed with boiled dinner pot liquor. Although traditionally cooked for 20 or 30 minutes or longer, this is a bit long for modern tastes.

If the greens are to be part of a boiled dinner, drain them when they are cooked, squeeze most of the water out, then pour some of the pot liquor from the boiled dinner onto them.

1 gallon turnip greens (about 1 pound)
about 1 to 2 quarts water, salted

Rinse the greens well in a bucket of water to get rid of any grit. Pick them over for weeds and slugs. Stuff the cleaned greens into a pot of boiling, salted water and cook about 20 minutes or to your liking.

Over: A store in rural Newfoundland, ca. 1905, possibly at Placentia, and possibly one of the Job Brothers & Company stores. *Maritime History Archive, Memorial University, PF-315.374.*

DRY GOODS
GROCERIES

Chapter 16

Steamed Puddings and Duffs

I have heard some cooks claim that puddings and duffs were different. Pudding, they said, was a lighter dish, cooked in a metal pudding basin and appearing with the main course and then again as dessert with a sweet sauce. In contrast, a duff was heavier, cooked in a pudding bag with boiled meat, and was never dessert. This distinction seems to be personal, not general, and I treat puddings and duffs as the same thing.

The pudding bag was the method of choice for both sweet and savoury puddings. It was made from any light cotton fabric, a cut-down flour sack for example, and filled no more than half to three-quarters full to allow for expansion of the pudding during cooking. The open end was tied off with cotton twine or closed with a drawstring sewn into the bag, and then either immersed in the pot in which meat was simmering or by itself in boiling water.

If the primary objective was to eat the duff with the meat main course, it would be simmered with the meat, even if it would later reappear as dessert. But if the primary objective was to create a sweet pudding to be eaten by itself, such as a Christmas pudding, the pudding would be simmered on its own. Savoury steamed puddings could also be cooked in an animal stomach, typically from a sheep or goat. The stomach was soaked and thoroughly scrubbed with baking soda, loosely filled with the pudding mixture, and the two openings tied off with cotton twine.

Ceramic pudding basins, which became widely available in the second half of the 19th century, were used for both sweet and savoury steamed puddings. These were imported from England and their use was very much from the English tradition. They came in various sizes, sometimes identified by a number, but there was little standardization between manufacturers. The essential pudding-basin attributes were a circular flat bottom with a peripheral ridge (sometimes notched to allow simmering water underneath to escape), sides gently flared to an open end about twice the diameter of the base, and a thickened band around the open end to keep the twine below the rim. The basin was only filled about half full to allow for pudding expansion, and a cloth draped over the top was tied tightly under the basin rim with a short length of twine. If the basin lacked notches in the base, it was placed on two or three short lengths of wood on the bottom of a saucepan large enough to hold the basin with some headroom. Any kind of wood was used, long enough to support the bottom of the basin. Water was put in the saucepan to come about halfway up the basin, brought to a boil, and then simmered with the lid on. The water was topped up if necessary with boiling water. Metal pudding basins with fluted sides were used the same as ceramic basins but had their own lids.

Of the traditional methods mentioned above, the pudding bag seems most popular in the 21st century. Many cooks make their own, and several sizes are available ready-made. The metal pudding basin has survived but is less popular, perhaps because few cooks took proper care of the tinned metal, and rust was inevitable. Stainless steel pudding basins, now available, need neither cloth nor twine. Many still use ceramic basins, which are available from specialist kitchen stores, and old ones turn up regularly in antique stores.

Any of the recipes below can be made in a pudding basin. As puddings can be difficult to turn out, grease the basin well before filling, and let it stand for a few minutes after it has finished steaming to allow the pudding to contract slightly as it cools. Run a small knife around the pudding, going as deep as you dare to loosen it. Alternatively, puddings can be cut and served straight from the basin.

Steamed puddings were well suited to Newfoundland because they were made of ingredients such as lard and flour which were on hand for many other purposes.

SAVOURY STEAMED PUDDINGS

The distinction between savoury and sweet steamed puddings was blurred, as mentioned above, because many puddings did double duty as both part of the main course and as dessert with a sweet sauce. Some main-course puddings were surprisingly sweet, such as figgy duff, so adapted easily for either purpose.

PLAIN STEAMED PUDDING

serves 6 to 8

This recipe comfortably fits a 5-cup pudding basin with plenty of room for expansion. If sugar was scarce, it could be left out of a plain steamed pudding because it would not be missed with the main course, and the sweetness of the dessert sauce (see Chapter 22) would offset any lack in the pudding itself.

1½ cups flour
6 tablespoons butter
1½ teaspoons baking powder
2 tablespoons sugar
¾ cup water

Grease a 5-cup pudding basin well. Rub the butter and flour together, then mix in the other dry ingredients. Stir in the water to make a medium dough. Put the mixture in the basin, tie a cloth over the top, and steam over simmering water in a large saucepan for about 1½ hours. Serve plain with a main course, as a dessert with a sweet sauce, or both. The sweet sauce could be any warm sauce, warm jam, or molasses.

PLAIN STEAMED MOLASSES PUDDING

serves 6 to 8

This recipe fits a 5- to 6-cup pudding basin with room for expansion. The sugar may be omitted—the molasses provides sweetness and a sweet sauce would make it dessert.

2 tablespoons sugar
2 tablespoons butter
1 egg
½ cup molasses
1½ cups flour
2 teaspoons baking powder
½ cup water

Mix the butter and sugar. Beat in the egg, molasses, flour, baking powder, and water. Scrape into a greased pudding basin, tie a cloth over the top, and steam over simmering water in a large saucepan for 1½ to 2 hours. To make this in a pudding bag, fill the bag about half full and simmer in boiling water for about 1 hour.

Serve with any sweet sauce.

PLAIN STEAMED MOLASSES PUDDING with currants

serves 6 to 8

Use an 8- to 10-cup basin for this recipe, which allows plenty of room for expansion. This pudding was often made just as a dessert and served with a sweet sauce.

- 2 tablespoons sugar
- 2 tablespoons butter
- 1 egg
- ½ cup molasses
- 1½ cups flour
- 2 teaspoons baking powder
- ½ cup water
- 1½ cups currants

Mix the butter and sugar, beat in the egg and molasses, mix in the flour, baking powder, and water, and add the currants. Scrape into a greased pudding basin. Tie a cloth over the top, and steam over simmering water in a large saucepan for 1½ to 2 hours. To make this in a pudding bag, fill the bag about half full and simmer in boiling water for about 1 hour.

FIGGY DUFF with bread crumbs

serves 6 to 8

Figgy duff or figgity duff (or other variations) is so called because in Newfoundland raisins were often called figs. This pudding was just as often called raisin pudding or raisin duff. The majority of modern figgy duff recipes are based on bread crumbs, but those without were also popular.

- 3 tablespoons butter
- 2 tablespoons molasses
- ¼ teaspoon salt
- 2 teaspoons baking powder
- 3 cups bread crumbs
- 2 cups flour
- ¾ cup milk
- 2 cups raisins

Cream the butter and sugar together. Mix in the molasses and salt. In a separate bowl, combine the flour and baking powder and add to the butter mixture. Stir in the bread crumbs and add milk gradually to form a dough. Stir in the raisins. Put into a large (10-cup), greased pudding basin, tie a cloth over the top, and steam over simmering water in a large saucepan for 2 hours.

FIGGY DUFF without bread crumbs

serves 6 to 8

- ½ cup sugar
- ¼ cup butter
- ¼ cup molasses
- ¼ teaspoon salt
- 2 teaspoons powdered ginger
- 3 teaspoons baking powder

2 ½ cups flour
1 cup milk
1 ½ cups raisins

Cream the butter and sugar together. Mix in the molasses, salt, and ginger. In a separate bowl, combine the flour and baking powder and mix this in, gradually adding milk to form a dough. Stir in the raisins. Put into a large (10-cup), greased pudding basin, tie a cloth over the top, and steam over simmering water in a large saucepan for 1 ½ hours.

STEAMED SAVOURY BREAD PUDDING with onions

serves 4

Bread puddings could be sweet or savoury. A savoury version was a typical side dish to a boiled dinner, and made great leftovers—slice the cold pudding and fry gently in butter for supper or a snack. My source for this recipe originally used a sheep's stomach in which to cook it. I found that the pudding became far too soggy in a bag, so, lacking a sheep's stomach, I prefer to use a pudding basin.

⅓ loaf stale bread
1 or 2 small onions, chopped
6 tablespoons flour, or just enough to bind the mixture
2 tablespoons finely chopped fatback pork
1 ½ teaspoons baking powder
1 teaspoon sugar
½ teaspoon salt
½ teaspoon pepper

Slice the bread. Soak, including crusts, in cold water for 5 minutes. Lightly squeeze out the surplus water, and break the slices apart. Mix in the onions, fatback, baking powder, sugar, salt, and pepper, stirring vigorously to further break up the bread. Sprinkle with flour and mix well, using just enough flour to form a soft dough. The exact amount will depend on the wetness of the bread. Place in a pudding bag, a well-scrubbed sheep's stomach tied off at the openings with cotton twine, or a greased 4- to 5-cup pudding basin. Simmer or steam over simmering water in a large saucepan for about 1 ½ hours. Serve with boiled dinner.

STEAMED SUET PUDDING

serves 6

Suet puddings proliferated in 18th-century England where different techniques and ingredients produced splendidly named examples such as spotted dog and drowned baby. Newfoundland got its puddings from England, but these robust names did not accompany them.

Suet is the hard fat around the kidneys of cattle or other animals (when moose became widespread on the island, moose suet was prized for baking). It was prepared by removing all the membranes and other extraneous matter and then chopping the fat, which when cold is quite hard and brittle. Suet has a savoury-sweet taste, suiting it to all styles of puddings. Raisins could be added to suet puddings (which then became spotted dog), but often suet puddings were kept plain to enjoy this particular flavour, although as dessert they would be accompanied by hot jam or molasses sauce (page 263).

- 1 ½ cups flour
- ¾ cup chopped suet
- ½ teaspoon salt
- 1 ½ teaspoons baking powder
- 1 cup water, or just enough to make a stiff paste

Chop the suet until there are no lumps bigger than about ¼ inch wide. Mix the flour, suet, baking powder, and salt. Stir in enough water to form a stiff dough. Grease a 4-cup pudding basin and add the dough. Tie a cloth over the top and steam over simmering water in a large saucepan for about 1 ½ hours.

SWEET STEAMED PUDDINGS

Sweet puddings were made from all wild berries. Crowberries, also called blackberries, if they were used at all, were most often made into puddings.

STEAMED CROWBERRY PUDDING

serves 6 to 8

Although my source for this recipe used a pudding bag, others specified a pudding basin, which I think is the better choice. Use a 3-quart basin and steam for the same length of time. This recipe is not particularly sweet, and as the crowberries have a mild flavour, it could be used as a plain pudding with a main course. With a sweet sauce it made a good dessert.

- ½ cup sugar
- 2 tablespoons butter
- 2 eggs
- ½ cup milk
- 2 teaspoons baking powder
- ¼ teaspoon salt
- 2 cups flour
- 1 ½ cups crowberries

Beat the sugar and butter together. Beat in the eggs, baking powder, and salt. Mix in the flour to form a loose dough. Stir in the crowberries. Put in a pudding bag and simmer in water for about 1 ½ hours.

STEAMED PARTRIDGEBERRY PUDDING

serves 6 to 8

4 tablespoons butter
½ cup sugar
¼ teaspoon salt
2 cups flour
3 teaspoons baking powder
1 ¼ cups milk
2 cups partridgeberries

Grease a 3-quart pudding basin. Cream together the butter and sugar. Combine the flour, salt, and baking powder, and mix into the sugar and butter. Beat in the milk to make a stiff batter. Fold in the partridgeberries. Scrape the batter into the prepared basin. Tie a cotton cloth over the top and steam over simmering water in a large saucepan for about 1 ½ hours.

STEAMED CHOCOLATE PUDDING

serves 4 to 6

Other sweet steamed puddings, such as this chocolate pudding, were popular. The 6 tablespoons of chocolate called for in the recipe equal only about 1 ounce, allowing several people to enjoy a limited amount of chocolate. Similar recipes were made with cocoa powder, using about half as much cocoa as chocolate.

2 tablespoons butter
6 tablespoons grated chocolate
1 egg
½ cup sugar
pinch salt
1 cup flour
1 ½ teaspoons baking powder
½ cup milk

Grease a 6-cup pudding basin. Melt the butter, add the chocolate and let it melt; keep warm but do not boil. Beat the egg and sugar together. Beat in the salt, flour, and baking powder. Beat in the milk to make a smooth batter. Beat in the melted chocolate and butter. Scrape into the prepared basin. Tie a cloth over the top and steam over simmering water in a large saucepan for about 1 hour.

STEAMED SWEET BREAD PUDDING with raisins

serves 4

Sweet bread pudding was often baked in an open pan, often a roasting pan. If cooked like that, bread puddings ended up with a crispy top and were not technically a steamed pudding. The same mixture was just as often steamed in a bag or pudding basin.

3 slices stale bread
½ cup raisins
2 eggs
¾ cup sugar
1 cup milk

Cut the bread, including the crusts, into ½-inch cubes. Put a layer of the bread in a 1-quart basin, sprinkle on a few raisins, then some more bread, then more raisins and so on, ending with a layer of bread. Pack down lightly. The basin should be half to three-quarters full. Beat the eggs, sugar, and milk until the sugar is dissolved; pour over the bread and raisins. Let soak for 5 minutes. Push down the top layers to make sure that all the bread is soaked in the milk mixture. Tie a clean cloth over the top of the basin and steam over simmering water in a large saucepan for 1 hour. Remove from the steamer and let it rest for a few minutes. The pudding is equally good hot or warm. Remove the cloth and scoop portions directly from the basin onto serving plates.

Sweet bread pudding was often served with a rum sauce, brown sugar sauce, or custard (see Chapter 23).

STEAMED PLUM PUDDING

serves 8 to 10

Although steamed suet puddings were often made without fruit, an exception was always made for plum pudding, also called Christmas or fruit pudding. Despite claims that plum puddings were made with plums "in the old days," no plums were in plum pudding (an obsolete meaning of plum in English is a raisin, still used in phrases like plum pudding or plum cake).

Traditionally, clumps of dried fruit had to be broken up before proceeding with a recipe, particularly if the fruit was old and stuck together. In the absence of suet, this pudding was made with butter or lard, although the taste and texture were slightly different.

If this was a Christmas pudding, many cooks preferred the English habit of flaming the pudding when serving it. Two or 3 tablespoons of brandy or rum were poured over the hot pudding and immediately lit before it evaporated. Christmas puddings were also served with hard sauce or rum sauce (page 264).

The combinations of dried fruits in plum puddings varied enormously, and within the total amount of dried fruit the components can be mixed according to taste and availability.

1 cup finely chopped suet
2 cups bread crumbs
1 cup flour
1 cup sugar
1½ cups raisins
1½ cups currants
1½ cups sultanas
2 teaspoons ginger
½ teaspoon cinnamon
1 teaspoon nutmeg
4 eggs, beaten well
½ teaspoon salt
2 teaspoons baking powder
¼ cup milk

Mix the dried fruit together, breaking up any clumps. Mix the flour, sugar, baking powder, salt, and spices, and toss with the mixed fruit. Mix in the suet and bread crumbs. Mix the eggs in thoroughly. Add the milk to form a stiff dough. Grease a large (10-cup) pudding basin, scrape in the mixture, tie a cloth over the top, and steam over simmering water in a large saucepan for about 3 hours.

Over: Berry picking on an unidentified hillside, ca.1930s. *The Rooms Provincial Archives Division, VA 94-36.1*

Chapter 17

Sweet Pies (or Tarts) and Pastry

The distinction between a pie and a tart depends on the culinary tradition of the speaker. In America a pie covers the gamut from sweet pecan pies with only bottom pastry, through apple pies with pastry top and bottom, to steak-and-kidney pies with pastry only on top. In the British tradition, a shallow, sweet dish with bottom pastry is usually called a tart, and Newfoundland, in its usual magpie fashion, adopted both usages. I am going to call everything in this chapter a pie, although many could be rightfully called tarts. Sweet pies in Newfoundland were made principally with fresh fruit, particularly wild berries, but also with dried fruit, jam, or no fruit at all.

FRESH FRUIT PIES

The traditional methods of making pies from wild berries (or any other fruit) differed only in detail. The amount of sugar was adjusted to both personal taste and the fruit used—sweet blueberries usually had less sugar than tart partridgeberries. Spicing also varied. Some cooks never put cinnamon in a blueberry pie; others always did. Every cook put spices of some sort in both apple and raisin pies. Pies were most often double-crust, with pastry top and bottom, but sometimes had only a bottom crust, and less frequently only a top crust. I do not know when the custom of using a lattice-work top crust became popular in Newfoundland, but it likely entered Newfoundland during or after World War II from the American tradition.

Any wild berries can be made into a pie using this recipe, with minor adjustments to the sugar.

BLUEBERRY PIE

makes one 9-inch pie

- 1 recipe of pastry, enough to make a top and bottom crust (page 198)
- 4 cups blueberries
- 1 cup sugar
- 6 tablespoons flour

Roll out half of the pastry into a thin circle about 10 inches in diameter. Line a pie plate with it, making sure it covers the rim of the dish. Mix the flour and sugar thoroughly. Toss the blueberries gently with this mixture and spread evenly over the pastry. Roll out the remaining pastry and lay it on the blueberries. Crimp together the edges to make a tight seal. Cut slits in the top pastry to let out the steam. Bake at 350°F for about 1 hour.

Serve warm or cold.

RHUBARB PIE

makes one 9-inch pie

Any domestic fruit, from apples to damsons, can be made into a pie using this recipe. Large pits, as those in damsons or plums, must be removed.

- 1 recipe of pastry, enough to make a top and bottom crust (page 198)
- 4 cups rhubarb, cut in ½-inch chunks
- 1½ cups sugar
- 6 tablespoons flour

Divide the pastry into two portions, and roll out one to line and cover the rim of a 9-inch pie plate. Combine the flour and sugar. Place a layer of rhubarb on the pastry in the plate, sprinkle with the flour and sugar mixture, then add more rhubarb and so on. Use all the flour and sugar mixture before getting to the last layer of rhubarb. Roll out the remaining pastry, wet the rim of the bottom pastry, and lay the top layer on top. Press the top and bottom rims of pastry together firmly, and crimp to make a tight seal. Cut slits in the top to let out the steam. Bake at 350°F for about 1 hour.

DRIED FRUIT PIES

A few dried fruits were commonly available, and frequently made into pies. The fruit was first rehydrated in simmering water, then put between pastry layers. Some cooks thickened the liquid with a little flour; others simply let all the water absorb into the fruit. These recipes for raisin pie and apricot pie illustrate the general methods used to make a pie from dried fruit.

RAISIN PIE

makes one 9-inch pie

- 1 recipe of pastry, enough to make a top and bottom crust (page 198)
- 2 cups raisins
- 1 cup water
- 1 cup sugar
- 2 tablespoons flour
- 1 tablespoon vinegar

Bring the raisins and water to a simmer; mix the flour and sugar and stir in. Simmer the mixture, covered, about 20 minutes. Stir in the vinegar, then set aside to cool. Divide the pastry into two portions. Roll out one portion and line a 9-inch pie plate with it, making sure the rim is covered. Spoon the cooled raisin filling into the pastry. Wet the rim of the pastry in the plate. Roll out the other half of the pastry and lay it on top of the filling. Press the top and bottom rims together and crimp firmly to make a tight seal. Cut slits in the top pastry to let out the steam. Bake at 350°F for about 1 hour, or until the pastry is browned.

APRICOT PIE

makes one 9-inch pie

- 1 recipe of pastry, enough to make a top and bottom crust (page 198)
- 3 cups dried apricots, chopped in ¼-inch cubes
- 1½ cups water
- ¾ cup sugar

Place the apricots in a small saucepan with the water and sugar and bring to a boil. Simmer gently with the lid half off until most of the water has been absorbed and a little syrupy liquid remains. Set aside to cool. Divide the pastry: roll out one portion and line a 9-inch pie plate, making sure to cover the rim. Spoon the cooled apricot filling into the pie plate. Wet the rim of the bottom layer of pastry.

Roll out the remaining pastry and lay it on the filling. Press the pastry edges together and crimp firmly to make a tight seal. Cut slits in the top pastry to let out the steam. Bake at 350°F for about 1 hour, or until the pastry is browned.

JAM PIES

Jam pies, a reliable standby, were widely popular. The method was straightforward: a thick layer of jam was sandwiched between two layers of pastry. Since jam pies are usually thinner than whole-fruit pies, there is less need to cover the rim of the plate with pastry because the two layers can be crimped together on the sloping side of the pie dish.

RASPBERRY JAM PIE

makes one 9-inch pie

1 recipe of pastry, enough to make a top and bottom crust (page 198)
2 cups raspberry jam

Divide the pastry: roll out one portion and line a 9-inch pie plate. Spoon the jam onto the pastry. Wet the rim of the pastry. Roll out the remaining pastry and lay it on the filling. Press the bottom and top rims together and crimp firmly to make a tight seal. Cut slits in the top pastry to let out the steam. Bake at 350°F for about 1 hour, or until the pastry is browned.

SWEET PIES NOT USING FRUIT

I first assumed that these pies were desperation food, for times when the jam had been eaten and the berry crocks empty. Wrong. These were enjoyed for their own sake, and often eaten when other supplies were still plentiful.

VINEGAR PIE

makes one 9-inch shallow pie

1 recipe of pastry, enough to make a single crust (page 198)
2 tablespoons butter, softened
1 cup sugar
2 tablespoons flour
½ teaspoon cinnamon
2 eggs
¼ cup milk
2 tablespoons vinegar

Cream the butter and sugar. Mix in the flour and cinnamon. Beat the eggs with the milk and then beat into the flour and butter mixture. Mix in the vinegar. Roll out the pastry and line a 9-inch pie plate. Trim the edges. Pour in the filling and bake at 350°F for 35 to 40 minutes, or until the filling is set.

Serve warm or cold.

MOLASSES PIE

makes one 9-inch pie

As this recipe makes a lot of filling, use a deep pie pan or plate. Be careful when pouring in the filling; discard any that won't fit in the pastry.

1 recipe of pastry, enough to make a single crust (page 198)
4 eggs
1 cup molasses
1 cup milk

Beat the eggs, milk, and molasses together until thoroughly mixed. Roll out the pastry and line a 9-inch pie plate. Trim the edges. Pour in the filling. Bake at 350°F for 1 to 1¼ hours, or until the filling is set.

Serve warm or cold.

PASTRY

Pastry was made of the usual combination of flour, fat, water, and a little salt. The principal fats were butter, lard, and rendered pork fat. Suet was also used, but as it was not as easily available, it was usually reserved for special occasions. When margarine became available, it was widely used, although many of my sources said they preferred the taste of butter or pork fat in pastry.

Apart from the different fats, little variation existed between recipes. The amount of fat was usually between one-half to one-third of the amount of flour (by volume). All pastries were used interchangeably for both savoury and sweet dishes, although sometimes about 2 tablespoons sugar were added to the mixture for a two-crust sweet pie. Newfoundland cooks were fond of adding a little baking powder to their pastry, just to give it a helping hand in puffing slightly. Any double crust recipe below can be halved to make a single-crust, and vice versa.

This is the richest pastry in that it has the most fat in proportion to flour. It may need to be rolled slightly thinner than the others because it has only 2 cups flour.

BUTTER PASTRY

makes two 9-inch crusts

2 cups flour
2 teaspoons baking powder
½ teaspoon salt
1 cup butter
about 8 to 10 tablespoons cold water

Mix the salt and baking powder with the flour. Rub in the butter. Stir in about 8 tablespoons water, adding more if necessary to bind the dough together. Gently press the dough into a ball.

BUTTER PASTRY

makes a thick single crust for savoury pies

1 ½ cups flour
3 teaspoons baking powder
½ teaspoon salt
½ cup butter
8 tablespoons cold water

Combine the flour, salt, and baking powder. Rub or cut in the butter. Stir in just enough water to bring the dough together; start with about 6 tablespoons and add 1 or 2 tablespoons more to just bind the dough.

LARD PASTRY

makes two 9-inch crusts

Two teaspoons of baking powder can be added. As lard makes a softer dough than butter, this pastry was often rolled slightly thicker for ease of handling.

3 cups flour
1 cup lard
1 teaspoon salt
about 10 to 12 tablespoons cold water

Mix the salt and flour. Rub or cut in the lard. Stir in about 10 tablespoons water, adding more if necessary to just bind the dough together. Gently press the dough into a ball.

SUET PASTRY

makes a single crust for sweet or savoury pies

1 ½ cups flour
1 cup finely chopped suet
½ teaspoon salt
7 to 8 tablespoons water

Mix together the salt, suet, and flour. Stir in about 7 tablespoons water, adding more as needed to just bring the dough together. Press into a fat disk and reserve in a cool place.

DUMPLING PASTE TOPPING

makes a single top crust

Dumpling paste toppings, usually called pastry, are more akin to the American biscuit topping. They were put on meat stews, which were then called pies by virtue of the "pastry" on top.

2 cups flour
3 teaspoons baking powder
½ teaspoon salt
¾ cup water, plus more as necessary

Mix the salt, baking powder, and flour, then stir in enough water to make a loose dough. Roll out to fit the pan being used for the stew. Lay on the meat stew and bake at 350°F for 30 to 40 minutes, or until the paste is lightly browned.

Over: Two free-standing cast-iron cookstoves, late 19th or early 20th century. Note the large ovens surrounding the flue at the back of each stove. *Archives and Special Collections Division, Memorial University, 27 02 001.*

Chapter 18

Cakes

Irish and English settlers brought their traditions of baking to Newfoundland, and after the introduction of baking powder, cakes and other baked goods proliferated wildly. Narrowing down the recipes for this chapter was difficult, but I hope the ones I have chosen illustrate the types of cakes that were traditionally baked.

BAKING POWDER

Before the introduction of baking powder, cakes were leavened in three ways, all of which presented difficulties for the cook. Baking soda, itself only in common use from the mid-19th century, was of limited use in sweet baked goods because it needs an acidic ingredient. Yeast-leavened cakes were of limited appeal because they were more bread- than cake-like. And the vigorous and lengthy beating of the egg mixture to incorporate as much air as possible was not for the weak of wrist, nor for busy cooks whose days were overfilled with the chores of running a household. The arrival of baking powder liberated the cook from time-consuming and laborious work, and from then on cake rising was a much simpler matter.

Mr. B.E. Dickinson of Halifax advertised Woodill's German Baking Powder in the St. John's press in 1879, exhorting readers to "ask your grocer for it." The idea caught on, and by 1885 both Perline and Royal baking powders were advertised by A.E.M.

MAGIC
BAKING POWDER
CONTAINS NO ALUM
MAGIC BAKING POWDER
CONTAINS NO ALUM
Users of this well known article have the assurance that food is made more wholesome and nutritious by its use.
"Magic" is a pure phosphate baking powder, and it is a well known fact that phosphate is a necessary constituent in food, while alum is a dangerous mineral acid.
"Magic" Baking Powder contains no egg albumen or other added ingredient for the purpose of making unfair and deceptive tests which have no value as a constituent of baking powder.
For economy buy the full weight 1-lb. size.
E.W.GILLETT COMPANY LIMITED
WINNIPEG TORONTO, ONT. MONTREAL

BOSTON BAKING POWDER.
Used by the leading Hotels in New England and New York.
We commend the QUALITY and REASONABLENESS of Price of this POWDER TO ALL PRUDENT Housekeepers, and assure the PUBLIC that a week's trial
Will Satisfy the Most Sceptical.
The time has come for the introduction of a High Grade Baking Powder at a RIGHT PRICE. Put up in 3-oz., 4-oz., 6-oz., 8-oz., 1-lb. and 5-lb. Tins. The leading GROCERS of St. John's sell it.
ARCHIBALD & CO.,
Sole Agents for Nfld.
dec27,4i

LOOK HERE! LOOK HERE
WOODILL'S
German Baking Powder,
Is the Cheapest and Best
FOR MAKING
Biscuits, Buns, Tea Cakes, Etc.
Address all orders to
B. E. DICKINSON,
Proprietor, Halifax, N. S.
To get the genuine observe my name, and the word "Registered." on each package.
Ask your Grocer for it.
Sept5

2 Good Things
EAGANS'
THE TEA
with a reputation, Black, Mixed or Natural Green.
COOKS' FRIEND Baking Powder,
worth 40c. lb.; our price, 20c. lb., 12c. ½ lb., 7c. ¼ lb., 2½ ounce tin, 5c.
The Leading Tea Stores.
C. P. EAGAN,
Queen's Road,
and corner Duckworth & Prescott Streets

ONCE
USED
ALWAYS
USED!
Ask Your Grocer for
Emerald Baking Powder
2 oz. Tins................5 cents.
¼ lb. Tins................10 cents.
½ lb. Tins................20 cents.

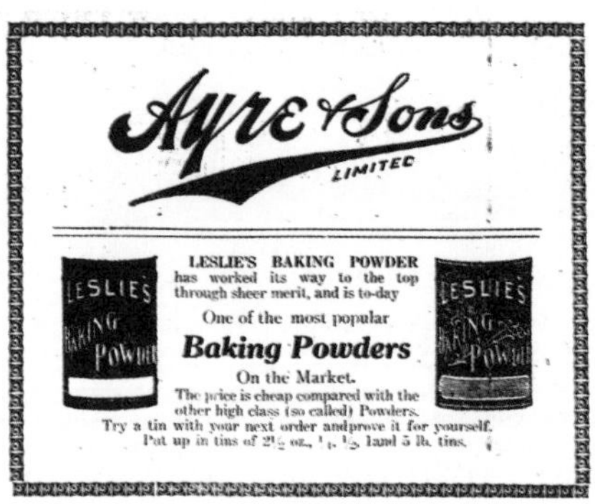
Ayre & Sons
LIMITED
LESLIE'S BAKING POWDER has worked its way to the top through sheer merit, and is to-day
One of the most popular
Baking Powders
On the Market.
The price is cheap compared with the other high class (so called) Powders.
Try a tin with your next order and prove it for yourself.
Put up in tins of 2½ oz., ¼, ½, 1 and 5 lb. tins.

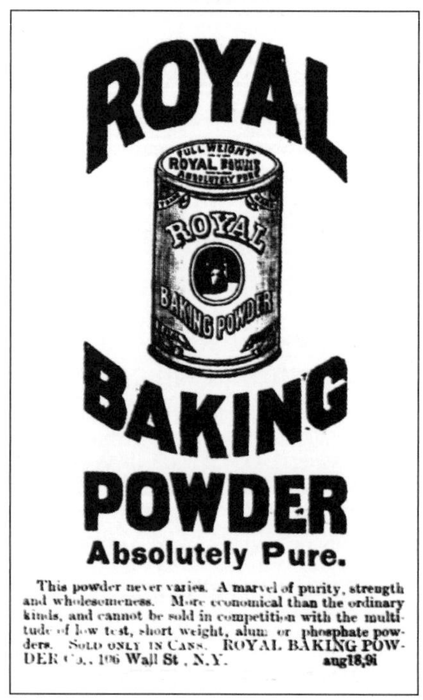
ROYAL
BAKING
POWDER
Absolutely Pure.
This powder never varies. A marvel of purity, strength and wholesomeness. More economical than the ordinary kinds, and cannot be sold in competition with the multitude of low test, short weight, alum or phosphate powders. SOLD ONLY IN CANS. ROYAL BAKING POWDER Co., 106 Wall St., N.Y.
aug18,9i

Archibald of 81 to 85 Water Street, St. John's. Soon after, at least five more brands were frequently advertised, and baking powder was firmly entrenched in Newfoundland kitchens before the turn of the century. Homemade baking powder was widespread because cream of tartar, of little use except in baking powder, was on the shelves by the end of the 19th century, and sodium bicarbonate was easily available. This recipe is from the 1905 cookbook.

BAKING POWDER

makes about 1 pound

¼ pound cornstarch
¼ pound bread soda
½ pound cream of tartar

Mix together well. Sift the mixture to ensure thorough mixing and remove any small lumps. Store in tightly stoppered jars in a cool, dry place.

DRIED GRAPES, FIGS, AND BROAD FIGS

Newfoundland cakes often contained dried grapes: currants, raisins, and sultanas. Distinctions vary, but in general, and in Newfoundland in particular, currants were the smallest, most shriveled, and blackest; raisins, dark brown and bigger than currants; and sultanas, larger and paler than raisins.

In Newfoundland, raisins were often called figs, so any food with raisins in it was a *figgy* something—figgy bread, figgy bun, figgy pudding. Some people used fig and raisin completely interchangeably, but often only larger raisins were called figs, the more expensive ones reserved particularly for cakes, while regular raisins were just that, and used for any recipe calling for them.

Just to confuse the issue, real dried figs were also imported from the late 19th century onward, and were called broad figs to distinguish them from raisin-figs. In addition, raisins were also called plums in the context of plum pudding (page 190).

CAKES

Bang belly has had diffuse and diverse meanings, everything from flat pancakes through dumplings to boiled puddings and cakes. I most often heard it in the sense of a lightly sweetened cake incorporating cubes of fatback, and that is how I use it here. This is one of the few cake recipes that uses baking soda, which works only in the presence of some acidic ingredient, molasses in this case.

BANG BELLY

makes one 9 by 9-inch cake

- 1 cup cubed fatback pork
- ½ cup molasses
- ½ teaspoon cinnamon
- 2 teaspoons baking soda
- 3 cups flour
- 1 cup water

Grease and flour a 9 by 9-inch cake pan. Mix the fatback, molasses, and cinnamon together well. Combine the flour and baking soda and stir into the molasses and fatback, adding water to form a soft dough. Scrape the dough into the prepared pan and level it off. Bake at 350°F for 40 to 45 minutes.

BLUEBERRY CAKE

makes one 8-inch cake

Blueberry cake was always a favourite, which means hundreds of recipes are out there. Most are much the same with differing quantities of blueberries. If baked in a bread pan, this was often called a blueberry loaf, but it's still a cake.

Fresh blueberries were traditionally used, so this was only a seasonal treat. Frozen berries work well, but bleed into the batter more than fresh ones do, giving the cake more of a purple cast than you might expect.

- ½ cup butter
- 1 cup sugar
- 2 eggs
- 1 teaspoon vanilla
- ¼ teaspoon salt
- 1½ cups flour
- 3 teaspoons baking powder
- ½ cup milk
- 1½ cups blueberries

Grease and flour an 8-inch round cake pan. Beat the butter and sugar. Mix in the eggs, salt, and vanilla, then beat well. Combine the flour and baking powder, and beat into the butter mixture alternately with the milk. Fold in the blueberries and scrape the batter into the prepared pan. Smooth the top and bake at 350°F for 60 to 75 minutes, or until a skewer comes out clean.

BOILED RAISIN CAKE
makes one 8-inch cake

Boiled cakes cause consternation for the uninitiated—surely cakes are baked, not boiled? But it was only a component of the cake that was boiled, not the cake itself, which was baked in the usual fashion. Boiled cocoa cakes and boiled fruit cakes were popular, but when a cake was simply called "boiled cake," it was usually a boiled raisin cake, the best of this style, and a popular variation of the basic raisin cake (page 214). Some cooks liked to bake this in a loaf pan; the following recipe is typical and can be baked either in a loaf pan or, as here, in a round cake pan.

½ cup butter
1 cup sugar
¼ cup molasses
¼ teaspoon cloves
½ teaspoon cinnamon
½ teaspoon nutmeg
1 cup raisins
1 cup water
1 egg, beaten
1 ½ teaspoons baking soda
2 cups flour

Put the butter, sugar, molasses, spices, raisins, and water in a small saucepan and bring to a boil. Take off the heat and let cool to room temperature. Grease and flour an 8-inch cake pan. Mix the beaten egg into the cooled raisin mixture. Mix the baking soda with about 1 teaspoon water and mix into the raisin mixture. Beat in the flour to make a loose batter. Pour into the prepared pan and bake at 350°F for 45 to 50 minutes, or until a skewer comes out clean.

CHOCOLATE CAKE with cocoa
makes one 8-inch cake

Chocolate was an early import into Newfoundland, but cakes made with solid chocolate can be tricky, so chocolate cake was likely less common before the arrival of powdered cocoa toward the end of the 19th century. Despite the ease offered by cocoa, cakes were still made with solid chocolate.

Many cooks I talked to specifically mentioned Fry's cocoa when talking about cooking in the earlier part of the 20th century. Fry's, and other cocoas, readily form little pebbles which can produce a measly looking cake. I was frequently admonished to sift it to break up any small clumps.

½ cup butter
1 ¼ cups sugar
3 eggs
¼ teaspoon salt
1 teaspoon vanilla
1 ½ cups flour
½ cup cocoa powder
3 teaspoons baking powder
¾ cup milk

Grease and flour an 8-inch cake pan. Cream the butter and sugar together. Add the eggs, salt, and vanilla and beat together. Sift the flour, cocoa, and baking powder together. Add this to the butter-sugar mixture alternately with the milk. Scrape the batter into the prepared pan. Bake at 350°F about 60 to 70 minutes, or until a skewer comes out clean.

CHOCOLATE CAKE with solid chocolate

makes one 8-inch cake

½ cup butter
1½ cups sugar
3 eggs
¼ teaspoon salt
¾ cup grated chocolate (about 2 ounces)
1 cup milk
2 cups flour
2 teaspoons baking powder

Grease and flour an 8-inch cake pan. Cream the butter and sugar together. Beat in the eggs and salt. Gently warm the chocolate in about ¼ cup milk in a saucepan and stir until it has melted. While stirring constantly, add the rest of the milk slowly to avoid curdling (a few specks of solid chocolate do not matter). Mix the flour and baking powder; add to the butter-sugar mixture alternately with the milk and chocolate, and stir until well combined. Scrape into the prepared pan. Bake at 350°F for at least 1 hour, or until a skewer comes out clean.

COTTAGE PUDDING

makes one 8-inch cake

Cottage pudding is from the American tradition, where it has been known since the end of the 19th century. Despite its name, it is very much a cake. Because it has less egg than many other cakes, it was often called plain cake in Newfoundland, particularly when served at room temperature. But when served warm, with hot sweet sauce, it was called cottage pudding.

This was often made in a square pan and cut in rectangles to serve. In American recipes the hot sauce served with cottage pudding was usually a brown-sugar sauce, but in Newfoundland any sweet sauce was used: molasses-rum, lemon, chocolate, simple hot jam, sugar-vanilla, plain custard, or molasses coady (see Chapter 22).

½ cup butter
1 cup sugar
1 egg
1½ cups flour
2 teaspoons baking powder
¼ teaspoon salt
¾ cup milk

Grease and flour an 8-inch round or square cake pan. Cream the butter and sugar together; beat in the egg. Mix the flour, baking powder, and salt, then beat in the flour mixture alternately with the milk until it has formed a smooth, even batter. Scrape the batter into the prepared pan and bake at 350°F for about 40 minutes, or until a skewer comes out clean. Serve warm, with a little sweet sauce over each portion.

CROWBERRY CAKE

makes one 8-inch cake

This crowberry cake used both baking powder and baking soda, even though either would leaven the cake. It is another relic from the days when the original soda of a recipe was retained just in case the new fangled baking powder turned out to be a dud.

½ teaspoon baking soda
¼ cup water
½ cup butter
½ cup sugar
1 egg
½ cup molasses
¼ teaspoon salt
½ teaspoon cinnamon
¼ teaspoon cloves
1¼ cups flour
2 teaspoons baking powder
2 cups crowberries

Grease and flour an 8-inch cake pan. Dissolve the baking soda in ¼ cup water. Cream the butter and sugar together; beat in the egg, molasses, salt, and spices. Mix in the dissolved baking soda. Mix the flour with the baking powder and mix into the butter-molasses mixture. Fold in the crowberries. Scrape into the prepared pan. Bake at 350°F for about 1 hour, or until a skewer inserted into the thickest part comes out clean.

LIGHT FRUIT CAKE

makes one 8-inch cake

Fruit cakes were really raisin (or sultana) cakes with other preserved fruit such as cherries or candied peel added or substituted. Both light and dark fruit cakes were made. A light fruit cake had more flour in proportion to other ingredients, while a dark fruit cake had less flour and proportionately more (and more varied) dried fruit and usually some spices. Fruit cakes, particularly at the dark end of the spectrum, had many other names: black cake, bride's cake, wedding cake, and Christmas cake. For celebratory occasions like Christmas, three or four cakes were made ahead of time, sprinkled with rum, and stored in tins in a cool place.

Fruit cake recipes were among the few I saw that had been written down, usually on a well-thumbed and kitchen-stained piece of paper, and I heard frequent claims that these recipes had been handed down through generations. No doubt such infrequently used recipes were difficult to keep in the memory like more everyday fare.

1 cup butter
1 cup sugar
3 eggs
1 cup sultanas
1 cup chopped glacé cherries
¾ cup milk
3 cups flour
2 teaspoons baking powder

Grease and flour an 8-inch cake pan. Cream the butter and sugar together. Beat in the eggs. Stir in the fruit and then the milk. Combine the flour and baking powder and mix into the butter and egg mixture. Scrape into the prepared pan. Bake at 350°F for 1¾ hours, or until a skewer inserted in the thickest part comes out clean.

DARK FRUIT CAKE

makes one 8-inch cake

Candied peel came in long strips and had to be chopped before use. Dark fruit cakes improved with time, so they were often wrapped in a light cloth drenched in rum to both enhance flavour and deter mould.

1 cup sugar
1 cup butter
4 eggs
3 tablespoons molasses
1 teaspoon cinnamon
1 teaspoon nutmeg
½ teaspoon ground cloves
1½ cups raisins
1½ cups dates, chopped
¾ cup mixed peel, chopped
¼ cup milk
1½ cups flour
1 tablespoon baking powder

Grease and flour a deep, 8-inch cake pan. Chop the peel and dates into raisin-size pieces. Beat the sugar and butter together until pale yellow. Beat in the eggs, molasses, and spices. Stir in the chopped fruit and raisins. Beat in the milk. Combine the flour and baking powder and mix into the batter. Pour the batter into the prepared pan. Bake at 300°F for about 2 hours, or until a skewer inserted in the thickest part comes out clean.

GINGER CAKE

makes one 8-inch cake

Ginger cake was a perennial favourite. This recipe makes a lightly spiced cake, but the ginger can be doubled if desired.

1 cup butter
1 cup sugar
3 eggs
¼ cup molasses
3 tablespoons powdered ginger
¼ teaspoon cinnamon
¼ teaspoon salt
2 cups flour
2 teaspoons baking powder
¼ cup milk

Grease and flour an 8-inch cake pan. Beat the sugar and butter together. Mix in the eggs, molasses, ginger, cinnamon, and salt and beat together well. Combine the flour and baking powder and beat into the butter mixture. Beat in the milk to make a smooth batter. Scrape the batter into the prepared pan and bake at 350°F for about 1 hour, or until a skewer inserted in the thickest part comes out clean.

INDIAN MEAL CAKE

makes one 8-inch cake

Indian meal was the same as cornmeal, and was often sold as cheap poultry feed. It also became associated with poverty, particularly when used as payment in government projects like the Indian Meal Line from Portugal Cove to Torbay. Despite these connotations, Indian meal (or cornmeal) cake has persisted simply because it tastes good. The problem of the lack of gluten in cornmeal was solved by adding gluten-rich regular white flour.

½ cup butter
¾ cup sugar
1 egg
¾ cup flour
1½ cups cornmeal
3 teaspoons baking powder
1 cup milk

Grease and flour an 8-inch cake pan. Cream the butter and sugar together. Beat in the egg. Combine the flour, cornmeal, and baking powder and mix with the butter mixture. Stir in the milk to form a soft dough. Put the dough into the prepared pan and bake at 350°F for 45 to 50 minutes, or until a skewer inserted in the thickest part comes out clean.

Serve warm or cold, sliced and spread with jam.

MOLASSES CAKE

makes one 8-inch cake

Molasses cake is another example in which the use of baking soda has persisted, although it works perfectly well with baking powder. Although raisins were usually part of molasses cakes, many cooks simply left them out.

½ cup butter
½ cup sugar
¼ teaspoon salt
¾ cup molasses
2 eggs
2 cups flour
1½ teaspoons baking soda
½ cup milk
1 cup raisins (optional)

Grease and flour a deep, 8-inch cake pan. Cream the butter and sugar together. Add the salt, molasses, and eggs and mix well. Combine the flour and baking soda and add to the creamed mixture alternately with the milk. Beat well, then fold in the raisins. Scrape into the prepared pan and bake at 350°F for 60 to 65 minutes, or until a skewer inserted in the thickest part comes out clean.

OLD-FASHIONED CAKE

makes one 8-inch cake

There are many variations of this cake with other local names, but the source of this particular recipe called it old-fashioned cake. The technique is unusual in that everything except the flour is mixed and beaten together first; the flour is mixed in last. Common additions were spices, nuts, and dried fruits.

Flavourings, sometimes called essences, were a feature of the traditional Newfoundland kitchen, so instead of using vanilla, this and other plain cakes could be changed into a lemon, peppermint, or almond cake by using the appropriate flavouring.

½ cup butter
1 cup sugar
3 eggs
3 teaspoons vanilla
3 teaspoons baking powder
1 cup milk
1 teaspoon vanilla flavouring (optional)
2½ cups flour

Grease and flour a deep, 8-inch cake pan. Beat together the butter, sugar, eggs, and vanilla. Mix in the baking powder, milk, and flavouring. Stir in enough flour to make a smooth, thick batter. Scrape it into the prepared pan. Bake at 350°F for 1 hour, or until a skewer inserted in the thickest part comes out clean.

ONE-TWO-THREE-FOUR CAKE

makes one 8-inch cake

One-two-three-four cake comes from the American tradition, and the name is the recipe by volume proportions (for example, 1 cup of butter, 2 of sugar, 3 of flour, and 4 eggs). This recipe makes an excellent basic cake. Flavourings were often added to turn this into a lemon or vanilla cake.

½ cup butter
1 cup sugar
2 eggs
1½ cups flour
2 teaspoons baking powder
½ cup milk
1 teaspoon vanilla or lemon flavouring (optional)

Grease and flour an 8-inch cake pan. Cream the butter and sugar together. Beat in the eggs. Mix the flour and baking powder, and beat into the butter and sugar. Add the milk and flavouring, and beat well. Scrape the batter into the prepared pan and smooth the top. Bake at 350°F for 40 to 45 minutes, or until a skewer inserted in the thickest part comes out clean. Turn out on a rack to cool.

PARTRIDGEBERRY CAKE

makes one 8-inch cake

This partridgeberry cake recipe is similar to the blueberry cake recipe except for the extra sugar to counteract the tartness of partridgeberries. The amount of partridgeberries is flexible—as little as ½ cup makes a good cake. If baked in a bread pan, it was called a partridgeberry loaf, but it is still a cake recipe. This cake was made both in season with freshly picked berries and throughout the winter using berries from a semi-frozen barrelful in the shed (see Chapter 20). Frozen berries bleed into the batter and give the cake a reddish cast.

½ cup butter
1 cup sugar
2 eggs
¼ teaspoon salt
1 teaspoon vanilla
1½ cups flour
3 teaspoons baking powder
½ cup milk
1½ cups partridgeberries

Grease and flour an 8-inch cake pan. Beat the butter and sugar together. Mix in the eggs, salt, and vanilla, and beat well. Mix the flour and baking powder, add to the butter mixture alternately with the milk, and beat well. Fold in the partridgeberries and scrape into the prepared pan. Smooth the top and bake at 350°F for about 60 to 75 minutes, or until a skewer inserted in the thickest part comes out clean.

POUND CAKE

makes one 8-inch cake

Pound cake was originally 1 pound each of butter, sugar, eggs, and flour. But equal weights got mixed up with volume measurements, particularly on the west side of the Atlantic, so some pound cake recipes are based on equal volumes, which is not quite the same thing. In other recipes, equal weights were more or less translated into volumes, as in the following example.

1 cup butter
1 ¼ cups sugar
4 eggs
¼ teaspoon salt
1 teaspoon vanilla
3 tablespoons milk
1 ½ cups flour

Grease and flour a deep 8-inch cake pan. Cream the butter and sugar together. Beat in the salt, vanilla, eggs, flour, and milk. Make sure everything is beaten together thoroughly. Scrape into the prepared pan. Bake at 350°F for about 1 hour, or until a skewer comes out clean.

RAISIN CAKE

makes one 8-inch cake

Raisin cakes were one of the best of a range of cakes using dried fruit such as currants, sultanas, dates, and candied citrus peel, etc. (for raisin cake using boiled raisins, see page 205).

¾ cup butter
1 cup sugar
3 eggs
½ teaspoon vanilla
2 ½ cups flour
2 ½ teaspoons baking powder
½ cup milk
1 ¼ cups raisins

Grease and flour an 8-inch cake pan. Cream the butter and sugar together. Add the vanilla and eggs and beat together well. Mix the flour and baking powder, and add to the butter and eggs alternately with the milk. When well beaten, mix in the raisins. Scrape into the prepared pan and bake at 350°F for 60 to 70 minutes, or until a skewer inserted in the thickest part comes out clean. Turn out on a rack and let cool completely.

SEED CAKE

makes one 8-inch cake

Seed cake was always caraway seed cake, and caraway seeds were stocked by stores across the island. Wild caraway is an introduced species found across Newfoundland and most of North America. Wild caraway plants could be gathered after the seeds had formed and laid on brown paper (or newspaper) or hung up to dry. When dry, the plants were rubbed to release the seeds, which were then stored in a cool dry place.

Seed cake was popular in Britain, America, and Newfoundland before World War II. Recipes varied, but the sugar was usually downplayed to suit the essentially savoury nature of caraway seed.

½ cup butter
¾ cup sugar
3 eggs
1 ½ cups flour
¼ teaspoon salt
1 teaspoon baking powder
½ cup milk
1 ½ teaspoons caraway seeds

Grease and flour an 8-inch cake pan. Beat the butter and sugar together, then beat in the eggs. Mix the flour, salt, and baking powder and beat into the butter mixture. Mix in the milk and beat well, then fold in the caraway seeds. Scrape into the prepared pan. Bake at 350°F for 40 to 45 minutes, or until a skewer comes out clean.

SPICE CAKE

makes one 8-inch cake

Spice cake was a useful standby—when the household was tired of cakes with berries or dried fruit, or had run out of them, spices were always available. Which spices were used in what amounts differed between cooks, but this typical recipe makes a mildly spiced cake. For a bolder flavour, double or triple the spices.

½ cup butter
1 cup sugar
2 eggs
½ teaspoon nutmeg
¼ teaspoon cinnamon
¼ teaspoon cloves
¼ teaspoon salt
2 cups flour
2 teaspoons baking powder
½ cup milk
1 cup raisins

Grease and flour an 8-inch cake pan. Beat the sugar and butter together. Mix in the eggs, spices, and salt and beat together well. Mix the flour and baking powder and beat into the butter mixture alternately with the milk. Mix in the raisins. Scrape into the prepared pan and bake at 350°F for about 50 minutes, or until a skewer inserted in the thickest part comes out clean.

SPONGE CAKE

makes one 8-inch cake

Real sponge cakes were not hugely popular, least of all among cooks, and most of my sources had never made them except perhaps for special occasions. Not surprising really, because these contain no baking powder and rely instead on the lengthy beating of the mixture, laborious and time-consuming before the advent of electrical mixers. Mrs. Beeton, for example, suggests beating the eggs for 15 minutes, an eternity with a whisk or wooden spoon. I doubt if many actually did that, to the detriment of the finished cake.

4 eggs
¾ cup sugar
¼ teaspoon salt
1 teaspoon lemon flavouring
¾ cup flour

Grease and flour an 8-inch cake pan. Beat the eggs vigorously for about 10 minutes or more until pale yellow. Stir in the sugar, salt, and lemon flavouring and beat for another 10 minutes until thick and foamy. Fold in the flour. Scrape into the prepared pan. Bake at 350°F for 40 to 45 minutes, or until a skewer inserted in the thickest part comes out clean. Turn out on a rack to cool.

WAR CAKE

makes one 8-inch cake

War cakes appeared under many names, such as Canada's War Cake, 1915 cake, eggless and butterless cake, or simply economical cake. This was a cake designed with frugality in mind—no eggs, no butter (but usually some other fat), and no milk. In Newfoundland, the official motive for war cake was "to encourage the baking by housewives of St. John's of bread, cake, buns etc., containing substitutes for wheat flour, so as to lessen the consumption of the latter and thereby release more for the use of the Allies." That explanation was part of an advertisement in the *Evening Telegram* for a "Victory War Bread Show" staged by the Newfoundland Food Control Board. It was likely more a matter of the gratifying glow of self-sacrifice rather than any tangible assistance to the war effort.

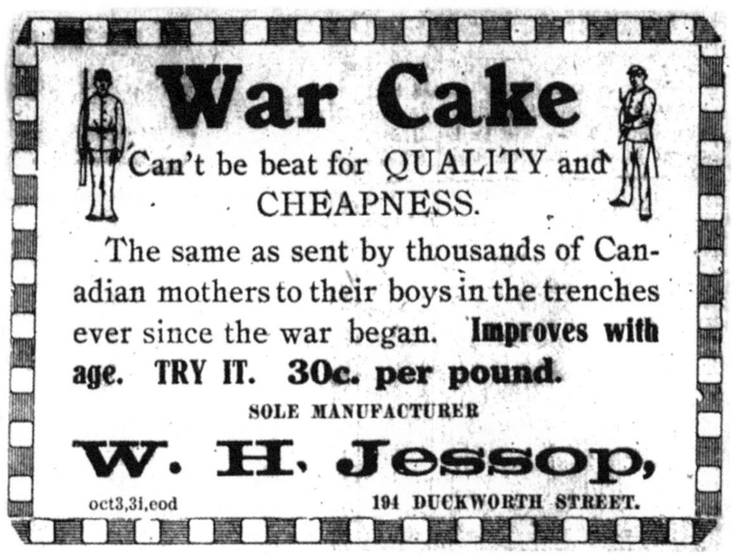

One real benefit of these cakes, however, was the lack of butter and eggs. These cakes lasted better than cakes with perishable ingredients and could be sent to the troops overseas. One enterprising baker in St. John's, W.H. Jessop of 194 Duckworth Street, advertised his War Cake as "The same as sent by thousands of Canadian mothers to their boys in the trenches ever since the war began. Improves with age. TRY IT. 30c. per pound."

War cake was essentially a boiled raisin cake without the butter and eggs.

VICTORY War Bread Show

(Under the auspices of His Excellency the Governor)

WILL BE HELD IN THE

British Hall, Wednesday, March 13th,

AT THREE O'CLOCK.

Object: To encourage the baking by the housewives of St. John's, of bread, cake, buns, etc., containing substitutes for wheat flour, so as to lessen the consumption of the latter and thereby release more for the use of the Allies.

Exhibits will be in five classes:

Class 1: Breads composed of wheat flour and not less than 20 per cent. of potatoes. First prize, a barrel of flour; second prize, a half barrel of flour.

Class 2: Bread composed of wheat flour and not less than 20 per cent. of oatmeal or rolled oats. First prize, a barrel of flour; second prize, a half barrel of flour.

Class 3: Bread composed of wheat flour and not less than 20 per cent. of any other substitute. First prize, a barrel of flour; second prize, a half barrel of flour.

Class 4: War cake, to contain not less than 20 per cent. of substitutes mixed with wheat flour. First prize, a barrel of flour; second prize, a half barrel of flour.

Class 5: Biscuits, tea buns, scones, etc., to contain not less than 20 per cent. of substitutes mixed with wheat flour. First prize, a barrel of flour; second prize, a half barrel of flour.

The factors which will influence the judges in their findings are palatability, appearance and cheapness.

The decision of the judges will in all cases be final.

Competitors can send loaves of bread of any size or shape, using their own baking equipment. Each exhibit should have attached to it a paper showing the recipe from which it is made, with the ingredients stated in pounds and ounces.

Exhibits will be received at the British Hall between the hours of 2 and 6 p.m. on Tuesday, March 12.

Each exhibit on presentation at the Hall will have affixed to it a number and the exhibitor will be given a similar number, and her name will be entered in a register kept for the purpose.

The judging will take place on Wednesday morning, and the names of the prize winners will be announced at the opening, when the prizes will be presented.

All exhibits will be turned over to charitable organizations for the benefit of the poor.

Admission, FREE.

NFLD. FOOD CONTROL BOARD.
mar6,11

---

1 cup sugar
1 cup water
1 tablespoon lard or pork fat
1 cup raisins
½ teaspoon salt
½ teaspoon cinnamon
½ teaspoon cloves
2 cups flour
1 teaspoon baking powder

Grease and flour an 8-inch cake pan. Combine all ingredients except the flour and baking powder and bring to a boil. Simmer for 5 minutes; remove from the heat and let cool. Combine the flour and baking powder and mix with the cooled raisin mixture to make a smooth, soft batter. Scrape into the prepared pan and bake at 350°F for about 40 to 45 minutes, or until a skewer inserted in the thickest part comes out clean.

WASHINGTON PIE

makes one 8-inch layer cake

Washington pie was not a pie but a layer cake, with jam in the middle and a decorative dusting of fine sugar on top. It was from the American tradition, where it was also called Martha Washington pie or Washington cake. The recipe has been in print since at least 1878, and American versions often had three or four layers of cake with a wide variety of jams, jellies, or marmalades between them. Newfoundland versions usually had only two layers of cake, with blueberry, partridgeberry, or bakeapple jam in the middle. Virtually any cake can be assembled in this fashion to make a Washington pie.

¾ cup butter
1½ cups sugar
3 eggs
2½ cups flour
3 teaspoons baking powder
1 cup milk
½ cup jam, or to taste
icing sugar for dusting on top

Grease and flour two 8-inch cake pans. Cream together the butter and sugar. Beat in the eggs. Combine the flour and baking powder and add alternately with the milk to the creamed mixture. Divide the batter between the prepared cake pans. Bake at 350°F for 40 to

45 minutes, or until a skewer inserted in the thickest part comes out clean. Turn out on a rack and cool. To serve, slice off the top of one cake to make a level surface. Spread with jam, and gently press the other cake on top. Dust with icing sugar.

BASIC WHITE CAKE

makes one 8-inch cake

White cakes were loosely related because they contained only egg whites, not the yolks. This seems extravagant, but was in fact economical—while the whites made a cake, the yolks could be used for a custard tart.

½ cup butter
1½ cups sugar
2 cups flour
2 teaspoons baking powder
¼ teaspoon salt
¾ cup milk
4 egg whites

Grease and flour an 8-inch cake pan. Cream the butter and sugar together. Mix the flour, baking powder, and salt; add to the butter and sugar alternately with the milk, and beat well. Whip the egg whites to peaks and fold into the batter. Pour into the prepared pan and smooth the top. Bake at 350°F for about 1 hour, or until a skewer inserted in the thickest part comes out clean. Turn out on a rack to cool.

WHITE CAKE

makes one 8-inch cake

Some cooks went one step less and did not beat the whites at all, relying totally on baking powder to rise the cake.

½ cup butter
¾ cup milk
2 egg whites
1½ cups flour
1 cup sugar
1 teaspoon baking powder

Grease and flour an 8-inch cake pan. Melt the butter. Stir in the milk and the egg whites (not whipped). Mix the flour, sugar, and baking powder. Mix the butter mixture with the flour mixture and beat until completely smooth. Pour into the prepared pan and smooth the top. Bake at 350°F for about 40 to 45 minutes, or until a skewer comes out clean. Turn out on a rack to cool.

ICING OR FROSTING

Two words meaning the same thing, with frosting preferred in America, icing the usual British term, and Newfoundland adopting both. Cakes were rarely iced except for special occasions—for every day, a dusting of sugar sufficed, if there was any decoration at all. Variations on these two icings were popular.

BUTTER-SUGAR ICING

enough for 1 cake

- 2 tablespoons butter
- 1 cup icing sugar
- 3 teaspoons milk, plus extra
- 2 or 3 drops vanilla, lemon, or other flavouring

Cream the icing sugar, butter, and 3 teaspoons milk. Continue to mix in small amounts of milk, about ½ teaspoon at a time, until the mixture is a soft, easily spreadable paste. Mix in the flavouring.

BOILED ICING

enough for 2 cakes

- 1 cup sugar
- ¼ cup water
- 1 egg white

Heat the sugar and water together until the sugar is dissolved. Boil gently until a small amount dropped into cold water will form a soft ball (around 240°F). Beat the egg white to stiff peaks. Pour the boiled sugar slowly into the beaten egg white in a thin stream, whisking constantly. Whisk until the mixture is stiff. When cool, spread on the cake.

Over: Wood's west-end candy store at 348 Water Street, St. John's, in the 1910s. Although styled a candy store, it was also a bakery, a confectionary, and a soda fountain, with dining rooms upstairs. *City of St. John's Archives, 01-23-007.*

OODS WEST END CANDY STO
WOOD'S
WEST END STORE
WOOD'S
FANCY BAKERY
& IMPORTED
PURE
FRUIT SODA
-ALL-
FLAVOURS
5 CENTS
PER GLASS
ICE
CREAM SODA
10 CENTS
PER GLASS

Chapter 19

Miscellaneous Sweet Things

The introduction of baking powder around 1880 allowed the proliferation of small baked goods so characteristic of the traditional Newfoundland kitchen. Most of the recipes in this chapter use it, but some use baking soda, reflecting an earlier time, and some use neither.

■ TEA BUNS

One of the best-loved items from the Newfoundland kitchen, tea buns are the same as British scones (and were often called that in Newfoundland) and similar to American biscuits, although biscuits are typically not sweet and are served with savoury foods. The examples in this chapter illustrate the range of recipes and inclusions.

My sources often mentioned that a glass or cup was a substitute for a metal cutter for the circles of dough, but they are far from ideal—the blunt rim of a glass compresses the dough and stops the rim from rising when baked. It is better to use a cutter made of thin metal, wiped frequently so that it cuts cleanly through the dough without undue compression.

PLAIN TEA BUNS

makes 12 to 18

- 3 cups flour
- ½ teaspoon salt
- 5 teaspoons baking powder
- ¾ cup butter, cut in small pieces
- ¼ cup sugar
- 1 cup milk, plus about another 3 to 4 tablespoons

Mix the flour, baking powder, and salt. Rub the butter into the flour mixture. Do not try to completely incorporate the butter: rub it in until all pieces are smaller than a split pea. Mix in the sugar, then stir in 1 cup milk and enough extra milk to make a soft dough. On a floured surface, press the dough into a flat disk, fold over, and press out again. Do this a few times just to make the dough stick together. Keeping the surface and rolling pin well floured, roll out the dough to about ¾ inch thick. Cut out circles with a 2- to 2½-inch round cutter and lay on a greased baking sheet. Press the leftover dough together and cut more disks. Bake at 350°F for 30 to 40 minutes, or until the tops are lightly browned.

RAISIN TEA BUNS

makes about 18

- 3 cups flour
- 3 teaspoons baking powder
- 3 tablespoons sugar
- ¾ cup cold butter, cut in small pieces
- 1 egg
- 1½ cups raisins

Mix the flour, baking powder, and sugar. Rub butter into the flour mixture. When there are no large pieces left, beat the egg and make it up to 1 cup with water (milk can also be used, but water makes a lighter bun). Stir the egg mixture into the flour and butter until it just holds together. Mix in the raisins. Roll out on a floured surface to about ½ inch thick. Cut out circles with a 2- to 2½-inch cutter and lay on a greased baking sheet. Bake at 350°F for about 35 minutes, or until lightly browned on top.

BLUEBERRY TEA BUNS

makes about 18

- 3 cups flour
- 4½ teaspoons baking powder
- ½ teaspoon salt
- ½ cup cold butter

6 tablespoons sugar
1 ¼ cups milk
1 ½ cups blueberries

Mix the flour, baking powder, and sugar. Cut the butter into small pieces, and rub into the flour mixture. Make a well in the centre and pour in the milk. Stir with a fork until well combined, then mix in the berries. Press the mixture together to make a loose ball. Turn out onto a lightly floured surface and pat out to about ½ to ¾ inch thick. Cut out circles with a 2- to 2½-inch cutter and lay on a greased baking sheet. Bake at 350°F for about 40 minutes, or until lightly browned on top.

PARTRIDGEBERRY TEA BUNS

makes about 18

3 cups flour
5 teaspoons baking powder
½ teaspoon salt
½ cup cold butter
½ cup sugar
1 ¼ cups milk
1 ½ cups partridgeberries

Mix the flour, baking powder, and sugar. Cut the butter in small pieces, and rub into the flour mixture. Make a well in the centre, pour in the milk, and stir together with a fork. Mix in the partridgeberries. Turn out onto a lightly floured surface and roll out to about ½ to ¾ inch thick. Cut out circles with a 2- to 2½-inch cutter and lay on a greased baking sheet. Bake at 350°F for about 40 minutes, or until lightly browned on top.

■ SQUARES

Making squares usually involved fruit (hence date, raisin, jam, partridgeberry squares), but virtually anything sweet—such as custard—was made into a square by pairing it with a flour-based mixture made like a cake, pastry, or crumble. Any of the sweet components were paired with any of the floury ones in a spectrum of possibilities with no hard distinctions between them.

PARTRIDGEBERRY SQUARES sandwich style

makes 9 to 12 squares

The partridgeberries in this recipe must be pressed firmly into the bottom layer of batter so that the top layer can be spread without shifting the berries. It is simpler to mix the berries with the batter before pouring it into the pan, which changes the style of square, and if the pan is greased and floured first, it will turn out like a cake.

¼ cup butter
¾ cup sugar
¼ teaspoon salt
2 eggs
1 cup flour
1½ teaspoons baking powder
¼ cup milk
1½ cups partridgeberries

Grease an 8 by 8-inch pan. Cream the butter, sugar, and salt together, then beat in the eggs. Combine the flour and baking powder, and beat them and the milk into the butter and egg mixture. Spread about half the batter in the prepared pan. Cover with a layer of partridgeberries and then with the remaining batter. Bake at 350°F for about 45 minutes, or until the top is golden brown and a skewer comes out clean. While still warm, cut into portions.

PARTRIDGEBERRY SQUARES berries on top

makes 9 to 12 squares

This recipe employs a similar cake mixture, but with the berries on top.

3 cups partridgeberries
1½ cups sugar
3 tablespoons butter
6 tablespoons sugar
¼ teaspoon salt
1 egg
¾ cup flour
1½ teaspoons baking powder
¼ cup milk

Mix the partridgeberries with 1½ cups sugar in a saucepan and put on a very low heat just until juice flows and the sugar has dissolved. Do not cook until the berries fall apart. Set aside to cool.

Grease an 8 by 8-inch pan. Cream the butter and sugar. Beat the eggs with the salt and beat this into the sugar and butter mixture. Mix the flour and baking powder and beat into the butter mixture alternately with the milk. Spread the batter in the prepared pan and bake at 350°F for about 25 to 30 minutes, or until the cake is well risen, lightly browning on top, and has started to come away from the sides. Poke 20 or 30 holes in the cake with a skewer or small knife. Spread the cooked partridgeberries and juice on top. Bake for another 20 minutes. Remove from the oven and let cool, but while it is still warm, run a small knife around the edge to make sure it does not stick, and score into small or large portions.

RAISIN SQUARES

makes 9 to 12 squares

These raisin squares use a pastry-like component in another top and bottom style.

1 ½ cups raisins
½ cup sugar
½ cup water
1 ½ cups flour
½ teaspoon baking powder
¼ teaspoon salt
½ cup butter
3 tablespoons cold water

Simmer the raisins, water, and sugar on a very low heat until most of the water has been absorbed (or evaporated) and the raisins are in danger of sticking. Let cool, but do not allow it to get cold and sticky. Mix the flour, baking powder, and salt. Rub the butter into this flour mixture. Stir in about 3 tablespoons cold water or enough to just bring the dough together. Divide the dough into two equal portions. Grease an 8 by 8-inch pan. Roll out one portion into roughly a 9 by 9-inch square. Line the bottom of the greased pan with this and let the pastry come up the sides. Spread the raisin mixture evenly over the pastry but do not let any raisins touch the sides because they will stick (the pastry running up the sides prevents them from sticking). Roll out the second portion of pastry, trim it to about 8 by 8 inches and lay it on top of the raisins. Press down lightly. Bake at 350°F for about 45 minutes, or until lightly browned. Cut into portions before it gets cold.

BLUEBERRY SQUARES flour-only crumble mixture

makes 9 to 12

The next two recipes use a crumble-style mixture, the first based only on flour. Although I use the term crumble mixture here, crumbles were not invented until World War II.

3 cups blueberries
1 tablespoon water
½ cup sugar
2 tablespoons flour
2 cups flour
¾ cup sugar
¼ teaspoon salt
¾ cup butter

Put the blueberries and about 1 tablespoon water in a small saucepan. Heat gently on a low heat until the berries start to release juice. Mix ½ cup sugar with 2 tablespoons flour and sprinkle over the berries and stir gently together. Heat until the mixture thickens and the berries start to burst. Remove from the stove and cool to room temperature. Grease and flour an 8 by 8-inch pan. Mix 2 cups flour with ¾ cup sugar and the salt, then rub in the butter until the mixture looks like coarse crumbs. Spread about half of this mixture in the prepared pan. Cover with the cooled blueberries, then with the rest of the crumble mixture. Bake at 350°F for 45 to 60 minutes, or until the crumble is lightly browned. Cut into portions.

DATE SQUARES with rolled-oat crumble mixture

makes 9 to 12 squares

This illustrates the rolled-oat crumble style of square, and to my mind this filling with this crust is the best possible square. Spreading the dates over the bottom layer is tricky because the sticky dates tend to pick up the crumble mixture. The easiest way is to drop small spoonfuls of the dates all over the bottom layer, to more or less cover it, and then gently nudge them together, finally smoothing it with the back of a spoon.

2 cups coarsely chopped dates, pits removed
¼ cup sugar
¾ cup water
1 ½ cups flour
¾ cup sugar
1 teaspoon baking powder
¼ teaspoon salt
¾ cup butter
1 ½ cups rolled oats

Bring the dates, ¼ cup sugar, and the water slowly to a gentle boil. Simmer on a very low heat until the mixture is thick, pasty, and in danger of sticking. Mix the flour, ¾ cup sugar, baking powder, and salt together. Rub the butter into this mixture until coarse crumbs. Mix in the oats. Divide this crumble mixture into two equal portions. Put one portion into an 8 by 8-inch pan and pat down gently in an even layer. Gently spread the date filling evenly over this layer. Spread the remaining crumble on top evenly, and pat down gently, but do not press down. Bake at 350°F for about 1 hour, or until the top is lightly browned and the edges are becoming crusty. Leave to cool. While still warm, run a thin knife around the edge to separate it from the pan where it has crusted, and cut into 9 or 12 squares.

■ OTHER SMALL CAKES

Parkin, a flat cake of oatmeal and molasses flavoured with ginger, has roots in the north of Britain. Originally an unleavened griddle cake, it became widely popular in early 19th-century Britain as a soda-leavened cake, which was particularly associated with Guy Fawkes night, November 5. When I first encountered parkin in one of the numerous, modern collections of Newfoundland recipes, I dismissed it as a recent addition. But then I found it in a handwritten recipe collection from 1917 (the Ayre manuscript), then in a column bylined "Betty" in the *Evening Telegram* in 1924, and there is a similar recipe in the 1928 cookbook. Here I give two versions.

PARKIN unleavened version

makes 8 or more pieces

This parkin is not an elegant cake; it is not suitable for a ladies' afternoon tea. The texture resembles a 21st-century granola bar, which makes this snack more suited to a long day outdoors. I have also made this with butter instead of dripping (the fat that drips from a roasting piece of meat).

2 cups oatmeal
¼ cup sugar
¼ cup dripping
2 teaspoons powdered ginger
½ cup molasses

Mix the oats, sugar, dripping, and ginger to make a crumbly dough. Work in the molasses until thoroughly incorporated. Spread in a thin layer in a greased 8 by 8-inch baking pan and smooth the top. Bake at 350°F for about 30 minutes, or until the surface is softly bubbling. Remove from the oven, let cool about 20 to 30 minutes, score into 6 or 8 rectangles, loosen the edges with a spatula, and carefully lift out and cool on a rack.

PARKIN leavened version

makes 9 to 12 pieces

This recipe makes a pleasantly dry and crumbly parkin, perhaps best eaten spread with butter. Other versions are made sweeter with more sugar, and less crumbly by the addition of an egg. But for my taste, both of these detract from the coarse texture of the oats set off by the light sweetness of the sugar and molasses.

½ cup butter
¼ cup sugar
¼ cup molasses
¼ cup milk
1 cup oatmeal
1 cup flour
¼ teaspoon salt
1 teaspoon baking powder
2 teaspoons powdered ginger

Gently heat the butter, sugar, and molasses. Stir until the butter is melted, then mix in the milk. Combine the oats, flour, salt, baking powder, and ginger and mix into the butter mixture. Mix thoroughly and turn out into a well-greased 8 by 8-inch baking pan. Smooth the top, and bake at 350°F about 25 minutes or until firm to the touch and pulling away from the sides of the pan. Turn out on a rack to cool.

SWEET POTATO CAKES

serves 4 to 6

For most people potato cakes are savoury, but sweet versions were made as well, from a sweetened dough of potato, flour, and dried fruit. I have heard them called Devonshire potato cakes, and a tradition of sweetened potato and dried fruit mixtures is prevalent in Devon, England, from where so many settlers originated.

Potato cakes were a good way of making a frugal dessert or lunch-box filler from leftovers and simple ingredients.

4 medium potatoes, peeled and cut in chunks
4 tablespoons butter
½ cup sugar
2 cups raisins
2 teaspoons baking powder
1 cup flour

Boil the potatoes in salted water until tender, drain well, and mash. Combine the butter, sugar, raisins, and baking powder. Mix in the potato and add the flour gradually to make a soft dough. Divide into 12 portions, roll each into a ball, and flatten on a greased baking sheet to about ¾ inch thick. Bake at 350°F for about 35 to 40 minutes, or until lightly browned.

BISCUITS

The range of biscuits baked in the Newfoundland kitchen was wide, derived from both American and British traditions. I have selected two of the more popular, ginger biscuits and jam-jams, and two which will be less familiar, Shrewsburys and kyffins.

GINGER BISCUITS

makes about 8 dozen

The more popular the biscuit, the more recipes in circulation—and recipes for ginger biscuits abound. The common threads were molasses, baking soda or baking powder, and of course powdered ginger, one of the spices widely available in the second half of the 19th century. This recipe uses baking soda rather than baking powder. Be careful with the flour. Initially, knead in just enough to make a dough which barely sticks to the surface, but be generous with the flour when rolling out the dough.

1 cup molasses
½ cup lard
2 teaspoons baking soda
3 teaspoons powdered ginger
1½ cups flour

Bring the molasses just to a boil, remove from the heat, and let cool a little. Mix in the lard and ginger, then baking soda, then stir in about half the flour. Turn out onto a lightly floured surface and knead in enough of the remaining flour to make a stiff dough that is reluctant to stick to your fingers. Roll out thinly, about ⅛ inch or less, on a well-floured surface, and sprinkle extra flour as needed to prevent the thin sheet of dough from sticking. Cut out 2½-inch circles and lay on a lightly greased baking sheet. Re-roll the scraps and cut out more. Bake at 350°F for about 10 minutes. The dark colour of the batter makes it difficult to tell the difference between perfectly cooked and starting to burn, so very often your nose is the best judge.

JAM-JAMS

makes 24 double biscuits

Jam-jams are pairs of thin, molasses biscuits held together by a layer of jam. Their origin is uncertain, but jams-jams are particularly associated with Newfoundland, although surprisingly enough some Mennonite communities also have a tradition of baking them. They were made commercially at least as early as 1925 when A. Harvey & Co. exhibited in the Industrial Fair in St. John's. The *Evening Telegram* noted that 37 varieties of biscuit were offered, jam-jams among them. In the 21st century, jam-jams are a popular product of Purity Factories. The hole in the middle of the top biscuit seems to be a Purity addition.

As the last of the flour can be difficult to mix in, turn out the dough and knead in the remaining flour before rolling it out. Slide the edge of a thin knife under each cut circle to pick it up and lay on the baking sheet as they are difficult to handle. If the circles crumple when the knife slides under, the dough needs more flour, gather it up and knead in an additional 1 or 2 tablespoons flour before rolling it out again.

A thick jam that sticks the two biscuits together without oozing out the sides is required. Spread jam on the underside (the side that was on the baking sheet) of the lower biscuit, then put the underside of the upper biscuit onto the jam, and squeeze them gently together. They are best if kept at least overnight before eating so that the jam softens the biscuits slightly.

1 cup butter
½ cup sugar
½ cup molasses
¼ teaspoon salt
2 teaspoons baking soda
3¼ cups flour, plus extra for rolling
jam as needed, about 1 cup

Beat the butter, sugar, and molasses together well. Mix the flour, salt, and baking soda, then beat into the butter mixture to make a soft dough. Turn out onto a lightly floured surface. Roll out thinly. Keep the surface well floured as this soft dough sticks easily. Cut out 2½-inch circles and re-roll the scraps. Lay the circles on a prepared baking sheet.

Bake at 350°F for 10 to 12 minutes, or until lightly browned. When cool, spread 2 teaspoons jam on half the biscuits, then lay another biscuit on top.

SHREWSBURY BISCUITS

makes 20 to 24 biscuits

¾ cup sugar
½ cup butter
1 egg
1½ cups flour
½ cup currants

Beat the sugar and butter together. Beat in the egg. Mix in the flour to make a soft dough. Turn out onto a floured surface and roll ¼ to ½ inch thick. Cut out 2½-inch circles and lay them on baking sheets. Re-roll the scraps and cut out more disks. Bake at 350°F for about 20 minutes until starting to brown at the edges, but do not let the biscuits brown all over.

KYFFINS

makes about 100 small biscuits

Kyffins are thin, brittle biscuits, good with a morning cup of coffee and not too sweet. Why they are called kyffins remains a mystery. The name is an old Welsh one, and there is a Mount Kyffin in Antarctica—but how did this name get applied to a biscuit in Newfoundland? This recipe is included not only as a curiosity but also because the mixture of baking soda and cream of tartar exemplifies the transition from baking soda to the widespread use of baking powder. The same result can be obtained by simply using baking powder.

I have had to interpret the original recipes more than usual in this case because both methodology and measuring were nebulous. For example, I'm sure Miss Cole (author of a recipe in the 1905 cookbook, copied in the Ayre manuscript) knew how much "a plate full of flour" was, but more than a century later it is not clear what she meant.

1 cup butter
1 cup sugar
¼ teaspoon baking soda
½ teaspoon cream of tartar
½ cup cold water
3¾ cups flour, plus more for rolling

Mix the butter and sugar. Stir the baking soda and cream of tartar into the water and pour over the butter-sugar mixture, scraping in all the solids. Beat together, and add about 3 cups flour (in ½-cup portions) until a soft dough has formed. Turn out and knead in the rest of the flour, or until a dough has formed that will not quite stick to a floured surface. Roll out to about ⅛ inch thick on a lightly floured surface and cut into small rectangles about 1 by 3 inches. Lay the rectangles on lightly greased baking sheets and bake at 350°F for about 20 minutes, or until lightly browned.

BAKED APPLES

serves 4

If you had an apple tree or the cash to buy apples from the store, baked apples were a popular dessert. They were often made in the residual heat of an oven heated for something else, so timing was variable.

4 large apples
about ¼ cup raisins
about 3 tablespoons sugar

Do not peel the apples. Cut out the cores with a small, narrow knife. Cut in from each end to remove a plug of the core, then cut out the middle with your knife. Stand the apples in a small baking dish. Divide about half the raisins between the apples, poking them down the holes you have made with a knife. Put about 2 teaspoons sugar on the raisins in each apple. Divide the rest of the raisins between the apples and push them down on the sugar. Sprinkle the remaining sugar in the bottom of the pan and add water to come about ¼ inch up the apples. Bake at 350°F (although they will cook at any temperature) for at least 1 hour, until the apples have started to split their skins and are completely soft; the time depends on the size of the apples and the oven temperature.

Spoon the pan juices over the apples. Serve hot or cold.

RICE PUDDINGS

These are sweet rice puddings, of which there were generally two different styles—with or without eggs. Raisins were often added to either version.

RICE PUDDING with eggs

serves 4 to 6

2 cups cooked rice
4 eggs
2 cups milk
½ cup sugar
1 cup raisins

Beat the eggs, milk, and sugar together until well combined; stir in the rice and raisins. Pour into an 8 by 8-inch baking dish. Bake at 350°F about 1 hour, or until completely set in the middle.

RICE PUDDING without eggs

serves 4

1 cup raw rice
¼ cup sugar
3 cups milk
1 cup raisins

Put the milk, rice, and sugar in a small saucepan and bring to a simmer over a low heat. Stirring frequently, simmer for about 20 minutes, or until the mixture is very thick. Stir in the raisins and simmer for 1 or 2 minutes more to heat the raisins.

BAKED CUSTARDS

These are not pouring sauces but baked, semi-solid desserts of milk, eggs, sugar, and vanilla.

BAKED CUSTARD

serves 4 to 6

This recipe was tricky—traditionally the oven temperature was difficult to regulate, and if cooked too hot or too long, baked custards ooze liquid in an unattractive fashion (water baths modulate the temperature and avoid this problem). Cooks often added other ingredients to stabilize the mixture. One simple addition was flour: mix 3 tablespoons flour with the sugar and beat into the eggs.

4 eggs
½ cup sugar
3 cups milk
½ teaspoon vanilla

Beat all the ingredients together. Pour into a shallow 8 by 8-inch pan. Bake at 250°F for 1 to 1¼ hours, or until the custard is barely set.

BAKED CUSTARD with porridge

serves 4 to 6

Other ways of stabilizing the mixture, or at least hiding any oozing liquid, was to mix in bread crumbs or leftover porridge, as in these recipes.

1 cup leftover porridge
2 cups milk
4 eggs
¾ cup sugar
½ teaspoon vanilla

Beat the porridge with the milk until smooth. Beat in the other ingredients. Pour into a shallow 8 by 8-inch pan. Bake at 350°F for 50 to 60 minutes, or until the custard is set.

BAKED CUSTARD with bread crumbs

serves 4 to 6

2 cups moist bread crumbs
2 cups milk
3 eggs
¾ cup sugar
½ teaspoon vanilla

Beat together the milk, eggs, sugar, and vanilla. Stir in the bread crumbs. Pour into a shallow 8 by 8-inch pan. Bake at 350°F for 50 to 60 minutes, or until the custard is set.

Over: Mrs. Jamie (Herb) and Mrs. W. Milley with a table of bottled preserves, probably at St. Anthony, ca. 1930. *The Rooms Provincial Archives Division, A 57-153.*

Chapter 20

Preserves: Jams, Jellies, and Pickles

JAM

Jam was an important way of preserving fruit. Large quantities were made in the fall, which then—apart from being slathered on tea buns—formed the basis of innumerable pies and puddings throughout the winter and spring.

Virtually any wild berry was made into jam, but the favourites were blueberries, partridgeberries, and bakeapples. Some berries, such as squashberries and high-bush cranberries, had large seeds and were generally made into jelly as the seeds were removed in the process. Jams from domestic fruit were also popular. Damsons were usually a reliable crop, and in years of abundance as much damson jam was made as blueberry. Jams from black, red, and white currants were all prized by those who grew them, as were gooseberry and plum jams. Jam was also made from dried fruit, particularly apples and apricots bought from the community store, and from vegetables such as pumpkin.

Before standardized preserving bottles (such as Mason) became widespread in the early 20th century, jams were put in whatever empty jars were handy. The problem with a random assortment of recycled jars was the risk of spoilage. I suspect that the penchant for very sweet jam, which persists to this day, particularly among older generations,

Newfoundland Wild Berries

About 59 species of edible wild berry grow in Newfoundland, but if closely related species (like the six chuckley pears) are grouped together, there are only about 30. Three were especially widespread, abundant, and flavourful, and thus of primary importance in Newfoundland kitchens. This Holy Trinity of Newfoundland wild berries—the blueberry, partridgeberry, and bakeapple—were essential ingredients of the traditional domestic economy. Rich in nutrients, they kept generations of Newfoundlanders not only alive but also (relatively) healthy.

Blueberries grow on heathlands and in woodland clearings and boggy areas. Where they are abundant, a special rake is used to gather them, a sort of narrow, deep dustpan with a comb of long, stiff wires projecting from the leading edge. The rake is scooped through the blueberry patch in a slow, swinging motion and the proceeds dumped into a bucket. Rakes collect berries far more quickly than hand-picking, but they also gather leaves and twigs, which must be sorted out later. In general people preferred to pick by hand, and if berry-picking was made a family or communal affair, large quantities that needed little or no cleaning were gathered in a pleasantly sociable fashion.

Partridgeberries are found in places similar to the blueberry but prefer more exposed conditions—rocky and dry soils and coastal headlands. They were gathered later in the season than blueberries, typically in late September or October after the tiny caterpillars of the partridgeberry fruitworm had vacated their premises. Unripe partridgeberries, gathered earlier in the season while still white and pink, were harvested less frequently.

Bakeapples are widespread on wetlands and are one of the first berries to ripen, typically by early August. They are a lot more work to pick than other berries because each plant only produces one berry, and plants do not grow in thick mats but are spaced out. Even though the picker is continually moving and bending down, considerable quantities of berries can be gathered where conditions are favourable.

Other berries varied in importance. The crowberry, for example, is abundant everywhere but was used in relatively few kitchens because it is not particularly flavourful. Crowberries were often called blackberries but should not be confused with the blackberry that looks like a big black raspberry.

Many of the tastiest wild berries were only locally abundant, and where they flourished people went out of their way to gather them. The list is long and includes raspberries, squashberries, marshberries, cranberries, chuckley pears, chokecherries, pin cherries, high-bush cranberries, wild redcurrants, skunk currants, wild gooseberries, huckleberries, wild raisins, rose hips, blackberries (not the crowberry), and sarsaparilla.

Other berries were only ever found in limited quantities. Although you might be lucky enough to find a bowlful for a dessert, there was never enough to preserve for the winter or make into wine. The supply of plumboys, for example, could never match demand. Strawberries were also usually in short supply, although the occasional bumper crop would enable a small batch of jam. The soapberry, in the few places where they were worthwhile picking, were eaten as a frothy mousse made from beating them with a little sugar. Snowberries were only of passing interest—at best a refreshing nibble in the woods—as were the bright orange crackerberries, which were widespread but dismissed as a snack for children at play.

Keeping berries was as necessary as keeping vegetables in the root cellar. Before home bottling technology (and later, freezers) became commonplace, there were only two ways of keeping berries over the winter: holding them uncooked in a cold place or boiling them into jam.

Partridgeberries, bakeapples, marshberries, and cranberries were worth keeping uncooked over the winter if more than a few gallons had been collected. A glazed earthenware crock or barrel was chosen that would hold the volume of berries, but different berries were never mixed in the same container. The berries squeezed out some juice under their own weight, but if the juice did not come near the surface of the berries, water might be added to do so. The container was covered by a lid or clean cloth or a well-scrubbed board was placed on the surface of the berries. Bakeapples, marshberries, and cranberries do not need freezing (although freezing wouldn't damage them), and barrels of these berries were often kept in a root cellar or a cool basement where they would not freeze and berries could be easily scooped out when needed.

Partridgeberries taste better for being semi-frozen and were not put in a root cellar. Containers of partridgeberries were kept in a cold back porch where they froze at least semi-solid in cold weather and had to be hacked in loose chunks with a large knife or small hatchet.

All other berries, in quantities great or small, if not made into jelly or wine, could only be kept over the winter as jam. Making enough jam to meet the needs of a large family was quite labour-intensive, so the ability to keep some types fresh in a barrel was a welcome relief.

comes from the traditional practice of maximizing the sugar in jam to minimize the risk of spoilage. Most of my sources advised boiling the jam for a span of time or "until done," which meant that traditional jams had a wide range of consistencies. Jellies required more care.

Traditional jam-making techniques were standard, as illustrated by the following recipes.

BLUEBERRY JAM

makes 1 gallon

2 gallons blueberries
14 cups sugar
1 cup water

Combine all ingredients in a large saucepan or stockpot and gently bring to a simmer. Simmer until thick. Pour into jars.

PARTRIDGEBERRY JAM

makes 20 cups

1 ½ gallons partridgeberries
12 cups sugar
8 cups water

Combine all ingredients in a large saucepan or stockpot and gently bring to a simmer. Simmer until thick. Pour into jars.

CRANBERRY JAM

makes 6 cups

8 cups cranberries
5 cups sugar
2 cups water

Combine all ingredients in a large saucepan and gently bring to a simmer. Simmer for about 30 minutes. Pour into jars.

GREEN PARTRIDGEBERRY JAM

makes about 3 cups

Green partridgeberries are only green in the sense of being unripe and immature. They are actually white on the underside and pink or red on the upper surface. This jam was rather unusual and not widely made.

My source warned me about the potential for small grubs (partridgeberry fruitworms, the larvae of a small moth) in partridgeberries, though I have never noticed any when making this jam.

4 cups unripe partridgeberries
1 cup water
2 cups sugar

Put the partridgeberries in a small saucepan with the water and sugar. Bring gently to a boil and simmer on a very low heat with the pot partly covered for 10 or 15 minutes, until the berries are soft and starting to break apart and some juice has formed. If any grubs float to the surface, skim them off. Turn the mixture into a shallow dish and leave to cool.

This will set into a very firm jelly which can be sliced with a small knife, or scooped with a spoon if you prefer.

PLUM JAM

makes 8 cups

Except for damsons, the identities of the various plums found in Newfoundland gardens are not clear, but they all made excellent jam. This recipe calls for the dark blue plum, but it will work on any garden plum from the smallest to the largest.

Removing the stones (or pits) is a major chore. Some people left them in, skimming off as many as possible while simmering, and then working around them in the jam pot. Fortunately, most larger Newfoundland plums are the freestone type, and the stone will almost fall out of a fully ripe plum cut around its natural groove. But getting the stones out of underripe fruit is a struggle.

1 gallon dark blue plums
4 cups water
6 cups sugar

Remove the stems and stones from the plums. Bring to a boil in a large saucepan or stockpot with the water and sugar, then simmer on a low heat until thick and at the setting point.

DRIED APRICOT JAM

makes 4 cups

Apricot jam was a popular jam made from store-bought dried fruit. I was always told to wash such fruit thoroughly, and one source told me to pick out any insects. A longer soaking period of two or even three days was advised by some, which could reflect differing degrees of fruit dryness.

2 cups dried apricots, coarsely chopped
3 cups water
3 cups sugar

Leave the chopped apricots to soak in the water for 24 hours. Bring the water, fruit, and sugar to a boil in a medium saucepan and simmer gently for 45 minutes to 1 hour or until the fruit is soft and translucent and the mixture has thickened.

MARMALADE

Until the middle of the 19th century the distinction between jam and marmalade was imprecise. Then marmalade became generally identified with citrus fruits, and eventually implied the use of Seville oranges unless a recipe specified otherwise. In Newfoundland the habit of making marmalade from diverse fruits and vegetables, with a little citrus included, persists into the 21st century. Marmalades could contain gooseberries, rhubarb, pumpkin, banana, and so on—as long as a little citrus was in there.

Seville oranges became available in Newfoundland around the beginning of the 20th century. The 1905 cookbook has three marmalade recipes, one of which calls for just oranges, while the other two specify Seville oranges (also known as bitter oranges). Tins of Seville orange pulp were advertised from about 1913. In practice, regular oranges, lemons, and grapefruit were used as the citrus in Newfoundland marmalades, possibly because Seville oranges have such a short season around February.

Most traditional Newfoundland citrus-based marmalade recipes called for soaking the sliced fruit for 12 to 48 hours. This practice, seen in recipes from the 17th to the 19th centuries, is supposed to remove some of the bitterness of the orange rind, but when I made the same recipe without the soaking I could detect no difference. The persistence of the method speaks to the conservative side of cooks who don't like to mess with a recipe with a proven track record.

RHUBARB MARMALADE

makes about 6 cups

The sharpness of the rhubarb in this recipe nicely complements the acidity of the citrus, while both are balanced by the sugar.

6 cups rhubarb, coarsely chopped
1 orange, halved, then sliced thinly
1 lemon, halved, then sliced thinly
3 cups sugar

Remove the seeds from the orange and lemon slices. Mix all ingredients and let stand overnight. Do not add any water; the rhubarb will release plenty of juice. Next day, bring the mixture to a boil in a medium saucepan and simmer until thick. It is important to stir frequently because the marmalade sticks and burns easily as it thickens. Pour into jars.

ORANGE and LEMON MARMALADE

makes about 7 cups

6 oranges, halved, then sliced thinly
2 lemons, halved, then sliced thinly
7 cups sugar
8 cups water

Remove the seeds from the orange and lemon slices. Place the slices and their juice in a medium saucepan with the water and let stand about 24 hours. Add the sugar, bring to a boil, and simmer for 1 to 2 hours or more until it is thick. Pour into jars.

JELLIES

Considerably more work and wastage is involved in making a jelly than a jam, so this was not the way to preserve large quantities of fruit. Traditionally, only a limited range of fruits and berries were used in jellies; particular favourites were squashberry, chokecherry, chuckley pear, high-bush cranberry, blackcurrant, crab apple, and damson. Some fruits are low in pectin and reluctant to set, which could be overcome by including some pectin-rich fruit, and crabapples were particularly prized for that purpose.

These recipes seem simple, but their results were good. Little measuring was done except that provided by cup, quart, and gallon vessels. Juice was strained through whatever fine-weave cloth was available, such as a piece of well-washed flour sack. Most of my sources advised squeezing the cloth to extract as much juice as possible, paying scant attention to getting the jelly absolutely clear.

Before domestic thermometers were available, determining the jelling point was usually done by dripping the hot mixture onto a cold plate to see if it jelled, or by holding a spoon dripping with the mixture over the pan to see if the last drips coalesced into a sheet.

The rule of thumb of ¾ cup sugar for every cup of fruit juice is generally applicable in all traditional jelly making.

DAMSON JELLY

makes 3 cups

8 cups damsons
3 cups water
about 2½ cups sugar

Bring the damsons and water to a boil and simmer in a large saucepan 30 minutes or until completely broken up, using a spoon to help. Strain the juice through a clean cloth, squeezing to obtain the last of the juice. For every cup of juice, add ¾ cup sugar. Bring to a boil and simmer until the jelly stage is reached. Pour into jars.

CRANBERRY JELLY

makes 5 cups

12 cups cranberries
6 cups water
4½ cups sugar

Bring the berries and water to a boil and simmer in a large saucepan 30 minutes, breaking up the berries with a spoon. Strain the juice through a clean cloth, squeezing to obtain as much juice as possible. Add the sugar to the juice and simmer another 30 minutes or more until the jelly stage is reached. Pour into jars.

SQUASHBERRY JELLY

makes 4 cups

One source called squashberries shirt-button berries because their large, flat seeds are about the size of small shirt buttons, although this name was not in general use. Those large seeds make the berries unsuitable for jam, but squashberry jelly is prized for its colour and flavour.

Once you have made this jelly you will appreciate why they are called squashberries—they are reluctant to break apart voluntarily and have to be squashed and mashed to release their contents.

- 8 cups squashberries
- 4 cups water
- 3 cups sugar

Simmer the berries in the water in a large saucepan for about 30 minutes. Mash the berries with a spoon to break them up. Strain through a coarse sieve or cloth while mashing or squeezing the berries. Discard the coarse pulp and seeds. Strain the juice through a clean, fine cloth, squeezing to obtain as much juice as possible. Bring the strained juice to a boil with the sugar and simmer until the jelly stage is reached. Pour into jars.

CHUCKLEY PEAR JELLY

makes 4 cups

Chuckley pears were more popular in Canada than in Newfoundland. For me, chuckley pears are inferior in taste and texture to other berries, so I tend to skip over them. Perhaps the lack of more flavourful alternatives elsewhere elevated the chuckley pear above its station in the berry hierarchy.

Although chuckley pear juice alone will set loosely, adding apples will make a stiffer jelly.

- 4 cups apples
- 4 cups chuckley pears
- 4 cups water
- 3 cups sugar

Peel the apples but leave in the cores and seeds. Chop coarsely and bring to a boil with the water and chuckley pears. Simmer about 30 minutes, mashing the fruit with a spoon. Strain the juice through a clean cloth, squeezing to obtain all the juice. Discard the pulp, add the sugar to the juice, and simmer until the jelly stage is reached. Pour into jars.

PICKLES

Pickle is simply a brine or strong salt solution used as a preservative. When vegetables were first preserved in brine, they were called pickles, but the name did not change when vinegar became the principal preservative.

Newfoundlanders made pickles from virtually every vegetable and many fruits, although there was a small range of perennial favourites, all with the common thread of vinegar and spices. Spices were usually a combination of cloves, cinnamon, allspice, mustard, ginger, and turmeric. Where available, pre-mixed pickling spices were used, which were proprietary mixtures of whole spices such as mustard seed, allspice berries, cinnamon stick, cloves, bay leaf, and so forth in various proportions.

These recipes illustrate the four principal approaches to making pickles: the ingredients could be cooked, then left to soak in vinegar and spices (for example, beets); all the ingredients, including vinegar and spices, could be stewed together (rhubarb, cabbage, partridgeberry); ingredients could be first salted, then stewed with vinegar and spices (chow-chow); or the ingredients were first salted, cooked briefly, then suspended in a flour-thickened sauce of vinegar, mustard, and other ingredients (mustard pickles).

"Simmer until reduced enough" was a frequent instruction from my sources, and I encountered pickles anywhere from loose and sloppy to thick and chunky. Before sterile bottling techniques appeared early in the 20th century, most pickles were heavily vinegared as a preservative.

PICKLED BEETS

makes 8 cups

8 cups sliced beets (about 6 pounds)
2 cups or more vinegar
4 pinches cloves

Trim the leaves and root from each beet but do not cut into the beet itself. Simmer for an hour or more, depending on size, until the beets are very tender. Remove from the pot. When cool enough to handle, trim off both ends, peel, and cut into ¼-inch slices. Place the slices into jars, pressing down lightly to pack them in. Sprinkle cloves into each jar, and pour in enough vinegar to just cover the beets.

RHUBARB PICKLES

makes 12 cups

1 ½ gallons coarsely chopped rhubarb (about 6 pounds)
8 cups chopped onion (about 2 pounds)
6 cups sugar
6 cups vinegar
1 teaspoon cinnamon
1 teaspoon cloves
1 teaspoon salt

Combine all ingredients and simmer until reduced by about one-third. Fill jars.

CABBAGE PICKLES

makes 8 cups

Most people made cabbage pickles with onion, using the flour-thickened sauce method. This is a much simpler version.

1 gallon finely shredded cabbage (about 2 medium heads)
2 cups sugar
2 cups vinegar
4 teaspoons salt
1 teaspoon cinnamon
1 teaspoon cloves

Mix all ingredients in a large saucepan or stockpot. Simmer gently until the liquid is reduced. Fill jars, dividing the liquid equally between them. Press the cabbage down into the liquid.

PARTRIDGEBERRY PICKLES

makes about 8 cups

9 cups partridgeberries
9 cups chopped onions
4½ cups sugar
1 ½ cups vinegar
1 ½ teaspoons salt
1 ½ teaspoons cinnamon

Mix all ingredients in a large saucepan or stockpot and bring to a boil. Simmer on a low heat for about 90 minutes until reduced by about one-quarter. Fill jars.

CHOW-CHOW

makes about 8 cups

Chow-chow, generally a pickle based on green tomatoes with other vegetables, appeared in America late in the 18th century. Commercial versions were advertised in the St. John's press from 1886 onwards, and it was very popular in Newfoundland from at least the beginning of the 20th century—four of the nine recipes in the pickle section of the 1905 cookbook are for chow-chow. The popularity of this pickle in Newfoundland was likely because it was a good way to use all those green tomatoes when the crop yet again failed to ripen.

1 gallon chopped green tomatoes (about 5 pounds)
8 cups chopped onion (about 2 pounds)
4 tablespoons salt
2 cups sugar
4 teaspoons mustard powder
1 teaspoon cloves
4 teaspoons ginger
2 cups vinegar

Mix the tomatoes, onions, and salt. Leave overnight. Next day, drain the liquid from the tomatoes and onions and add the rest of the ingredients. Bring to a boil and simmer on a low heat until the tomatoes are very soft and the liquid has been reduced to a minimum. Fill jars.

MUSTARD PICKLES

makes about 10 cups

10 cups coarsely chopped vegetables: equal amounts of cucumber, cabbage, cauliflower, onion
3 tablespoons salt
6 tablespoons flour
½ cup sugar
3 tablespoons mustard powder
1 tablespoon turmeric
1 cup water
2 cups vinegar

Mix the vegetables with the salt in a pot, and add water just to cover. Leave overnight, then drain. Bring about 3 quarts water to a boil and add the drained vegetables. Bring back to a boil and simmer 1 or 2 minutes to barely cook the vegetables. Drain and reserve the vegetables.

Combine the flour, sugar, mustard, and turmeric. Slowly add 1 cup water and the vinegar to the flour mixture to make a smooth batter, mashing any lumps as you go. Bring to a simmer and stir until thickened. Combine this sauce with the reserved vegetables and fill jars.

Mustard

My sources rarely specified which mustard they were talking about. The widely available mild ground mustard, sold simply as mustard or mustard powder, was most often used. Hot English mustard sold under the brand Colman's was available in Newfoundland from at least 1898. It is hotter and more pungent than the regular issue, to be used sparingly, particularly by the uninitiated. To substitute hot English mustard in any recipe calling for mustard, use about one-quarter the amount to start.

Vinegar

Vinegar was an essential ingredient in the traditional kitchen, whether homemade or store-bought. It was a necessary part of pickles and a general-purpose condiment, sprinkled on cooked salt fish or baked potatoes. Barrels of vinegar were imported from the early days of settlement, and from the late 19th century onwards there were plenty of advertisements for retail amounts of different vinegars, including red (presumably red-wine vinegar), white-wine, malt, and simple white vinegar.

Homemade vinegar was widely used around the island. Although none of my sources was still making vinegar, most had done so between the wars. The engine behind homemade vinegar is the vinegar plant, also called a mother of vinegar or simply vinegar-mother. This is not a leafy plant but a complex mixture of microorganisms which form a gelatinous mass. The mother was taken from the previous batch of vinegar or begged from a neighbour who had one growing. This was then fed a sugary mixture and left to ferment. The sugary mixture was often a solution of molasses, but any sweet liquid would work, such as blueberry juice with added sugar.

If no pre-existing vinegar plant is available, you have to make your own. Mix 2 cups molasses with 8 cups water and divide between about five clean containers (each about 3- or 4-cup capacity). Cover these with clean cloth but do not seal with a lid. Leave for about a month. If any go mouldy, discard them (if all go mouldy, start again). With luck, at least one of the containers will start to grow the characteristic jelly-like layers of the vinegar plant. Use pieces of that to start larger batches of vinegar.

MOLASSES VINEGAR

makes about 8 cups

8 cups water
2 cups molasses
1 piece of vinegar plant

Dissolve the molasses in the water and place in a clean crock. Do not seal with a lid but cover with a clean cloth. Add the vinegar plant and leave for a month at room temperature. After a month, taste the liquid. For a stronger vinegar taste, leave for another month or more. When ready, according to taste, strain through a clean cloth into clean containers, and use bits of the plant to start another batch.

Vinegar keeps well, so accumulate it through the year to have enough on hand for making pickles in the fall.

BULK PRESERVATION: SHREDDED SALTED CABBAGE (SAUERKRAUT) AND BRINED CABBAGE

Cabbage in a root cellar was prone to rot, so two other methods of bulk preservation involving salt were used. Shredded salted cabbage, sometimes called sauerkraut, used just enough salt to discourage unwanted microorganisms and foster those that manufactured the acidic environment that preserved the cabbage. Brined or pickled cabbage was not such a finely balanced business. It relied on the brute force of the strongest possible salt solution (pickle) to kill any and all microorganisms.

SALTED SHREDDED CABBAGE (SAUERKRAUT)

makes 4 gallons

6 medium cabbages
1 ½ cups coarse salt

Trim the cabbages and cut off any damaged leaves. Cut into quarters lengthways, remove cores, and sliver finely. Place a thick layer of shredded cabbage into a crock and sprinkle a small spoonful of salt over it. Continue adding layers of cabbage and salt, pressing each layer down firmly, and make sure you have enough salt left at the end for a good sprinkle on top. Place a plate on top of the cabbage and use a clean beach rock on the plate as weight. Press down firmly. After about two days the salt will have drawn water out of the cabbage. If the salty water does not cover the cabbage, dissolve about 2 tablespoons coarse salt in 4 cups water and gradually add to the crock until the cabbage is covered. Keep the plate and weight on top to keep the air out. If it goes mouldy or starts to smell foul, discard the batch.

Rinse the cabbage well and drain before eating, and eat either hot or cold as a side dish.

BRINED (PICKLED) CABBAGE

makes about 4 gallons

Salt cabbage should not spoil if you make sure the original pickle is saturated (no more salt will dissolve—it's as strong as it can be) and that the cabbage is kept submerged. I was frequently told to use the floating-potato method as an indicator of brine saturation. It is at best imprecise. Potatoes will float in any solution of salt down to about 50 per cent saturated, at which point some still float and others do not. Better to start with a solution that is definitely saturated, as in the method explained below. Although the solution will be diluted by water drawn out of the cabbage, it will remain strong enough to preserve it.

2 gallons water
8 cups coarse fishery salt
8 medium cabbage
 (about 16 pounds trimmed)

First, make the pickle. Bring the water to a boil and add salt. Remove from the heat and let cool, stirring occasionally. Don't worry if the salt won't all dissolve; that means it's saturated. Cut coarse or damaged leaves from the cabbage and trim the stalk close to the bases of the leaves. Cut each trimmed head lengthways into quarters (bigger cabbage into six or eight sections, and smaller ones just in half). Pack cabbage tightly into a 5-gallon crock, leaving 1 to 2 inches of space at the top. Pour in enough cool pickle just to cover the cabbage. Put a weight on top to hold the cabbage under the pickle (a clean piece of board with a beach rock on top is good). Every other day for a week, push down on the board so that the cabbage slides down. After about two weeks the cabbage will be ready, and will keep almost indefinitely. Before eating, soak as many pieces of cabbage as you need in several changes of fresh water for 24 hours or more.

Over: Five women outside a canning shed in St. Anthony, 1932. The woman second from the left holds a hand-cranked device that clamped to a table-top and crimped and sealed the lids on the cans. Two on the right are holding another can-lid sealer. *The Rooms Provincial Archives Division, VA 92-305.*

Chapter 21

Canning and Bottling

Canning and bottling are potentially confusing terms, particularly in North America, where canning means putting things in glass jars even though cans are metal. In this chapter, "canning" refers to preserving food in metal containers and "bottling" is preserving in glass jars.

Industrial canning arrived in Newfoundland in the 1870s, brought in to preserve lobster for a wider market in the days before modern transportation made the distribution of live lobsters a possibility. Canneries were established around the island, proving a boon to the local economy. Some were of significant size, like the one in St. Barbe that employed 40 people and processed 5,000 lobsters per day in 1890.

But most canneries were small-scale commercial productions. Two of my sources described this type of cottage industry from between the wars. Lobsters were boiled in fresh water in a 40- to 50-gallon boiler. The meat was extracted from the tails and two large claws of cooked lobsters; meat from the small legs would only be used if the lobster was large enough. An entire family could form an assembly line to take out the meat and pack it into cans. A 1-pound can typically held two tails, four claws, and some bits and pieces, but the tomalley (liver) and coral (egg sacs) from the bodies were not put in the cans. One-pound cans, 24 to the case, were most often used, but sometimes half-pound cans at 48 to the case were used.

The lids and sealing machine were key to the process. A lid was placed on the open end of each filled can and stamped with an identifying number. The lid rims were lined with a thin rubber gasket which ensured a tight seal when the sealing machine rolled and crimped the lid over the upright edge of the can. Meanwhile, the boiler had been emptied and filled with clean water. Filled cans were packed in the boiler, and the cans boiled for 2½ to 3 hours. The cans were lifted out, placed in rows on a wooden rack, and, while they were still hot, two men finished the process: the first man punctured each lid with a quick tap of a little hammer with a short, sharp spike on it. Each can spurted a little steam and spray as the pressure released. The second man soldered this hole shut. The merchant would eventually arrive and buy the cans, and a label was applied elsewhere.

DOMESTIC CANNING

The small-scale commercial canning process was a basic technology easily adapted to home production and provided a welcome alternative to preservation by salting. Domestically, fruit and vegetables were not canned, but many different fish were, including eel, capelin, mackerel, and tuna. Meat, such as rabbit, seal, and beef, was also canned.

Home canning and bottling of non-acidic foods such as fish or meat is potentially deadly. Do not attempt this unless you have both the knowledge and specialized equipment to do so safely. These recipes describe how canning was done in the early 20th century—not the preferred methods of today.

CANNED EEL

makes six 1-pound cans

6 eels, skinned and cleaned

Cut the eels into approximately 2-inch logs, a length that will stack vertically in the can. Fill each can with vertical lengths of eel. Typically, six to eight pieces will fill a can. Seal and process in a boiling water bath for 3 hours. Store in a cool, dry place.

CANNED SALMON
makes six 1-pound cans

1 whole salmon (about 12 pounds, enough to yield 12 cups cubed salmon)
6 teaspoons salt
water

Fillet the salmon. Remove all small bones and skin. Cut the trimmed salmon meat into approximately 1-inch chunks. Fill each can loosely with salmon chunks and 1 teaspoon salt per can sprinkled between the layers of salmon. Add water to just cover the salmon. Seal and process in a boiling water bath for 3 hours. Store in a cool, dry place.

CANNED BEEF
makes six 1-pound cans

6 pounds beef, off the bone
6 teaspoons salt
water

Trim the beef by removing all large lumps of fat and all the gristle. Cut the meat into 1- to 2-inch chunks. Fill each can with the beef chunks and 1 teaspoon salt per can sprinkled between layers. Add water to each can to just cover the beef. Seal and process in a boiling water bath for 3 hours. Store in a cool, dry place.

BOTTLING IN GLASS JARS

Glass preserving jars, of the Mason jar style, arrived in Newfoundland in the 1880s and were very popular by the early part of the 20th century. Vegetables were never bottled; the sheer volume necessary for a family made a root cellar the only viable option. Berries, unless made directly into jam or kept fresh in barrels (see Chapter 20), were often bottled, as were damsons and plums, and the general method below can be widely applied.

Fish and meat were also bottled, most frequently eel, capelin, cod liver, cod tongues, salmon, mussels, mackerel, chicken, turr, seal, rabbit, and beef. Just as for canning, the method was uniform except for minor variations in the preparatory stages.

BOTTLED PLUMS

makes six 1-quart jars

24 cups fresh plums
3 cups sugar

Cut the plums in half and remove the pits. Cut the halves into two or four pieces, depending on size. Pack the jars with plum pieces, pressing down firmly because they will shrink during the processing, and sprinkle ½ cup sugar into each. Seal jars and boil in a large pot of water for about 1 hour.

BOTTLED MUSSELS

makes six 1-quart jars

9 or 10 gallons fresh mussels in the shell

Clean the mussels by removing the beards and weeds clinging to the shells. Put about half an inch of water in the bottom of a large pot and fill the pot about one-third full with cleaned mussels. Cook until the mussels are all fully open, in as many batches as required. Discard any that do not open. Pour off the cooking liquid and reserve. Remove the cooked mussels from their shells and pack into the jars, leaving at least 1 inch of space at the top. Divide the reserved cooking liquid between the jars; if necessary top with fresh water to just cover the mussels. Seal jars and boil in a large pot of water for 3 hours. Store in a cool place.

BOTTLED CHICKEN

makes about six 1-quart jars

Most chicken was eaten fresh, but occasionally supply exceeded demand. The meat from old, tough laying hens was sometimes bottled in the hope that the long processing would tenderize it. Any domestic or wild bird (turrs being a favourite) of any size can be bottled; just adjust the number of jars used.

9 small chickens
(about 2 pounds each, whole trimmed weight)
6 teaspoons salt
water

Cut off the chicken heads, feet, and outer two joints of the wings. Peel off the skin, taking all the feathers with it. Remove the guts and clean the cavity. Cut the legs off close to the body and cut each leg into two pieces (thigh and drumstick). Cut off the wings. Cut out the backbone. Cut down each side of the breastbone and cut each breast from the ribs. Cut each breast into at least two portions. Pack each jar with portions of chicken, sprinkling in 1 teaspoon salt per jar, filling to about 1 inch from the top. Pour water into each jar to come just to the top of the chicken. Shake and tap the jars to remove air bubbles. Seal jars and boil in a water bath for at least 3 hours.

BOTTLED RABBIT

makes about six 1-quart jars

12 rabbits
12 slices of fatback,
  each about 1 by 6 inches
6 small onions
6 teaspoons salt
water

Remove the rabbit heads, feet, and entrails. Peel off the skin. Cut each animal into six portions: front legs, back legs, and the meaty loin behind the ribs split in two along the backbone (keep the rest of the backbone, the rib cage and the head for soup). In each jar place the parts of about 2 rabbits, 2 slices of fatback, 1 onion peeled and cut in quarters, and 1 teaspoon salt. Each jar should be loosely filled to no more than about 1 inch below the top. Fill each jar with water to barely cover the meat. Seal the jars and boil in a water bath for at least 3 hours.

Over: A man selling fish on the St. John's waterfront, 1939. *The Rooms Provincial Archives Division, VA 14-58.*

Chapter 22

Sauces

DRAWN BUTTERS

Drawn butter in Britain has an obsolete meaning of plain melted butter, but in the US the term has persisted to mean both plain melted butter and butter melted and clarified. I don't know which country contributed the name to Newfoundland's drawn butters, which are flour-thickened water and melted butter sauces. Newfoundland drawn butter is derived from similar British sauces, but there they were not called drawn butter in the 19th century. In 1861 Charles Francatelli described a sauce to pour over salt fish and parsnips which is essentially Newfoundland drawn butter, but gives it no particular name. Mrs. Beeton has three recipes for melted butter, all of which resemble Newfoundland's drawn butter, and an Egg Sauce for Salt Fish which is essentially the same as the Newfoundland drawn butter with egg.

In Newfoundland, drawn butters were served most often with fish, and less commonly spooned over cooked vegetables. The four basic recipes—plain, with fried onion, with boiled onion, or with hard-boiled egg—have significant differences in taste. In general, the plainer the fish (or vegetable) being dressed, the more complex the sauce chosen to go with it. For example, plain boiled salt fish with no scrunchions benefits from the fried onion or egg version, whereas fish pan-fried in rendered pork fat and served smoking hot needs at most the plain version.

DRAWN BUTTER plain
serves 4 to 8

½ cup butter
1 tablespoon flour
½ cup water
¼ teaspoon salt or to taste
¼ teaspoon pepper or to taste

Melt the butter in a small saucepan on a medium heat. Stir in the flour to make a smooth paste. Add the water, salt, and pepper and stir while bringing it back to a boil. Simmer about 5 minutes. Taste and adjust seasonings.

DRAWN BUTTER with fried onions
serves 6 to 8

This was one of the more popular versions of drawn butter, used with salt fish, fresh fish, salmon, or on the potatoes or brewis served with the fish.

½ cup butter
2 onions, chopped
2 tablespoons flour
salt and pepper
1 ½ cups water

Melt the butter in a small saucepan on a medium heat. Fry the onions gently in the butter for about 10 minutes or until they are lightly golden and soft. Sprinkle on the flour and mix thoroughly. Stir in some salt and pepper and about half the water, and stir while bringing back to a boil. Simmer and continue stirring until the sauce is shiny and smooth. Slowly add the remaining water until a desired consistency has been reached. Simmer on a low heat for 5 to 10 minutes. Taste and adjust seasonings.

DRAWN BUTTER with boiled onions
serves 6 to 8

2 onions, chopped
2 cups water
¼ cup butter
1 tablespoon flour
salt and pepper

Place the onions in a small saucepan with the water and bring to a boil. Simmer until the onions are soft and the water has been reduced to about 1 cup. In a separate small saucepan melt the butter and stir in the flour. When the onions are cooked, stir them and their water into the flour and butter and bring back to a boil. Simmer until thickened. Add salt and pepper to taste.

DRAWN BUTTER with hard-boiled eggs

serves 6 to 8

Egg sauce could mean either chopped eggs in drawn butter or chopped eggs in a white sauce. They were both used for similar purposes and were considered interchangeable, even though they have distinctively different tastes and textures.

½ cup butter
1 tablespoon flour
½ cup water
½ teaspoon salt
¼ teaspoon pepper
2 hard-boiled eggs

Melt the butter in a small saucepan and stir in the flour until smooth. Add the water, salt, and pepper, and stir until smooth again. Bring back to a boil and simmer 5 minutes. Coarsely chop the hard-boiled eggs, stir them into the sauce, and simmer 5 minutes. Taste and adjust seasonings.

SAUCES FOR SAVOURY DISHES

APPLESAUCE

serves 4 to 6

Applesauce was made almost exclusively for a meal of roast fresh pork. Those with an apple tree likely had apples in the cellar, and a few were made into sauce when pigs were killed in December.

4 cups peeled apples,
  chopped into ½-inch chunks
  (about 4 apples)
½ cup water
½ cup sugar
2 pinches cinnamon
1 pinch cloves

Simmer apples with ½ cup water and ½ cup sugar until soft. If the apples have not fallen apart after about 10 minutes, mash with a spoon or potato masher. Add spices to taste and additional sugar if desired.

If the apples were not sharp enough, 1 or 2 teaspoons vinegar was often added, and 2 tablespoons butter was sometimes stirred in at the end of the cooking.

BREAD SAUCE

serves 6 to 8

Stiffening liquids with bread was a common technique in the Middle Ages which has largely died out, surviving only in things like bread sauce. This recipe is of British origin, where crumbled bread is combined with flavoured stock or milk to make a thin paste, then finished with seasonings and butter.

Do not use completely dry bread crumbs or the resulting texture will be too sticky. As you add the crumbs, aim for a critical consistency: neither thick enough to keep a spoon upright, nor thin enough to flow off a spoon. It is better to have the sauce a little thick to start as it is easily thinned at the finishing stage.

This is a traditional sauce with roast pheasant in Britain, and as my source mentioned, she liked it with roast partridge. Even if you don't have a brace of partridge to cook, this is good with any kind of poultry, so try it with a simple roast chicken.

1 small onion, peeled
4 whole cloves
2 cups milk
2 cups bread crumbs
¼ teaspoon grated nutmeg
¼ teaspoon black pepper
½ teaspoon salt
2 tablespoons butter

Stick the whole cloves into the peeled onion. Put into a small saucepan with the milk and bring to a simmer. Remove from the heat, cover, and set aside. After about 30 minutes, remove the onion and cloves. If the onion falls apart, scoop it all out with a slotted spoon along with the cloves. Squeeze the onion gently to remove the milk. Discard the onion and cloves and put the milk back on a low heat. Gradually stir in the bread crumbs, salt, and spices. Do not add all the crumbs at once—add them in portions, mixing constantly, adding more as needed. When it is heated through and thickened, stir in the butter. Serve warm.

CHEESE SAUCE

serves 6 to 8

Cheese sauce was used as the basis of macaroni cheese (page 170), and sometimes on potatoes, carrots, and other vegetables.

3 tablespoons butter
4 tablespoons flour
½ teaspoon hot English mustard
½ teaspoon salt
¼ teaspoon pepper
1 ½ cups milk
1 cup grated cheese

Melt the butter in a small saucepan on a medium heat. Stir in the flour and mustard to make a smooth paste. Add the salt, pepper, and milk, and bring to a simmer while stirring constantly. Simmer about 10 minutes. Add the grated cheese and stir until completely melted.

MINT SAUCE

serves 4–6

Mint sauce was only made to go with lamb and was never particularly popular in Newfoundland, despite wild mint being widespread and locally abundant. Mint was used fresh in season but was also dried for year-round use—then a special trip to Mint Brook (Mint Brooks abound in Newfoundland) was not necessary whenever a little mint was needed. A British-style mint sauce, a liquid mixture of mint and vinegar tempered with a little sugar, was more popular than a thickened sauce. The habit of making mint jelly is a later addition to the Newfoundland kitchen.

To make this with fresh mint—a far superior taste—use about 4 tablespoons chopped fresh mint.

2 tablespoons crumbled dry mint
3 tablespoons vinegar
1 tablespoon sugar
1 tablespoon water

Mix all ingredients together and let stand for about ½ hour. Stir well before using.

MUSTARD SAUCE

serves 8

Mustard sauce was made almost exclusively for dabbing on ham, pork, or beef. This recipe is made with regular mild ground mustard. The same sauce can be made with hot English mustard powder, in which case far less should be used, about 1 tablespoon for a pungent sauce; only 1 or 2 teaspoons if you are unfamiliar with this style of mustard.

2 tablespoons butter
2 tablespoons flour
½ cup milk
2 teaspoons sugar
3 tablespoons mustard
(1 tablespoon or less hot English mustard)
2 tablespoons vinegar
¼ teaspoon salt
pepper

Melt the butter in a small saucepan on a medium heat. Stir in flour to make a smooth paste. Add the milk and bring to a boil, stirring continuously while it thickens. Stir in the mustard and salt and simmer for about 10 minutes. Thin with more milk if desired. Sprinkle with pepper.

MUSTARD PASTE

serves 8

Personally, and for many of my sources, a simple mustard paste was preferable to mustard sauce. Spread sparingly on meat—very sparingly if using hot English mustard. Wealthier households often had special little mustard pots, complete with a miniature spoon.

3 tablespoons mustard
(1 tablespoon or less hot English mustard)
1 tablespoon milk (or water)

Combine ingredients into a paste.

PLAIN WHITE SAUCE

serves 8

White sauce (later known as béchamel) was milk thickened with a mixture of butter and flour and seasoned simply with salt and pepper. As a plain sauce, its use was restricted to dressing cooked vegetables. It was either poured over the boiled onions or parsnips often served with salt fish, for example, or mixed with cooked, chopped vegetables such as carrot or cabbage, which some families called creamed vegetables. Adding other ingredients turned this into cheese, mustard, or egg sauce to be used for other purposes.

3 tablespoons butter
3 tablespoons flour
1 ½ cups milk
¾ teaspoon salt
¼ teaspoon pepper

Melt the butter in a small saucepan on a medium heat. Stir in the flour to make a smooth paste. Add the milk, salt, and pepper, and bring to a simmer, stirring constantly until thickened. Simmer for about 10 minutes. Taste and add more salt if desired.

EGG SAUCE

serves 8

Egg sauce made with a milk-based white sauce was very popular on boiled salmon, and some families reserved it exclusively for that. It was also served with salt fish, or salt turbot, and sometimes on fresh, poached codfish. Rarely, it was used to dress cooked potatoes or other vegetables.

3 tablespoons butter
2 tablespoons flour
1 cup milk
2 hard-boiled eggs
¾ teaspoon salt
¼ teaspoon pepper

Melt the butter in a small saucepan on a medium heat. Stir in the flour to make a smooth paste. Add the milk, salt, and pepper, and bring back to a simmer, stirring constantly until thickened. Simmer about 10 minutes. Chop the hard-boiled eggs finely and stir into the simmering sauce. Simmer another 5 minutes. Taste and add more salt if desired.

SAUCES FOR SWEET DISHES

CHOCOLATE SAUCE

serves 4 to 6

Chocolate sauces were made with cocoa or chocolate according to availability and preference. This general-purpose chocolate sauce uses solid chocolate. It can be thinned with milk.

4 tablespoons butter
2 tablespoons flour
1 cup milk
½ cup grated chocolate
½ cup sugar

Melt the butter on low heat and stir in the flour. Add the milk and stir on a low heat until thick. Add the salt, sugar, and chocolate and stir until the chocolate has melted and the sauce is smooth.

CUSTARD SAUCE

serves 4 to 6

Custard as an egg-thickened pouring sauce appeared in the mid-19th century and was a traditional part of Newfoundland food. When custard powder (a cornstarch-thickened, yellow mixture) arrived in Newfoundland around 1890 it was widely adopted, and the old skill of making real custard thickened with egg yolks became a rarity. But it survived, and I have a vivid memory of one of my sources demonstrating—on a wood-fired cookstove no less—the art of finding the exact place on the stovetop where custard would slowly thicken without curdling prematurely. Most of today's top chefs wouldn't have a hope.

2 eggs
½ cup sugar
1 cup milk

Beat the sugar and eggs together. Beat in the milk. Warm gently over a low heat, stirring constantly, until the custard thickens. Do not overheat or it will curdle.

HARD SAUCE

serves 8

Hard sauce was a solid, cold confection, cut into pieces to serve. Each portion of warm dessert was crowned with a piece of hard sauce, which then melted and was scooped up with each spoonful. This was the traditional sauce for steamed puddings, Christmas pudding in particular (page 190), and was also served with hot mince pies. It is of British origin, and Elisabeth Ayrton, the British food historian and cookery writer, mentions recipes for this back to the early 18th century.

½ cup butter, room temperature
½ cup sugar
1 tablespoon dark rum

Beat the butter, sugar, and rum together. Press it into a small bowl and place in a cool place where the butter will harden. To serve, cut portions from the dish and place each on top of a serving of warm pudding.

JAM SAUCE

serves 4 to 6

Hot jam sauce was a reliable standby. Even when supplies were getting low, there was almost always enough flour and a handful of raisins to make a steamed pudding, and any jam could be heated and poured over it. If plenty of jam was available, it was simply warmed up, maybe with a little water, but if the jam shelf was getting empty, it was best to stretch what was available.

1 cup jam
½ cup water
1 tablespoon flour

Mix the flour with 1 tablespoon of the water, mashing it carefully together to avoid any lumps. Heat the jam with the rest of the water. Stir in the flour mixture and bring to a boil. Simmer the mixture for 2 or 3 minutes and then remove from the heat.

Serve warm over any pudding.

LEMON SAUCE

serves 4 to 6

Lemon sauce was a general-purpose sauce used to liven up plain steamed puddings.

¾ cup sugar
2 tablespoons flour
1 cup water
1 lemon

Mix the flour and sugar thoroughly in a small saucepan. Add the water in large drops, mixing well to avoid any lumps. Mash any small lumps with a spoon. Bring to a boil and then simmer 3 or 4 minutes. Grate the lemon rind into the sauce. Cut the lemon in half, squeeze out the juice, discard the pits, and add it to the sauce. Serve warm over plain pudding or plain duff.

MOLASSES COADY

serves 4 to 6

Molasses coady was also known as lassy coady, lasses coady, or simply molasses sauce. At its simplest this was plain molasses warmed until it would pour easily over a dessert such as a steamed pudding. Usually it was embellished a little, with a spoonful of butter and a pinch of nutmeg or cinnamon, according to what was on hand.

1 cup molasses
2 tablespoons butter
¼ teaspoon cinnamon

Warm the molasses to nearly boiling point. Stir in the butter and cinnamon. Pour over portions of steamed pudding or another dessert of your choice.

MOLASSES SAUCE

serves 4 to 6

Molasses-rum sauces appeared in many forms. If the rum was omitted or was only a minor element, then it was simply called molasses sauce, but if the rum was emphasized, then it was rum sauce. These sauces were poured over any sweet pudding, particularly those enriched with raisins, currants, or other dried fruit.

2 tablespoons butter
3 tablespoons flour
½ cup sugar
¼ cup molasses
¼ teaspoon salt
1 cup water
1 tablespoon dark rum (optional)

Melt the butter, stir in the flour, and mix well. Stir in the sugar, molasses, and salt, then stir in the water and bring to a simmer until it thickens slightly. Add rum to taste.

RUM SAUCE

serves 4 to 6

Rum sauce is simply a molasses-rum sauce heavy on the rum. Some people reserved these alcohol-rich sauces for celebratory food like Christmas pudding, but other households poured it on any kind of sweet pudding.

2 tablespoons butter
2 tablespoons flour
½ cup water
1 cup sugar
1 tablespoon molasses
¼ cup rum

Melt the butter. Stir in the flour, then add the water, and bring to a boil to thicken it. Add the sugar and molasses, mix well, and simmer briefly. Add rum to taste.

SOFT SAUCE

serves 8

Soft sauce was a popular variation on hard sauce, using milk or cream instead of liquor, and usually served warm and semi-liquid. It was often flavoured with vanilla, but many versions omit it. Like hard sauce, it was served on steamed puddings and duffs but was considered less celebratory. It was also called butter sauce and sweet white sauce.

½ cup butter, at room temperature
½ cup sugar
3 tablespoons milk
1 teaspoon vanilla

Place the milk, sugar, and vanilla in a small saucepan and warm over a low heat. When the sugar has dissolved, beat in the butter to make a smooth sauce. If the butter will not combine properly, continue warming and beating until it does. Serve warm or at room temperature.

SUGAR SAUCE

serves 4 to 6

Sugar sauce came in a variety of forms. At its simplest it was sugar dissolved in warm water, but it was usually thickened with flour or cornstarch and flavoured with vanilla. Sometimes butter was stirred in at the last minute. If brown sugar was used, it was called brown sugar sauce.

1 cup sugar
2 tablespoons cornstarch
1 ½ cups water
2 teaspoons vanilla
3 tablespoons butter

Combine the sugar and cornstarch together thoroughly. Stir in the water and bring to a boil. Simmer briefly. Take off the heat and stir in the vanilla and butter.

Over: An order from Mr. Grippe of HC (Heart's Content?) in 1885 for 5 pounds of tea, at about 2 shillings per pound, with instructions to despatch the goods on the schooner *Two Brothers. The Rooms Provincial Archives Division, MG 956.29.*

MG 956.29
HC 30/9/85
Please send by Schr "Two Brothers" 5 lbs of tea at about 2/-
Chas Grippe
NEWFOUNDLAND
POST CARD
THE ADDRESS ONLY TO BE WRITTEN ON THIS SIDE
ONE CENT
TO
Mr Peters
Ayre and Sons
St Johns

Chapter 23

Drinks

■ BEER

Early in the 18th century, spruce beer was the first commercial brew in Newfoundland. The first brewery that used malt was established in 1802 near Mundy Pond, St. John's, and several more were built in St. John's through the 19th century. At the same time, beer was imported from Europe, particularly Britain, as illustrated by the range advertised in St. John's in the 19th century (see Appendix 3).

Not everyone could afford the local or imported product, so there was a long tradition of home brewing. Domestically, molasses beer (often simply called beer, or regular beer) and spruce beer were the favourites, with nettle or dandelion-leaf beer also being made. No doubt Prohibition in Newfoundland from 1917 to 1924 encouraged home production.

Molasses beer was a natural fit for Newfoundland. Molasses and yeast, the two primary ingredients, were widely available and relatively cheap. Even before the arrival of commercial yeast in the 1880s, yeast-laden froth could be had from a neighbour brewing beer, or barm for bread-making was used. Beer was frequently flavoured with hops, either bought dry from the store or picked fresh from the hops that were found around most communities. Sometimes beer was flavoured with apples or other ingredients.

MOLASSES BEER

makes about 2 gallons

2 gallons water
6 cups molasses
2 tablespoons yeast

Stir the water and molasses together in a large 4- or 5-gallon container, until it is all dissolved. Stir in the yeast, cover the container with a clean cloth, and put it somewhere warm. Let the yeast work for a week or more, then decant into a clean crock through a piece of clean flour sack.

The beer can be stored in the crock or poured into bottles. Hops can be added to the fermenting beer.

SPRUCE BEER

makes about 2 gallons

Spruce beer was brewed by the earliest European settlers in North America. In 1796, for example, Amelia Simmons, author of the first American cookbook, published a recipe calling for "eight ounces of essence of spruce." The fact that such an essence was a regular item of commerce indicates that spruce beer was widely brewed.

The ways of making spruce beer were legion, but always used black spruce, never white. Black spruce often has a bush of small branches at the top, which is why many sources suggest only using the tops of the spruce. However, others used the young green cones of the black spruce. The amounts of molasses and sugar varied, as did the time left to brew.

the top 18 inches or more
of a young black spruce
2 gallons water
2 cups sugar
1 cup molasses
2 tablespoons yeast

Cut the smaller branches off the trunk at the top of the spruce. Boil these in the water for about 1 hour. Strain off the water and discard the spruce branches. Add the molasses and sugar to the water and stir well to dissolve. Cool to room temperature. Stir in the yeast. Cover with a clean cloth and leave in a warm place for about a week. Strain through a fine, clean cloth into a clean container.

CALLIBOGUS
serves 2 to 4

Callibogus is a word of mysterious origin and multiple spellings—see the *Dictionary of Newfoundland English*. It was a mixture of spruce beer, dark rum, and molasses, but variations abounded. The drink probably originated in colonial America, and reached Newfoundland by the 18th century. It is seldom seen anymore. I have experimented with callibogus, and it's not something I would go out of my way to find or make. While it has curiosity value, it was likely only a device to make rather weak spruce beer slightly more alcoholic and a more attractive drink for many.

The taste is marginally better if the molasses is the "fancy" grade, but probably more authentic if made with dark, blackstrap molasses.

4 cups spruce beer
½ cup dark rum
¼ cup molasses

Mix well. Can be consumed immediately.

DANDELION-LEAF BEER
makes about 2 gallons

Dandelion-leaf beer was a popular brew, made from either the water left from boiling the leaves to eat as a green vegetable or from leaves boiled up just to make beer. Other abundant wild greens, such as nettles, could be made into beer in a similar fashion.

1 gallon dandelion leaves
2 gallons water
4 cups sugar
2 tablespoons yeast

Bring the water and dandelion leaves to a boil. Simmer about 10 minutes and then strain. Add the sugar to the water, stir until dissolved, and let cool to room temperature. Stir in the yeast. Leave to ferment for at least 2 days or up to a week.

WINE

Newfoundland imported large quantities of wine in the 19th century (see Appendix 3). Wealthier merchants and the rising middle class must have bought most of it, because it would have been out of reach for the average Newfoundlander. Most wine was made at home, not from grapes but from other fruit, a few vegetables, and a lesser number of flowers. Wine was made primarily from wild fruit, particularly blueberries, partridgeberries, and bakeapples. No doubt wines made from them were popular because of the sheer abundance of those berries, but also because they are among the better tasting of homemade wines. Raspberry wine and squashberry wine, held by many to be the best of the wild-fruit wines, were made less frequently because those berries were less abundant. Dogberry, crowberry, wild sarsaparilla berry, and dandelion flower wine were less common. From cultivated fruit and vegetables, wine was made from damsons, blackcurrants, redcurrants (particularly popular), beets, parsnips, rhubarb, and others.

Although recipes for wine differed greatly in detail, there were only two fundamentally different methods. The first was to let wild yeasts found on the fruit skins ferment the wine. The fruit was not boiled (which would kill the yeasts) but was either crushed or left whole and mixed with water and sugar, then left to allow the wild yeasts do their work. Some fruit, such as blueberries, are particularly well suited to wild-yeast fermentation because the bloom on the skin is loaded with yeasts. Wild yeasts can be unpredictable, however, and could result in an unpalatable mess, so many people preferred to boil the fruit in water first, which killed the wild yeasts and also released the juices from the fruit. The juices were then strained off and fermented by adding sugar and yeast. Some used a hybrid approach and boiled the fruit but then added fresh berries or even dried fruit such as raisins to re-introduce wild yeast. Before the 1880s, the source of yeast for the second method was lees from someone else's brewing, or barm which was on hand for bread-making. After the 1880s yeast could be purchased at the community store.

Using these basic techniques, wine can be made from virtually any fruit or vegetable. These recipes outline traditional ways of making wine before easy access to specialized equipment such as airlocks and hydrometers. The use of flour sacks for straining was common because their fine weave, necessary to contain the flour, made ideal general-purpose straining cloths.

BLUEBERRY WINE using natural yeasts

makes 2 gallons

1 gallon blueberries
2 gallons water
6 cups sugar

In a 4-gallon glazed earthenware crock, dissolve the sugar in the water. The water may be heated to speed up the dissolving process, but it must then cool to room temperature before proceeding. Stir the blueberries into the sugar solution, cover with a clean cloth, and leave at room temperature to ferment for about 3 weeks, or until it has completely stopped bubbling. Do not put the wine in a cool or drafty place. Strain through a double layer of flour sacking into bottles or other small containers.

PARTRIDGEBERRY WINE made by adding your own yeast

makes 2 gallons

As molasses was cheaper than sugar, it was used whenever possible. However, molasses makes any wine dark and gives it a pronounced flavour, so many people preferred to substitute the same amount of sugar. Crowberry and raspberry wines were made in the same fashion.

1 gallon partridgeberries
2 gallons water
6 cups molasses
4 tablespoons yeast

Bring the partridgeberries and water to a boil and simmer for about 10 minutes or until the berries are falling apart. Strain through a clean cloth into a 4-gallon crock, squeezing the cloth to get the maximum amount of juice. Discard the solids in the cloth. Add the molasses and mix thoroughly. Add the yeast, cover the crock with a clean cloth, and leave to ferment for 2 to 3 weeks or until it has completely stopped bubbling. Do not put the crock in a cold or drafty place. Strain through a clean cloth into bottles or other small containers.

PARSNIP WINE

makes 1 gallon

1 gallon parsnips
1 gallon water
8 cups sugar
¼ cup yeast

Wash and trim the parsnips but there is no need to peel them. Chop them small, and bring to a boil in the water. Simmer about 30 minutes. Strain off the liquid through a fine, cotton cloth, squeezing to get the last drop. Dissolve the sugar in the liquid. When cool, add the yeast, and cover with a clean cloth. Leave to ferment for 3 to 4 weeks or until it has completely stopped bubbling. Carefully pour the wine into bottles or other small containers, leaving the sediment behind.

DANDELION FLOWER WINE

makes 1 gallon

½ gallon dandelion flowers
1 gallon water
6 cups sugar
2 tablespoons yeast

Remove all dandelion stems. Measure the flowers by packing them lightly so they spring back a little under the pressure of your hand. Boil in the water for about 30 minutes. Strain off the liquid through a cloth into a crock. Add the sugar and stir until dissolved. When cool, add the yeast. Cover the crock with a cloth and leave it to ferment for several weeks until it has completely stopped bubbling. Pour the wine into clean bottles or other small containers and keep in a cool place.

SPIRITS

Newfoundland imported large quantities of spirits in the 19th century (see Appendix 3). But alongside the legal spirits came those from two additional sources: smuggling (spirits made elsewhere but landed illegally) and domestically and illegally distilled spirits, usually called moonshine, an American term adopted in Newfoundland somewhere in the 19th century.

Moonshine was any beer or wine, low in alcohol, distilled to make a strongly alcoholic drink. The percentage of alcohol varied but was usually more than today's commercial standard 40 per cent. In 1920 a woman on Prince of Wales Street, St. John's, was convicted of making a 55.7 per cent alcohol moonshine.

In much of the English-speaking world domestic distilling has long been illegal, not so much to protect the health of the people but to preserve the tax revenue for the government. But no government restriction has ever stopped an underground culture of distillation, and in that tradition, making moonshine was widely practiced in Newfoundland. Everyone I have spoken to on this topic has known someone who made moonshine, or has confided that they used to be something of an expert but had of course given it up long ago. Moonshine was (and still is) widely available in both rural and more urban parts of the island.

Home-distilling was a science, and great care was taken to get the heating and cooling processes exactly right. Everyone was aware of the dangers of getting it wrong, and the possibilities of illness, blindness, and death were the stuff of legend. The technique for distillation was adjusted to allow for differences between beer and wine. Those who made a specialty of distilling usually brewed batches of "beer" from molasses or potatoes especially for the purpose, just to make a uniformly alcoholic mixture to use in a standardized procedure.

Quite apart from being illegal, and the real dangers if not properly made, moonshine is a harshly unpleasant drink unless matured properly and carefully diluted to temper the high alcohol content. If you are offered a bottle, my advice is to politely decline on these grounds, unless you are certain of the provenance.

TEA

The English started drinking tea in the second half of the 17th century, and the Irish followed suit in the middle of the 18th. At first a drink only for the wealthy, the removal of tariffs toward the end of the latter century helped spread tea-drinking across all social classes, from the poorest manual labourer to the wealthiest merchant. No matter their station in life, 19th-century English and Irish immigrants brought a firmly entrenched tea-drinking habit. In the first half of that century, those settlers mostly purchased congou and bohea, two Chinese black teas, although the more expensive Souchong, a large-leaf congou from South China, was also for sale. Green teas, those dried straight from the bush without fermentation, were also available. Before about 1890, when Indian tea appeared in Newfoundland, all tea in Newfoundland was Chinese, and tea from Sri Lanka (then Ceylon) was advertised in Newfoundland from around 1897.

In the second half of the 19th century in Newfoundland, there was a general shift to brand-named tea such as Jubilee, Golden Cross, and Golden Tip, and the names congou and bohea slowly fell out of general use. Any commonly available black tea (unless qualified by a brand) was simply called tea. Two grades of tea were usually available, common and best, with the former around 3s 6p per pound, and best tea slightly more expensive at 4s per pound. Relative value shows teas were expensive in the 19th century. In the 1880s, for example, the price of 2 or 3 pounds of tea would buy a new pair of top-of-the-line leather boots. Nevertheless, merchant's account ledgers were full of sales of tea, as they were for tobacco; plainly the populace was addicted to both.

In general, when Newfoundlanders talk of tea, they mean black tea, be it a mug at breakfast or a boil-up in the woods. Some brewed it very strong, often called barking-kettle tea by those who preferred a milder brew. Teapots of varying sizes were widely employed and there was general agreement on how a good pot of black tea should be brewed. The following is how one source told me in no uncertain terms how she brewed a good pot of tea.

A POT OF PROPERLY BREWED TEA

serves 6 to 8

- 8 teaspoons tea, each heaped if you like strong tea, otherwise about level
- boiling water

Never put the tea leaves into a cold teapot; it must be heated first. Bring the water to a boil, and pour about ½ pint into an 8-cup teapot. Swirl it around for about 1 minute to heat the pot. Pour out this water. Spoon the tea leaves into the pre-heated pot. Bring the water back to a full rolling boil. Bring the teapot to the kettle (not the other way around) and pour the boiling water directly onto the tea leaves. Stir for a few seconds, put the lid on the pot, and put a tea cozy on the pot (or wrap one or two kitchen towels around it). Let it steep for about 5 minutes. Pour into mugs or cups, and let each person add sugar and milk according to taste. If making tea in the woods or on a small boat where there is no teapot, spoon your tea leaves directly into the kettle just as you take it off the fire, then cover the kettle and let it steep.

These instructions are as valid today as they were in the 1920s—using less-than-boiling water results in an insipid and inferior brew. Sugar was available from the earliest days of European settlement, but fresh milk was not so easily obtained. If you were brewing tea at home, you were lucky if you had milk from your own cow. If you were away from home on the boat, you might take a bottle of milk with you, but it was the arrival of tinned milk late in the 19th century that ensured a reliable supply.

COFFEE

Coffee reached the British Isles around the same time as tea but did not spread so evenly across the social classes. In general, coffee became a drink of the middle classes, the merchants, and the professionals, who brought coffee drinking to Newfoundland. Both roasted coffee beans and green (unroasted) beans were available, but home roasting green beans is a tricky business, so ready-roasted were far more in evidence, and both coffee mills and coffee pots were frequently advertised. It was not until 1883 that ready-ground coffee was advertised in Newfoundland, and instant coffee appeared in Newfoundland in 1919, after its invention and marketing in the US in circa 1900–1910.

The proliferation of coffee-making gadgets started in the late 18th century, but except for the occasional mention of a percolator (invented in the 1890s), I have only heard about the basic coffee pot in Newfoundland. The following is based on an old description but still applies exactly today.

A POT OF COFFEE
serves 4 to 6

a 4-cup coffee pot
6 to 8 level tablespoons ground coffee, depending on how strong you like it
boiling water

Put the ground coffee in the pot. Pour the boiling water onto this slowly, while stirring. Put on the lid and let steep for no more than 5 minutes. Stir again, give the grounds a few seconds to settle, and then carefully pour out into cups, leaving behind as much of the grounds as possible.

The traditional coffee pot tapered from a wide base to a narrower top, a shape that helped trap the grounds in the angle of the base while pouring.

DRINKING CHOCOLATE AND COCOA

Chocolate was an early import, but it was not until the 1880s that something clearly identifiable as a drink, "Pure Soluble Cocoa," was advertised. Making cocoa was straightforward: just add boiling water to 1 or 2 tablespoons of soluble cocoa in a mug and sweeten to taste. Drinking chocolate was a little fussier because of the risk of making the chocolate seize if it was improperly handled.

DRINKING CHOCOLATE made from solid chocolate
serves 4 to 6

about 2 cups grated chocolate
4 cups milk

Mix the grated chocolate with about ½ cup milk. Warm gently, stirring until the chocolate has all melted and the mixture is smooth. Add the rest of the milk and heat until hot and nearly boiling. Divide between cups and add sugar to taste.

Bibliography

Anaïs, Seantel. "(Mal) Nutrition and the 'Informal Economy' Bootstrap: The Politics of Poverty, Food Relief, and Self-Help." *Newfoundland and Labrador Studies* 24, no. 2 (2009): 239–260.

Andrews, George. Merchant's Ledgers. Port de Grave. 1866–1883. MG871. The Rooms Provincial Archives, St. John's, NL.

Ayre, Agnes. Manuscript Recipe Collection. 1917. Private collection of Agnes Murphy, Fredericton, NB.

Ayrton, Elisabeth. *The Cookery of England*. Middlesex, UK: Penguin Books, 1977.

Beeton, Isabella. *Mrs. Beeton's Book of Household Management*. 1861. London, UK: Chancellor Press, 1982.

Carter, George. Merchant's Ledgers. Herring Neck. 1887–1898. MG477, Box 1. The Rooms Provincial Archives, St. John's, NL.

The Columbus Ladies Association. *The C.L.A. Cook Book. Compiled and Contributed by the Members of The Columbus Ladies Association.* St. John's, NL, 1926.

The Daily News. St. John's, NL. 1894–1940.

Dale, Linda. "A Woman's Touch: Domestic Arrangements in the Rural Newfoundland Home." *Material History Bulletin* 15 (1982): 19–26.

Davidson, Alan. *North Atlantic Seafood*. Middlesex, UK: Penguin Books, 1980.

Davidson, Alan. *The Oxford Companion to Food*. Oxford, UK: Oxford University Press, 1999.

Driver, Elizabeth. *Culinary Landmarks: A Bibliography of Canadian Cookbooks, 1825–1949*. Toronto, ON: University of Toronto Press, 2008.

Ellis, Eleanor, ed. *Northern Cookbook.* Ottawa, ON: Indian Affairs and Northern Development, 1967.

The Evening Telegram. St. John's, NL. 1879–1926.

Farmer, Fanny. *The Boston Cooking-School Cook Book.* 1896. Facsimile of the first edition. New York, NY: Plume Books, 1974.

Francatelli, Charles. *A Plain Cookery Book for the Working Classes*. 1861. Facsimile of the first edition. Whitstable, UK: Pryor Publications, 1993.

George, Niki. "An Investigation of Jigg's Dinner." *Culture and Tradition* 21 (1999): 80–89.

Glasse, Hannah. *The Art of Cookery Made Plain and Easy*. 1747. Facsimile of the first edition. Totnes, Devon, UK: Prospect Books, 1995.

Grigson, Jane. *Fish Cookery*. Middlesex, UK: Penguin Books, 1975.

Grigson, Jane. *English Food*. Middlesex, UK: Penguin Books, 1977.

Grigson, Jane. *The Observer Guide to British Cookery*. London, UK: Michael Joseph, 1984.

Guy, Jeannie. "Newfoundland Cooking." *Newfoundland Quarterly* 102, no. 2 (2009): 10–11, 31.

Halstead, Byron. *Barn Plans and Outbuildings*. 1889. Reprint. Ottawa, ON: Algrove Publishing Ltd., 1999.

Hartley, Dorothy. *Food in England*. London, UK: MacDonald, 1954.

Jesperson, Ivan, ed. *Fat-Back & Molasses. A Collection of Favourite Old Recipes from Newfoundland and Labrador*. St. John's, NL: Jesperson Press, 1980.

The Ladies' Aid Society of St. Andrew's Presbyterian Church. *The P.L.A. Cook Book Arranged from Tried and Proven Recipes.* St. John's, NL: Manning and Rabbitts, Printers, 1925 (a retitled edition of Presbyterian Ladies' Aid, 1924).

The Ladies' Aid Society of St. Andrew's Presbyterian Church. *The P.L.A. Cook Book (Second edition) Arranged from Tried and Proven Recipes.* St. John's, NL: Manning and Rabbitts, Printers, 1928.

The Ladies' Aid Society of St. Andrew's Presbyterian Church. *The P.L.A. Cook Book (Third edition) Arranged from Tried and Proven Recipes.* St. John's, NL: The Evening Telegram, 1939.

The Ladies' College Aid Society of the Methodist Church. *The L.C.A.S. Cookbook. Arranged from Tried and Proven Recipes.* Robinson and Currie, 1905.

The Ladies' College Aid Society of the United Church. *The L.C.A.S. Cookbook. Arranged from Tried and Proven Recipes.* Dicks and Co. Limited, 1930.

Ladies of Toronto and Chief Cities and Towns in Canada. *The Canadian Home Cook Book. Compiled by Ladies of Toronto and Chief Cities and Towns in Canada.* 1877. Facsimile edition. Toronto, ON: Coles Publishing Company, 1971.

Lillico, Mary. Manuscript Recipe Collection, ca. 1925–1930. Private collection of the author, St. John's, NL.

MacDonald, Janet. *Feeding Nelson's Navy. The True Story of Food at Sea in the Georgian Era.* 2004. Yorkshire, UK: Frontline Books, 2014.

Mariani, John. *Encyclopedia of American Food and Drink*. New York, NY: Lebhar-Fredman, 1997.

Memorial University of Newfoundland. *Recipes of Newfoundland Dishes.* St. John's, NL: Memorial University of Newfoundland, 1971.

Moore, Sarah. "Fish and Brewis: A Historical and Contextual Analysis." *Culture and Tradition* 28 (2006): 15–29.

Morris and Ryan. Merchant's Ledgers, St. John's. 1815–1826. MG472, Box 1. The Rooms Provincial Archives, St. John's, NL.

New England Grocer Office. *The Grocer's Companion and Merchant's Handbook*. 1883. Facsimile edition. Whitefish, MT: Kessinger Legacy Reprints, 2010.

Neve, Ray. *Hops*. London, UK: Chapman and Hall, 1991.

O'Dea, Shane. "The Development of Cooking and Heating Technology in the Newfoundland House." *Material History Bulletin* 15 (1982): 11–18.

Overton, James. "Brown Flour and Beriberi: The Politics of Dietary and Health Reform in Newfoundland in the First Half of the Twentieth Century." *Newfoundland Studies* 14, no. 1 (1998): 1–27.

Presbyterian Ladies' Aid. *Tested Recipes by Presbyterian Ladies' Aid. St. John's, Newfoundland*, 1924 (retitled and reissued as *The P.L.A. Cookbook, Arranged from Tried and Proven Recipes, by the Ladies' Aid Society of St. Andrews Presbyterian Church*, 1925).

Ryan, Glen. *Native Trees and Shrubs of Newfoundland and Labrador*. Parks Division. Department of Culture, Recreation and Youth. Government of Newfoundland and Labrador, St. John's, NL, 1978.

Scott, Peter. *Edible Plants of Newfoundland and Labrador*. Portugal Cove-St. Philips, NL: Boulder Publications, 2010.

Sexty, Suzanne. "The Brehms. Newfoundland's First Family of Margarine." *Newfoundland Quarterly* 101, no. 2 (2008): 30–49.

Sheridan, Monica. *The Art of Irish Cooking*. 1965. New York, NY: Hippocrene Books, 1996.

Shortis, Henry. Shortis Papers. Unpublished manuscript, ca. 1920. Typewritten copy held at Centre for Newfoundland Studies, Memorial University Libraries, St. John's NL.

Simmons, Amelia. *American Cookery*. 1796. Reprint. Facsimile edition. New York, NY: Dover Publications, 1984.

Smallwood, Joseph and Robert Pitt, eds. *The Encyclopedia of Newfoundland*. 5 vols. St. John's, NL: Newfoundland Book Publishers and Harry Cuff Publications, 1981–1994.

Smith, Andrew, ed. *The Oxford Encyclopedia of Food and Drink in America*. 2nd ed. 3 vols. Oxford, UK: Oxford University Press, 2013.

Story, George, William Kirwin, and John Widdowson, eds. *Dictionary of Newfoundland English*. 2nd ed. Toronto: University of Toronto Press, 1982.

Tavenor, Joshua. "Early Newfoundland and the Atlantic World: Imports to Newfoundland in the Late Seventeenth and Early Eighteenth Centuries." Master's thesis, Memorial University of Newfoundland, 2010.

The Toronto Branch of the Grenfell Mission. *The Grenfell Mission Cook Book*. Kansas City, MO: North American Press, ca. 1950.

Tulloch, Judith. *Goods and Services Advertised in St. John's Newspapers, 1830–1840*. Research Bulletin no. 220. Ottawa, ON: Parks Canada, 1984.

The Twillingate Sun and Northern Weekly Advertiser. 1884–1908.

APPENDIX 1

Formal Names of Animals and Plants with Common Names, Alternate Names, and Notes

Common names for living things are notoriously confusing: the partridge in Newfoundland is a ptarmigan elsewhere, and our bakeapple is their cloudberry. A list of internationally recognized, formal (Latin) names of species mentioned in the text may be useful to those unaccustomed to local names. I have omitted the Latin names of most of the familiar domesticated vegetables such as potatoes and carrots, only including those such as turnips where it might add clarity.

MAMMALS

Arctic Rabbit = Arctic Hare *Lepus arcticus.*
Beaver *Castor canadensis.*
Black Bear *Ursus americanus hamiltoni.*
Caribou = Woodland Caribou *Rangifer tarandus.*
Harp Seal *Pagophilus groenlandicus.*
Harbour Seal = Bay Seal *Phoca vitulina.*
Moose *Alces alces.*

Muskrat *Ondatra zibethicus.*
Rabbit = Snowshoe Rabbit = Snowshoe Hare *Lepus americanus.*

BIRDS

Alcids = birds of family Alcidae; in Newfoundland mainly Dovekie, Murre, and Puffin, but there are others.
American Black Duck *Anas rubripes.*
Arctic Ptarmigan = Rock Ptarmigan *Lagopus mutus.*
Bull-bird = Dovekie q.v.
Canada Goose *Branta canadensis.*
Common Eider Duck *Somateria mollissima.*
Dovekie = Bull-bird *Alle alle.*
Greater Black-backed Gull *Larus marinus.*
Herring Gull *Larus argentatus.*
Kittiwake = Black-legged Kittiwake *Rissa tridactyla.*
Loon = Great Northern Diver *Gavia immer.*
Mallard Duck *Anas platyrhynchos.*
Murre = both the Common Murre *Uria aalge*, and the Thick-Billed Murre *Uria lomvia.*
Partridge = Ptarmigan q.v.
Pintail Duck *Anas acuta.*
Ptarmigan = Willow Ptarmigan *Lagopus lagopus.* Locally called Partridge.
Puffin = Atlantic Puffin *Fratercula arctica.*
Red-breasted Merganser = Shell-bird *Mergus serrator.*
Ring-necked Duck *Aythya collaris.*
Saddle-back Gull = Greater Black-backed Gull q.v.
Shell-bird = Red-breasted Merganser q.v.
Turr = both species of Murre q.v.

FISH

Brim = Redfish q.v.
Capelin *Mallotus villosus.*

Codfish *Gadus morhua.*
Eel *Anguilla rostrata.*
Eel Pout *Macrozoarces americanus.*
Flounder, Black-back = Common Flounder = Winter Flounder *Pseudopleuronectes americanus.*
Flounder, Yellow Tail = Yellow Tail Dab = Rusty Flounder *Pleuronectes ferruginea.*
Grenadier *Macrourus berglax.*
Halibut *Hippoglossus hippoglossus.*
Herring *Clupea harengus.*
Lumpfish *Cyclopterus lumpus.*
Mackerel *Scomber scombrus.*
Redfish = Ocean Perch *Sebastes marinus.* Locally called Brim or Bream (which it isn't).
Salmon, Atlantic *Salmo salar.*
Scad *Trachurus trachurus* or *Selar crumenophthalmus.* Both called Horse Mackerel.
Sculpin usually applied indiscriminately to both the Shorthorn Sculpin *Myoxoceph alus scorpius* and the Longhorn Sculpin *Myoxocephalus octodecemspinosus.*
Trout Included under this general heading are the Brook Trout = Speckled Trout = Mud Trout *Salvelinus fontinalis,* and the Arctic Char *Salvelinus alpinus,* both native to the island. It can also include the European Brown Trout *Salmo trutta* and the Rainbow Trout *Onchoryncus mykiss,* both introduced to the Avalon Peninsula of the island in the 1880s.
Tuna, Blue-fin *Thunnus thynnus.* Locally called Horse Mackerel (not to be confused with scad).
Turbot = Greenland Halibut = Greenland Turbot *Reinhardtius hippoglossoides.* Simply called turbot in Newfoundland, not to be confused with the European Turbot.
Turbot, European *Scophthalmus maximus.*
Winter Flounder = Flounder, Black-back q.v.
Wolf Fish *Anarhichas lupus.*

INVERTEBRATES

Clam, Soft Shell *Mya arenaria.*
Coucou = Coo-Coo = Whelk q.v.
Crab, Snow = Long Legged Crab *Chionoecetes opilio.*
Cuttlefish *Sepia officinalis.*

Lobster, Western Atlantic *Homarus americanus.*

Mussel = Common Mussel = Blue Mussel *Mytilus edulis*. There is at least one other species which may occur with *M. edulis*, but since it is indistinguishable except by experts, for the cook they are all the same.

Oyster, American = Western Atlantic Oyster *Crassostrea virginica.*

Oyster, European = Eastern Atlantic Oyster *Ostrea edulis*.

Partridgeberry Fruitworm *Grapholita libertina.*

Periwinkle = Wrinkle *Littorina littorea*. There are at least two other similar species which may be found together with *L. littorea* which are distinguishable by experts if not by cooks; they are all wrinkles in the pot.

Shrimp mostly *Pandalus borealis.*

Snow Crab = Crab q.v.

Soft Shell Clam. = Clam q.v.

Squid *Illex illecebrosus.*

Whelk *Buccinum undatum.*

Wrinkle = Periwinkle q.v.

PLANTS

Bakeapple = Cloudberry *Rubus chamaemorus.*

Bean, White or Navy = Haricot Bean *Phaseolus vulgaris.*

Bean, Calavance = Cavalance. The identity of this bean is not clear. The *Dictionary of Newfoundland English* says it is *Dolichos barbadensis* or *D. sinensis*, the latter now considered a synonym of *Vigna unguiculata*, which includes the cow-pea and black-eye pea. However, other sources say it is simply any small bean or the Hyacinth Bean, *Lablab purpurea* (previously *Dolichos lablab*). Solvong this taxonomic labyrinth is beyond the scope of the present work.

Bean, Lima = *Phaseolus lunatus.*

Bilberries *Vaccinium* spp. Around four species in Newfoundland, and all can be mistaken for blueberries, but are less common. In the kitchen treat as blueberries.

Blackberry = Canadian Blackberry *Rubus canadensis*. The most common of a taxonomically confused group, which may include up to seven species in Newfoundland. All look like a black raspberry and can be treated the same in the kitchen.

Blackberry = Crowberry q.v. Do not confuse this black berry (so called because it is jet-black) with the above species.

Blueberry = Lowbush Blueberry *Vaccinium angustifolium*. This is *the* blueberry of Newfoundland, found all over the island in great abundance. There are two very similar but much less frequent species, and they and their relatives the bilberries (q.v.) can all be treated the same in the kitchen.

Cabbage (regular smooth-leaved) *Brassica oleracea* var. *capitata*.

Cabbage, Savoy (with crinkled leaves) *Brassica oleracea* var. *bullata*.

Calavance = Bean, Calavance q.v.

Caraway *Carum carvi*.

Chick Weed *Stellaria* spp., most frequently *S. media*.

Choke Cherry *Prunus virginiana*.

Chuckley pear = Serviceberry = Saskatoon Berry = Wild Pear = Indian Pear *Amelanchier* spp. There may be five (or more) closely related species in Newfoundland; the taxonomy is confused but the cook should not be. Treat them all the same.

Crackerberry = Bunchberry *Cornus canadensis*.

Cranberry = Large Cranberry *Vaccinium macrocarpon*.

Cranberry, high-bush (not a true cranberry) = Jointwood Berry *Viburnum opulus* var. *americanum*.

Crowberry = Blackberry q.v. = Heath Berry = Curlew Berry *Empetrum nigrum*. There are also two other related species which are far less common.

Currants, Wild. Three closely related species, Black Bristly Currant *Ribes lacustre*, Skunk Currant *Ribes glandulosum*, and Northern Red Currant = Wild Red Currant = Swamp Red Currant *Ribes triste*.

Dandelion *Taraxacum officinale*.

Dock = Curled Dock *Rumex crispus*.

Dogberry *Sorbus americana* or *S. decora*. Two almost-identical species, separable by experts; can be treated the same.

Elderberry = Red Elderberry *Sambucus pubens*.

Gooseberry, Northern = Wild Gooseberry *Ribes oxyacanthoides*.

Haricot Bean = Bean, White q.v.

Hop, European *Humulus lupulus* var. *lupulus*. An introduced species.

Hop, Native American *Humulus lupulus* var. *lupuloides*.

Huckleberry. Two related species, the Black Huckleberry *Gaylussacia baccata*, and the Dwarf Huckleberry *Gaylussacia dumosa*. Can be treated the same in the kitchen, although the former is better tasting than the latter.

Hyacinth Bean = Bean, Calavance q.v.

Jointwood Berry = Cranberry, Highbush q.v.

Marshberry = Small Cranberry *Vaccinium oxycoccus*. Also often called a Cranberry, but this is a different species from the usual Cranberry q.v.

Mint = Wild Mint *Mentha arvensis*, or Heart Mint *M. cardiaca*. Identical for culinary purposes.

Mushroom, White Field (an honourary plant) *Agaricus* spp., usually *A. campestris.*

Navy Bean = Bean, Navy q.v.

Partridgeberry = Mountain Cranberry = Red Berry = Lingonberry *Vaccinium vitis-idaea.*

Pin Cherry *Prunus pensylvanica.*

Plumboy = Hairy Plumboy = Dewberry = Ground Raspberry *Rubus pubescens.*

Raspberry *Rubus idaeus.*

Sarsaparilla = Wild Sarsaparilla = False Sarsaparilla *Aralia nudicaulis.*

Snowberry = Creeping Snowberry = Maidenhair Berry *Gaultheria hispidula*. Also called Wintergreen after the taste of its white berries.

Soapberry *Shepherdia canadensis.*

Spruce, Black *Picea mariana.*

Spruce, White *Picea glauca.*

Squashberry *Viburnum edule.*

Strawberry = Wild strawberry *Fragaria virginiana* or *Fragaria vesca*. These two closely related species can be treated the same.

Turnip (in Newfoundland) = Swedish Turnip = Swedes (in Europe) = Rutabaga (in the US) *Brassica napobrassica* or *Brassica napus rapifer*, depending on the authority consulted. This is the ubiquitous turnip of Newfoundland. Do not confuse this with the Eurasian turnip *Brassica rapa.*

Witherod = Northern Wild Raisin *Viburnum nudum* var. *cassinoides.*

APPENDIX 2
Measures: Volume, Weight, Currency, Oven Temperature, and Barrels

■ VOLUME

Newfoundland used a mixture of measures taken from both the American and the British systems. But in general differences between the two can be ignored because no great precision is needed when using old recipes, and the following US measures can be safely used.

1 teaspoon = ⅓ tablespoon = ⅙ fluid ounce (about 5 millilitres)
1 tablespoon = 3 teaspoons = ½ fluid ounce (about 15 millilitres)
1 cup = 8 fluid ounces = 16 tablespoons (about 250 millilitres)
1 pint = 2 cups = 16 fluid ounces (about 500 millilitres)
1 quart = 2 pints = 4 cups = 32 fluid ounces (about 1 litre)
1 gallon = 4 quarts = 128 fluid ounces (about 4 litres)

■ WEIGHT

Until the 1970s the unit of weight in Newfoundland was the pound, subdivided into

16 ounces, with multiples of the stone, quarter, hundredweight, and ton. The quintal, in Newfoundland understood to be 112 pounds, was the same as a hundredweight.

Hundredweights, quintals, quarters, and pounds were used in the weighing of fish, particularly salt fish.

1 ounce (oz) = 1⁄16 pound (about 28 grams)
1 pound (lb) = 16 ounces (about 450 grams)
1 stone = 14 pounds (about 6.3 kilograms)
1 quarter (Qtr) = 2 stone = 28 pounds (about 12.6 kilograms)
1 hundredweight (Cwt) = 1 quintal = 112 pounds (about 50.5 kilograms)
1 ton = 20 hundredweight (1,008 kilograms)

CURRENCY

Until 1865 Newfoundland used the British currency of pounds, shillings, and pence, abbreviated £.s.d. There were 20 shillings to the pound, and 12 pence to the shilling. In addition were half-pence, farthings (quarter pence), and guineas (21 shillings). In 1865 the first decimal currency of Newfoundland dollars and cents was put in circulation, but the use of the British £.s.d. system persisted late into the 19th century.

Since dry salt fish was measured in Cwt, Qtr, and lb, and valued in shillings per quintal, the mental agility involved in calculating the value of a given weight of dry salt fish was amazing, even if pencil and paper were involved. You want to sell 25 Cwt, 3 Qtr, 17 lb of salt fish to the merchant, and the value of this grade of fish is 17s 6d per quintal. How much will you get? Sounds like a nightmare high school arithmetic test.

OVEN TEMPERATURE

Most of my sources talked about slow, medium, or hot ovens, a survival from the days before dials when oven temperature was estimated by feel, or sometimes by the time taken for a scrap of paper to darken. The following are the approximate equivalents used in this book.

Slow oven = 300°F (about 150°C)
Medium oven = 350°F (about 180°C)
Hot oven = 400°F (about 205°C)

BARREL SIZES

Barrel sizes are notoriously confusing because the volume varied from commodity to commodity, from place to place, and from time to time. The British system was rationalized when the Imperial Standard was introduced in 1824, but at that point the American system diverged, retaining many of the old measures from colonial times but also setting some new standards of its own.

The following barrel sizes were widely accepted in Newfoundland in the period after the middle of the 19th century that concerns us here. But many of the old standards such as the British wine barrel of 32 imperial gallons persisted, and there will be many differences of opinion about this. Note that because Newfoundland was part of Britain's Empire when the Imperial measures were standardized, the barrel sizes below are in British imperial gallons, where 1 gallon = 160 imperial fluid ounces = 4.55 litres.

1 firkin = 9 gallons (¼ barrel; 41 litres)
1 barrel = 36 gallons (164 litres)
1 Tierce = 42 gallons (191 litres)
1 hogshead = 54 imperial gallons (1.5 barrels; 246 litres)
1 puncheon = 100 gallons (about 3 barrels; 490 litres)

The puncheon was one of the largest wooden barrels and had a particularly confusing range of nominal sizes, from about 40 to 140 gallons.

APPENDIX 3
Food in the Stores

Although not an exhaustive list, these are the principal foods advertised in the St. John's press up to the end of 1918.

VEGETABLES

Beets, new beets. Cabbage, large white cabbage, green cabbage, Nova Scotia cabbage. Carrots, white carrots. Celery. Fresh corn. Cucumbers. Lettuce. Onions, Bermuda onions, Oporto onions, Norfolk onions, silverpeel onions, red onions. Parsnips. Potatoes, P.E.I. potatoes, new potatoes, choice Newfoundland potatoes, dry potatoes, potatoes (Prolifics), Nova Scotia Blue potatoes. Sweet potatoes. Turnips, Swedish turnips, best Newfoundland turnips. Tomatoes (fresh) for table use, fresh tomatoes for pickling.

FRESH FRUIT

Apples, crab apples, choice American and Nova Scotian apples, Gravenstein, Kings, Baldwin, Canada apples, table apples, no.1 choice cooking apples, no.1 apples, choice winter keeping apples, red apples, Siberian Crabs for preserving, King of Tompkins, Ribston Pippins, Bishop Pippins, northern spy, russet, 5-points, Vandeniers. Bananas.

Coconuts. Cranberries. Damsons. Grapes, Spanish grapes, large green grapes, Muscatel grapes. Lemons. Oranges, choice oranges, sweet oranges, large sweet oranges, Florida oranges, Oporto oranges, Seville oranges. Partridgeberries. Peaches. Pears, Bartlett pears, Medford pears, Bell pears, sugar pears. Pineapples. Plums, choice preserving plums, large egg plums, greengages, apricot plums, sugar plums. Rhubarb. Strawberries. Watermelons.

DRIED FRUIT AND NUTS

Almonds. Dried apples, evaporated apples. Dried apricots. Broadfigs. Currants, Palermo currants. Dates. Dried figs (real figs), dough figs (real figs). Nuts, hazel nuts, assorted nuts, walnuts. Peel, lemon peel, orange peel, citron peel. Prunes. Raisins, seedless raisins, Valencia raisins, Denia raisins, loose muscatel raisins, London raisins, Layer's raisins, Dehesa's raisins, sultana raisins. Sultanas.

TINNED GOODS

Anchovy paste, Gorgona anchovies. Asparagus. String beans. Boiled beef, corned beef, roast beef. Bloater paste. Brawn. Smoked capelin. Boned chicken. Cod tongues. Sugar corn. Findon (sic) haddock. Fruit. Ham, lunch ham. Herring, smoked Loch Fyne herring. Lamb tongue. Lard, leaf lard. Lobsters. Condensed milk. Meat, potted meat. Mushrooms. Mussels. Oysters. Ox tongue. Peaches. Peas. Pears, Bartlett pears. Pineapples. Rabbit. Salmon. Sardines, Albert sardines. Sausages, Oxford sausage, Frankfurter's sausages. Soup, ox tail soup, chicken soup, tomato soup. Tomatoes. Tripe.

PRESERVES, JAMS, JELLIES, AND CONDIMENTS

Mango chutney. Honey. Assorted jams, large tumblers of jam, apricot jam, blackcurrant jam, cranberry jam, damson jam, greengage jam, gooseberry jam, plum jam, raspberry jam, strawberry jam. Jellies, peach, pineapple, quince and strawberry jellies, Keiller and Son's jams and jellies, Hartley's jams and jellies. Marmalade, Scotch marmalade, homemade marmalade. Sweet pickles, pickles, chow-chow. Pan Yan pickles, Lazamby's pickles and sauces, Batty's pickles and sauces. Preserves, assorted preserves. Tomato sauce, tomato catsup, Beefeater sauce, Lee and Perrins sauce, Yorkshire relish, Mushroom ketchup.

DRY GRAINS, DRY BEANS, PASTA, DRY PEAS, RICE, SAGO, AND TAPIOCA

Barley, pearl barley. Beans, Lima beans, haricot beans, white beans, navy beans, calavances. Macaroni, Naples macaroni, Marvelli macaroni, macaroni and vermicelli in boxes and tins, spaghetti. Peas, yellow split peas, split green peas, dry green peas, dry marrowfat peas, green peas, blue peas. Rice, Japan rice, Rangoon rice. Sago, pearl sago. Tapioca.

BISCUITS, BREAD, CAKES, AND CONFECTIONARY

Biscuits (not bread), fresh baked biscuits, soda biscuits, Jacob's cream crackers, Royal afternoon tea biscuits, Kiel, finger, Marie, ginger, wafer. Bread (hard bread), Harvey's no.1 and 2 hardbread, Browning's No. 1 hardbread, biscuit, pilot biscuit. Soft bread. Christmas cakes in season, cakes, cakes and tarts. Assorted confectionary, assorted candy, beefsteak candy, lamp-wick (striped) candy, peppermint (red and white striped), caramels, Neilson's chocolates, chocolate.

BUTTER, CHEESE, EGGS, AND MARGARINE

Butter, choice Canada butter, Nova Scotia butter, creamery butter, splendid butter, American Butter, choice Townships Butter, selected Eastern Townships, good Kamouraska butter, table butter, dairy butter, choice dairy butter, butter carefully selected, Cork butter, Cork pickled butter. Cheese, good cheese, choice cheese, very good cheese, prime Canadian cheese, new Canadian cheese, English cheese, English Cheddar cheese, Cheshire cheese, Gloucester cheese, Wiltshire cheese, Wiltshire loaf cheese, Stilton Cheese, Gorgonzola cheese, Dutch cheese. Eggs, P.E.I. corn-fed eggs, egg powders. Oleomargarine, cooking butter, butterine, Cottolene.

FLOUR, CEREALS, SUGAR, AND MOLASSES

Arrowroot. Cornmeal, Indian meal, yellow corn meal. Cornflour, cornstarch. Buckwheat flour. Graham flour. Rye flour. White flour, Surprise, Gold Seal, Five Roses, Pillsbury's Best, Our Own Country, Jennie, Acme, Pansy, S. D., Gold Leaf, Queen of Roses, M., Diamond, Three Roses, White Blossom, Sweet Briar Sunlight, White Star, Columbia, Rangoon flour, Atlantic Mills, Volunteer, Sensation, Royal Standard, Stock's Patent, Northwestern, Galaxy, Devon, Sunbeam, Our Country, Imperial, Gold Seal, Ogilvie's, Centennial, Pride of the State, Major Mills, Ethel Mills, Magnolia, Strathroy Mills, White Star, White Eagle, Ambrosial Pastry flour, Centennial, Pride of the State, Eden's best, Superfine flour, New York no.2 superfine and extra, superior extra flour, good family flour, very choice flour. Cream of wheat. Rolled wheat. Rolled oats, oatmeal, Scotch oatmeal. Hominy. Molasses, best Barbados molasses, choice molasses, bright heavy molasses. Sugar, loaves of sugar, crystal sugar, cane sugar, pure white sugar, granulated sugar, cube sugar, brown sugar, light brown sugar, bright brown sugar, icing sugar.

BAKING POWDER, ESSENCES, SPICES, CONDIMENTS, VINEGAR, AND YEAST

Baking powder, Royal, Emerald, Boston, Dunn's, Borwick's, Freeman's. French capers. Desiccated coconut. Stafford's Essences, lemon, vanilla, almonds, peppermint, ginger wine. Hops. French olives. Table salt. Bread soda. Spices, allspice, caraway seed, cinnamon, whole cloves, ground cloves, curry powders, ground ginger, mustard, English mustard, ground nutmeg, whole nutmegs, pepper, black pepper ground, white pepper ground, turmeric, mixed pickling spices, savory, thyme, cream of tartar. Vinegar, table vinegar, raspberry vinegar, white-wine vinegar, red vinegar, white vinegar, malt vinegar. Fruit wines and syrups, lime juice, lime juice cordial, Rose's lime juice, hop cordial. Yeast cakes.

TEA, COFFEE, COCOA, AND DRINKING CHOCOLATE

Our best tea, Crown, Royal, Moning, Singha Tea, Congou, Bohea, Indian, scented caper, dooars, cachar, sylhst, darjling, gunpowder, orange pekoe, Parnell's Tea, Tetley tea, Bulldog Tea, Red Rose Tea, pure Ceylon, Lipton's Ceylon teas. Coffee, coffee beans, ground coffee, finest Ceylon planation coffee, green coffee, superior ground coffee, very choice ground coffee, best procurable coffee, Camp and Elder's coffee. Chocolate, cocoa, cocoa essence, Epp's cocoa, Fry's cocoa, instantaneous chocolate.

FISH AND SHELLFISH, FRESH, SMOKED, AND FROZEN

Fresh cod, cod tongues, halibut, herring, lobsters, oysters, turbot. Salt herring, bloaters, kippers, red herring, saltcod, salt turbot, finnan haddock, superior smoked Digby herring, Nova Scotia smoked herring. Frozen cod, cod tongues, herring, oysters, lobsters.

FRESH MEAT AND POULTRY

Beef, Chicago beef, steaks, roasts, brisket, oxen. Chickens. Ducks. Geese. Lamb. Mutton. Partridge. Pork. Rabbits. Turkeys. Venison.

SALT MEATS

Choice family beef, salt beef, mess beef, beef cuttings, boneless beef cuttings, plate beef, cooked corned beef, corned beef, Yorkville packet beef, Halstead's packet beef, Hill's packet beef, Tuthill's packet beef, ox tongue, boiled beef. Corned mutton. Pork, choice pork, jowls, choice jowls, pig's heads, loins, hocks, small hocks, heavy mess pork, family pork, mess pork, family mess pork, butt pork, clear and butt pork (Johnson's brand), clear and butt pork (Kenwood brand), salt fatback, tongues, boneless pork cuttings, spare ribs. Sheep tongues.

■ BACON, HAM, AND SAUSAGE

Bacon, Irish bacon, English bacon, Ayreshire bacon, Baltimore bacon, Canadian bacon. Hams, Ferris's hams, English hams, Scotch beef ham, Choice boiled ham, new Canada hams, choice sugar-cured hams, Belfast ham, York cut hams, Canadian hams. Fresh sausages, Halifax sausages, fresh Montreal sausage, Oxford sausages, Bologna sausage, tongue sausages, homemade sausages.

■ BEER, CIDER, AND SHRUB

Bass ale, Edinburgh ale, lager beer, amber ale, barrels of Bass ale, bottles of Burton's ale, amber ale, hogsheads of Devonshire ale, hogsheads of Edinburgh ale. Cider, barrels of cider. New York lager. Porter, Barclay's bottled porter, scotch porter, hogsheads of porter, old brown stout, cases of Guinness stout. Casks of shrub.

■ WINE

Bordeaux claret, cases of Margeaux [sic] and St. Julien claret, pipes and hogsheads of good French red wine, red wine in cask, red wine, Burgundy. Champagne, Adolphe Collins' Champagne, superior pink Champagne. Ginger wine. Italian wine. Moselle, Rhine wines, light Rhenish wines, sparkling and still hock in cases. Spanish red wine, sherry, golden sherry, sherry in cask, superior pale sherry, superior amontillado, very superior Manzanilla wine, Spanish red wine, Vidonia wine, Catalonia wine, Madeira, Malaga, kegs of Old Dry Malaga Wine, Canary wines, Teneriffe [sic] wines. Port in bottle, old port wine, choice old port wine, choice old port wine in hogsheads and quarter casks, Newman's port.

SPIRITS

Brandy, dark brandy, pale brandy, hogsheads of brandy, Martell's brandy, Cognac brandy, cherry brandy. Gin, Geneva, Holland gin. Rum, puncheons of rum, casks and puncheons of high-proof rum, choice Jamaica rum, St. Jago rum, Jamaica (first shot) rum, Old Tom rum. Scotch Whisky, Barley Bree Scotch whisky, Peeble's rye and Cairn Dhu whisky, Peeble's Irish whiskey, Thom and Cameron's Buchanan blend whisky.

Index

alcids 147
American-style pancakes 156
apples 13
    baked 229
applesauce 257
apricot (dried) jam 238
apricot pie 195

baked apples 229
baked beans 174
baked beef liver 108
baked beets 175
baked cod tongues 64
baked custard 230–231
baked seal carcass with mustard 137
baked stuffed fresh trout 86
baking powder 203
bang belly 203
barley 44
barm 26, 27
basic white bread 29
beans, baked 174
beans (dried) 173
beans (fresh) 175
beans, green 10
bear 127
beaver 127
beef 102–109
    bone soup 43
    canned 252
    heart, stuffed 107
    kidney 104
    and kidney pie 105
    and kidney pudding 105
    liver 108
    minced, stew or pie 106
    roast 102
    salt 122
    stew 103
    tongue 107
    and vegetable pie 104
beer 267–269
    dandelion-leaf 269
    molasses 268
    spruce 268
Beeton, Mrs. (Isabella) 34, 58, 66, 177, 213, 255
beets 10
    baked 175
    pickled 242
birds, wild 146
biscuits, ginger 226
biscuits, Shrewsbury 228
black pudding 113–116
blue-lumps 80

blueberries 234
- cake 204
- jam 236
- pie 194
- squares 223
- tea buns 220
- wine 270

boiled clams 92
boiled dinner 122–123
boiled fish 56
boiled fresh herring 77
boiled fresh salmon 84
boiled fresh salmon with salt beef 84
boiled icing 217
boiled lobster 93
boiled mussels 94
boiled raisin cake 205
boiled salt cod tongues 65
boiled salted sounds 66
bottled chicken 252
bottled mussels 252
bottled plums 252
bottled rabbit 253
bottling in glass jars 251–253
braised seal 137
brawn 113–114
bread leavened with soda 34
bread pudding
- steamed savoury, with onions 187
- sweet, with raisins 189

bread sauce 258
bread
- basic white 29
- Christmas sweet 33
- corn 36
- leavened with commercial yeast 29
- pork 30
- quick currant 35
- raisin 32
- soda 35
- sweet 32
- white leavened with barm 28
- whole wheat 33

bream 82
brewis 37, 39, 40, 59–60
- and cheese 40
- with meat and gravy 39
- and scrunchions 39
- and steak 40

brim 82
brined (pickled) cabbage 247
britches, cod 67
buns, pork 31, 156–157
butter 165
butter pastry 198
butter-sugar icing 217

cabbage 10, 175
- brined (pickled) 247
- pickles 243
- salted 176
- salted shredded 246

cakes 204–216
- blueberry 204
- boiled raisin 205
- chocolate with cocoa 205
- chocolate with solid chocolate 206
- crowberry 207
- dark fruit 208
- ginger 208
- Indian meal 209
- light fruit 207
- molasses 209
- old-fashioned 210
- one-two-three-four 210
- partridgeberry 211
- pound 211
- raisin 212
- seed 212
- spice 213
- sponge 213
- war 214
- white 216

callibogus 269
Cameron, Ruth 106
canned beef 252

canned eel 250
canned salmon 251
canning 249–251
capelin 71–73
    fried fresh 73
    salt dried 73
caribou 127
carrot and parsnip hash 154
carrots 10, 176
cattle 102
cauliflower 11
celery 11
cheese 167–170
    brewis and 40
    fingers 169
    sauce 258
    toasted 167
chicken 141–143
    bottled 252
    stew 143
    roast 143
    and vegetable soup 44
chocolate cake with cocoa 205
chocolate cake with solid chocolate 206
chocolate pudding, steamed 189
chocolate sauce 261
chow-chow 244
Christmas sweet bread 33
chuckley pear jelly 241
clams 91–92
    boiled 92
    fried 92
clam soup 44
cod 53–68
    boiled 56

    britches 67
    cheeks, pan-fried 62
    fish stew 55
    gills 68
    heads 62
    hearts 68
    liver 68
    pan-fried fish fillets 55
    sounds 65–67
    stomachs 68
    tongue pie 64
    tongues 62–65
    tongue stew 65
    tongues, baked 64
    salt 53
coffee 274–275
colcannon 153
commercial yeast 29
coo-coo 99
corn bread 36
corned herring, roasted 77
corned turbot 89
cornish pasties 151
cornmeal 36, 209
cottage pudding 206
cranberry jam 236
cranberry jelly 240
creamed oysters on toast 96
croquettes, oyster 97
crowberry cake 207
crowberry pudding, steamed 188
cuckoos 99
cucumber 11
currant bread, quick 35
custard sauce 261
custard, baked 230–231

damper bread 152
damson jelly 240
dandelion flower wine 272
dandelion-leaf beer 269
dandelions 176
dark fruit cake 208
date squares 224
dock 176
dole flour 22, 26, 33
doughboys (see also dumplings) 48
drawn butter 255–257
    with boiled onions 256
    with hard-boiled eggs 257

with fried onions 256
plain 256
dressing 159–160
dried apricot jam 238
dried beans 173
drinking chocolate 275
ducks 145, 148
dumplings 48, 49, 50
as pie topping 50
suet 50
dumpling paste topping 199

eels 74–75
canned 250
fried 75
stewed 75
eggs 143–144
pickled 145
preserving in salt 144
preserving in waterglass 144
egg sauce 260
salt fish and parsnips with 58
English-style pancakes 155

Farmer, Fanny 37
fatback pork, salt 121
figgy duff 186
figs 203
fillet of sepia and macaroni 99
fish, boiled 56
fish and brewis 59–61
fishcakes 58
fish stew 55
flippers (see also seal flippers) 133
flour, dole 22, 26, 33
Francatelli, Charles 82, 178, 180, 255
fresh britches 67
fresh oysters on the half shell 96
fried beef liver with onions 108
fried clams 92
fried eel 75
fried fresh capelin 73
fried fresh herring 76
fried lamb kidneys 112
fried lumpfish 81
fried mackerel 81
fried seal carcass 136
fried seal flippers 133
fried seal liver 138
fried tuna slices 88
fried veal 108
fruit cake, dark 208
fruit cake, light 207

geese 146, 148
gills, cod 68
ginger biscuits 226
ginger cake 208
Glasse, Hannah 78
goat 112
green beans 10
green partridgeberry jam 236
greens, turnip 180–181
gulls 147

ham 110
hard bread 37, 38, 39, 40, 59–60
hard sauce 262
hash 153–154
cod sound 67
using mixed, cooked vegetables 153
salt fish 59
heart, beef, stuffed 107
hearts, cod 68
hearts, stuffed lamb 111
herbs 11
herring 75–80
boiled fresh 77
fried fresh 76
plain boiled salt 79
roasted corned 77
roasted fresh 77
salt, nine-hour 79
vinegared 78
hops 11, 177

icing 217
  boiled 217
  butter-sugar 217
Indian meal cake 209

jam-jams 227
jam pies 196
jams 236–238
jam sauce 262
jellies 239–241
Jiggs' dinner 122–123

kidney
  beef kidney 104
  beef and kidney pie 105
  beef and kidney pudding 105
  fried lamb kidney 112
kyffins 228

lamb 111
lamb hearts, stuffed 111
lamb kidneys, fried 112
lard pastry 198
leggies 59
lemon sauce 263
lettuce 11, 177
light fruit cake 207
liver, beef, fried with onions 108
liver, cod 68
loaf, salmon 85
lobster 92–93
lumpfish 80–81

macaroni cheese set with eggs 170
macaroni cheese with plain cheese sauce 170
macaroni, fillet of sepia and 99
mackerel 81–82
  fillets, rolled, vinegared 82
  stuffed 81
margarine 166
marmalade 238–239
marrow 179
mashed turnip 180
milk 163
minced beef stew or pie 106
mint sauce 259
molasses 22, 23, 33
  beer 268
  cake 209
  coady 263
  pie 197
  sauce 263
  steamed pudding 185–186
  vinegar 246
moonshine 272
moose 127–128
mushroom soup 45
mushrooms on toast 154
muskrat 127
mussels 93–94
  boiled 94
  bottled 252
  pie 94
mustard 245
mustard paste 260
mustard pickles 244
mustard sauce 259
mutton 111

nine-hour salt herring 79

ocean perch 82
old-fashioned cake 210
one-two-three-four cake 210
onions 11, 177
orange and lemon marmalade 239
ox liver 108
ox tongue 107
oysters 95–97
  creamed, on toast 96
  croquettes 97
  on the half shell 96
  soup 46

pancakes 6, 155–156
pan-fried cod cheeks 62

pan-fried cod heads 62
pan-fried cod tongues 63
pan-fried fish fillets 55
pan-fried fresh sounds 66
pan-fried fresh trout 86
pan-fried whale steak 139
parkin 225
parsnips 11, 58, 177
parsnip wine 271
partridgeberry cake 211
partridgeberry jam 236
partridgeberry jam, green 237
partridgeberry pickles 243
partridgeberry pudding, steamed 189
partridgeberry squares 222
partridgeberry tea buns 221
partridgeberry wine 271
pasta 156
pastry 197–199
pear 13
pea soup 46
peas (dried) 178
peas (fresh) 178
perch, ocean 82
periwinkles (see also wrinkles) 97–98
pickles 242–244
    cabbage 243
    mustard 244
    partridgeberry 243
    pickled beets 242
    pickled eggs 145
    rhubarb 243
pies
    apricot 195
    beef and kidney 105
    beef and vegetable 104
    blueberry 194
    jam 196
    minced beef 106
    molasses 197
    mussel 94
    rabbit 130
    raisin 195
    rhubarb 194
    salmon 85
    seal flipper 134–135
    vinegar 197
    Washington 215
plain boiled salt herring 79
plain potato cakes 158
plain salt fish with pork fat 57
plain steamed molasses pudding 185, 186
plain steamed pudding 185
plain tea buns 220
plain white sauce 260
plum jam 237
plum pudding, steamed 190
plums, bottled 252
pork 109–111
pork bread 30
pork buns 31
pork buns with fried fatback 157
pork buns with raw fatback 156
pork, salt 120
pot of properly brewed tea 274
potato cakes 157–158
potato cakes with fatback 158
potato cakes, sweet 226
potatoes 178
potatoes, smothered 179
pound cake 211
puddings
    beef and kidney 105
    black 113–116
    chocolate, steamed 189
    cottage 206
    partridgeberry, steamed 189
    plum, steamed 190
    steamed, crowberry 188
    suet, steamed 187
    white 116
pumpkin 12, 179
Purity Factories 37

quick currant bread 35

rabbit 128–130
bottled 253
pie 130
soup 46
stew 129
raisin bread 32
raisin cake 212
raisin cake, boiled 205
raisin pie 195
raisin squares 223
raisin tea buns 220
raspberry jam pie 196
redfish 82
red-lumps 80
rendered fatback 121
rhubarb 13
marmalade 239
pickles 243
pie 194
rice puddings
savoury 158
sweet 229–230
ripped herring 75, 79
roast beef 102
roast chicken 143
roasted corned herring 77
roasted fresh herring 77
roasted lobster 93
roast salt fish 59
roast tuna 88
roast turr 147
rolled salt herring in vinegar 80
rolled vinegared mackerel fillets 82
root cellars 13–17
rosefish 82
rum sauce 264

salmon 83–86
boiled fresh 84
boiled fresh with salt beef 84
canned 251
loaf 85
pie 85
salted 85
salt beef 122
salt cod (see also salt fish) 53, 57–59
tongue pie 64
tongues, boiled 65
salt dried capelin 73
salted cabbage 176
salted shredded cabbage 246
salt fatback pork 121
salt fish 57–59
with drawn butter 57
fishcakes 58
hash 59
with parsnips and egg sauce 58
roast 59
salt meat 119–124
salt pork 120
salt salmon 85
sauerkraut 246
savory 11
savoury rice pudding 158
Scotch-packed herring 75, 79
scrunchions 121
seal 130–138
braised, 137
carcass, baked, with mustard 137
carcass, fried
carcass, roast 136
head 137
liver, fried 138
soup 47
seal flippers 132–135
fried 133
with mustard 133
pie with dumpling-paste topping 134
pie with pastry on top 135
with vinegar 134
seal harvest 130–131
seed cake 212
sepia, fillet of, and macaroni 99
shallots 12, 179
sheep 111
shellfish 91–99

Shrewsbury biscuits 228
smothered potatoes 179
soda bread 35
soft sauce 264
sound hash 67
sounds, boiled salted 66
sounds, pan-fried fresh 66
soup
    beef bone 43
    chicken and vegetable 44
    clam 45
    mushroom 45
    oyster 46
    pea 46
    rabbit 46
    seal 47
spice cake 213
spirits 272
sponge cake 213
spruce beer 268
squares 221–224
    blueberry 223
    date 224
    partridgeberry 222
    raisin 223
squash 12, 179
squashberry jelly 241
squid 98–99
steak 40
steak and brewis 40
steamed puddings
    chocolate 189
    crowberry 188
    molasses with currants 186
    molasses, plain 185
    partridgeberry 189
    plain 185
    plum 190
    savoury bread pudding with onion 187
    suet 187
    sweet bread with raisins 189
stew
    beef 103
    chicken 143
    cod tongue 65
    fish 55
    minced beef 106
    rabbit 129
stewed eel 75
stomachs, cod 68
stuffed beef heart 107
stuffed lamb hearts 111
stuffed mackerel 81
stuffing 159–160
    for beef, lamb, or other animal heart 160
    for birds and fish 159
    with thyme 159
suet dumplings 50
suet pastry 199
suet pudding, steamed 187
sugar sauce 264
sweet bread pudding with raisins 189
sweet breads 32
sweet potato cakes 226

tea 273–274
tea buns 219–221
toasted cheese 167
tomatoes 12
toutons 160
trout 85–86
    baked, stuffed 86
    pan-fried 86
tuna 87–88
    fried, slices 88
    roast 88
turbot 89
    corned 89
turnip 12, 13, 180
    and potato hash 154
    mashed 180
turnip greens 180–181
turr, roast 147

veal, fried 109
vinegar 245

vinegared herring 78
vinegar pie 197

war cake 214
Washington pie 215
Welsh rabbit (rarebit) 168–169
whale 138–139
whelks 99
white bread leavened with barm 28
white cake 216
white pudding 116
white sauce, plain 260
whole wheat bread 33
wine 269–272
    blueberry 270
    partridgeberry 271
wrinkles, boiled on the beach 97
wrinkles, as a main meal 97

yeast, commercial 29

Roger Pickavance was raised in the Welsh Borders, where his life-long interest in food and cooking started with fruit and vegetables from his parents' garden, trout from local rivers, and Welsh lamb from the hills behind his home. His memories of those tastes are still the benchmarks by which he judge food today. His father was a keen ornithologist, his mother knowledgeable about wild flowers, and it was their love of the natural world that started Pickavance on the path to a PhD in biology, which in turn led to a faculty position at Memorial University.

Pickavance arrived in Newfoundland in 1968, a pivotal time. The fishery had peaked and was starting its long, slow decline. The traditional way of life outside St. John's was entering a period of very rapid change. Roads were reaching ever-more isolated communities, so people could drive to the bigger centres where supermarkets were springing up, hastening the decline of the small community store, and bringing new and unusual foods into the traditional kitchens of Newfoundland.

But many traditional foods were still in evidence, many of which Pickavance had neither seen nor heard of before, including saltfish, cod tongues, britches, partridgeberries, and bakeapples. Seeing these in the kitchens of his new-found home opened his eyes to cooking traditions that had lasted for many generations, but which—along with the way of life—were being rapidly diluted by the modern world. And that was the impetus behind this book.